Labor Union Theories in America

Background and Development

Labor Union Theories in America

Background and Development

MARK PERLMAN

Department of Political Economy
The Johns Hopkins University

ROW, PETERSON AND COMPANY

Evanston, Illinois   White Plains, New York

To Naomi

Preface

This book examines the major explanations of American unionism written long enough ago to have ripened sufficiently for
analysis, and arranges them into natural theoretical groupings.
It is both a stocktaking of the wealth of literature on the subject
and a discussion of the relevance of that literature to present
thinking.

The justification for this study lies principally in the usefulness
which older studies have for an understanding of the current
American labor movement. A knowledge of the literature provides a necessary background. And if the literature is presented
properly, students in the field can also acquire an insight into
their own intellectual antecedents, and thereby obtain perspective
about their period and themselves—surely a most necessary step
in any objective analysis. In other words, examination of the old
literature is generally necessary and always desirable when for-
mulating sophisticated current assessments of the functions, policies, and goals of unionism.

Although American unionism itself is an old institution, having
appeared first in the seventeenth century and had its formal beginnings as a movement in Philadelphia in 1827, only in the last
nine decades has it begun seriously to affect the structure and
operation of American industry. During this latter period it has
experienced several waves of growth, has penetrated into virtually
every sector of community life, and has come to affect the thinking as well as the economic well-being of most Americans. Quite
obviously, it has had to adapt to its environment, and in so doing
has modified its form, reoriented its objectives, and reshaped its
policies. Because of the growing social importance of unionism,
numerous writers have sought to "explain" it—to narrate the

story of its origins and growth, to discuss its functions and operational techniques, and, generally, to analyze its ultimate role in society.

As a rule, present-day writers have neglected this legacy of earlier analyses because of two factors, the first of which stems from the complexity of unionism as an institution. Great differences exist between schools of thought regarding the relevant questions that should be asked. And because unionism has many sides, answers to one set of questions have been relatively meaningless when presented as responses to another set.

The second factor relates to an all but inescapable tendency of research workers to overlook data unearthed in projects, the general value of which is to them meaningless. The practice has been to formulate "new" explanations, resulting in a jungle of individual interpretations. The jungle has expanded, and each generation has found itself doing the same or similar tasks over and over again.

The Plan of the Work

In this book the term "theory" is used as synonymous with what others might call "basic interpretation"; hence, five "theories" of unionism. The term "interpretation" is used as applying to differences within any one of the five theories.

The book presents five basic theories of unionism. In this connection the work of approximately twenty significant individuals is discussed. Five basic theories evolved because in reviewing the literature it was found that there are five basic ways in which unions have been viewed. Further analysis revealed that each of these approaches was associated in its formation with characteristics or premises peculiar to a particular academic discipline or a particular general social movement. Each of the five tended to emphasize certain aspects of unionism, because each was seeking in unionism an answer to the questions framed within the academic discipline or social movement. The five are (1) the Protestant Christian Socialist and the Roman Catholic Christian social movements, (2) the Marxian Socialist movements, (3) the environmental psychology discipline, (4) the neoclassical economics discipline, and (5) the legal or jurisprudential history discipline.

Each of the five basic theories is presented in a separate chapter, where the discussion is developed in three steps. First, there is an introductory statement relating to the cultural or intellectual setting in which or from which the theory developed. Because these statements are necessarily general and brief, it is perhaps useful to draw attention to their importance. It is largely because of the differences in setting that the various theories developed— each stemming from a particular configuration of ideas and events.

Following the reference to the setting, an attempt is made to isolate the key ideas that provide the theme of the theory. At that point it is relatively simple to identify the relevant or critical postulates employed by each of the writers within the theory. Discussion of the major works—those best illustrating the development of the theory—make up the third part of each "theory" chapter. Needless to say, the object of this book is not principally to evaluate ideas. Quite the contrary; the purpose is to suggest the range of ideas and to analyze the course of their development. Consequently, virtually no attempt has been made in the body of the work to assess the "value" of each theory.

However, in the last chapter an attempt is made to bring the theories into contemporary (post–Great Depression) perspective, in order to facilitate discussion of current unionism. Here there is discussion of why the theories are not complementary to each other and why one cannot incorporate all the different ideas into a single general theory. An indication is also given of why two of the five seem to be irrelevant for current uses and why a third appears to have only limited value. In this last section there is also a discussion of the author's own position, that is, why two of the theories seem to him to be most useful in answering the critical questions of the past two and a half decades. The last chapter, therefore, ends with the identification of the author's value judgments which, it is hoped, did not materially affect the presentation of any of the material.

The Appendix is an outline of some of the views of several leaders of organized labor, presented in the context of four public investigations of the industrial-relations problem. Some attention is given also to the scope and results of the investigations.

Acknowledgments

The writing of this book came as an indirect result of a course given more than six years ago at the University of Hawaii—when I became acutely aware of the price being paid by research people because of the lack of any systematic discussion of the great American interpretative masterpieces on unionism.

When I joined the faculty of the New York State School of Industrial and Labor Relations at Cornell University, I was encouraged to concentrate my research on the subject of comparative theories of trade-unions. The present book was prepared largely as an integral part of my Cornell duties. For this reason I want to acknowledge the excellent opportunity Dean Martin P. Catherwood gave me to read, to reflect, and to write. I want also to thank collectively my colleagues at Cornell for their encouragement and stimulation; in particular I must single out the excellent ILR library staff, of which Professor J. Gormly Miller is the head.

Grateful acknowledgment is also to be expressed to the staff of the National Archives, Industrial Records Division, and to Miss Angela Lavarello, who, long before I joined the Johns Hopkins faculty, prepared for me a complete bibliography of the works of the late George Ernest Barnett.

Mrs. Arthur Misener very kindly and very carefully read a draft of the manuscript and made hundreds of excellent suggestions, most of which I readily accepted, and a few which I probably should have accepted, but did not. For her interest, this word of appreciation can only be a token.

Above all, I want to acknowledge the aid given me by four scholars who read the last draft and recommended some important revisions. Again, while I can lay claim to having acted on most of them, I must also admit to the sole responsibility for not having accepted all. The four are Merle Curti (Frederick Jackson Turner Professor of American History at the University of Wisconsin), Joseph Dorfman (Professor of Economics at Columbia University), John T. Dunlop (Professor of Economics at Harvard University), and Edwin E. Witte (Professor of Economics at the University of Wisconsin).

MARK PERLMAN

Baltimore
February, 1957

Acknowledgments of Permission to Quote

From H. C. Adams, "Economics and Jurisprudence," *Economic Studies*, Vol. II, copyright 1897, American Economic Association, by permission of the association.

From George Barnett, "American Trade Unionism and Social Insurance," *American Economic Review*, Vol. XXIII, copyright 1933, American Economic Association, by permission of the association.

From G. K. Chesterton, "Notebooks," *Illustrated London News*, c. 1895, copyright presently held by Miss D. E. Collins; by permission of Miss Collins.

From John R. Commons, *Documentary History of American Industrial Society*, copyright 1910, The Arthur H. Clark Company, by permission of the publisher.

From John R. Commons, *Industrial Goodwill*, copyright 1919, McGraw-Hill Book Company, Inc., by permission of the publisher.

From John R. Commons, *Labor and Administration*, copyright 1913, The Macmillan Company, by permission of the publisher.

From John R. Commons, *Myself*, copyright 1934, The Macmillan Company, by permission of the publisher.

From John R. Commons and Associates, *History of Labour in the United States*, copyright 1918, The Macmillan Company, by permission of the publisher.

From William Z. Foster, *From Bryan to Stalin*, copyright 1937, International Publishers, by permission of the publisher.

From Florence Harriman, *From Pinafores to Politics*, copyright 1923, Henry Holt and Company, Inc., by permission of the publisher.

From Jacob H. Hollander and George E. Barnett, *Studies in American Trade Unionism*, copyright 1906, Henry Holt and Company, Inc., by permission of the publisher.

From Robert F. Hoxie, *Trade Unionism in the United States*, copyright 1917. Permission to quote not denied by Allan D. Hoxie, to whom copyright was assigned in 1950.

From Carleton H. Parker, *The Casual Laborer and Other Essays*,

Table of Contents

ONE

The Awakening

A judicious man, says [the "crabbed satirist"] looks at Statistics, not to get knowledge but to save himself from having ignorance foisted on him.

—Thomas Carlyle
Chartism, 1839
Chap. 2, "Statistics"

The emergence of a distinct body of literature on trade-unionism in America should be placed at about 1886–89, when five major treatises appeared. By then an effort was being made to satisfy a demand for statistical facts, and this demand was, in part at least, being replaced by a demand for interpretations of the social movements of the "working population." To understand the significance of this shift in interest, one must first consider what preceded both of these demands.

The absence of specific information about wages and working conditions had given rise as early as 1867 to a movement leading to the establishment of numerous state bureaus of labor statistics. The collection of such data on a national scale was first suggested by William H. Sylvis (1828–69) at the 1867 convention of the National Labor Union. Sylvis, a reformer and labor leader, was active in the molders' union and the leading spirit in the National Labor Union. His proposal was developed the following year to embrace a concrete plan for "a new department at Washington to be called THE DEPARTMENT OF LABOR, the head of said department to be called the Secretary of Labor, and to be chosen directly from the ranks of workingmen. To this department should be referred all questions of wages and hours of labor in the navy-yards and all other government workshops, the registry and regulations of trades'-unions and co-operative associations . . . and all other questions directly concerned with and affecting labor" (cf. **16**, pp. 74, 293, and particularly 316–17).[1] Although the idea was not adopted nationally for some time, it was taken up almost immediately in several of the states.

Massachusetts, one of the leading industrial states, was the first to respond to this proposal. In June, 1869, the Massachusetts General Court (the legislature) resolved that the governor should biennially in May appoint a chief for a bureau of labor statistics. Provision was made for him to choose a deputy, and the two were ". . . to collect, assort, systematize and present in annual reports to the legislature . . . statistical details relating to all departments of labor . . . especially . . . to the commercial, industrial, social, educational and sanitary condition of the laboring classes, and to the permanent prosperity of productive industry . . ." (**6**).

Why Massachusetts initiated this action is an amazing story of political maneuvering. The action was intended partly to minimize the consequences of the legislature's refusal to grant a charter of incorporation to the Knights of St. Crispin, who had wanted to operate as a co-operative purchasing unit so that they could buy household items for members and thus lower the cost of living. The new law was also a consequence of the legislature's refusal to enact legislation to limit hours of work, which was being sought by the Boston Eight-Hour League. Partly, too, it was the recognition by the legislators themselves that passage of effective compulsory school legislation would be impossible as long as social data on the laboring population were inadequate.

In any event, the newly established bureau was run during its first four years (1869–73) by Henry Kemble Oliver (1800–1885), who had played a major role in the public school movement in Massachusetts, and George E. McNeill (1837–1906), active in the ten- and eight-hour movements and founder of the International Labor Union. Although neither man was trained in statistics,

[1] The references will be found at the end of each chapter.

and despite their lack of a clear knowledge of social problems and the efficient ways to solve them, Oliver and McNeill set out immediately to reform what they privately considered to be the most iniquitous social evils of the time. Dissatisfaction with their crusading zeal soon manifested itself, and by 1873 they were dropped from the bureau. What was most remarkable, perhaps, was the decision of the conservative Republican leaders of the time to retain the agency at all. Their confidence, however, was reflected in the appointment of Carroll Davidson Wright (1840–1909), a statistician, party regular, and former state senator, as the new and more responsible bureau head. Wright, recognizing the existence of political shoals, ran the agency more circumspectly, emphasizing the collection rather than the interpretation of data. Eleven years later, after twelve states had established similar bureaus, he was called to Washington to organize what is now the federal Bureau of Labor Statistics.

As a result of the work of Wright and his professional contemporaries, the decade of the seventies produced a number of factual studies of wages, hours, and working and living conditions, as well as surveys of factory legislation, estimates of the growth of corporate enterprises, discussions of levels of education and sobriety among working people, and general essays on social integration of minority groups in factory towns. If the treatment of these varied topics seems prejudiced and the measuring techniques inadequate to modern observers, it is wise to recall that these were pioneer efforts.

Perhaps a typical example of the best work done in the period was a lengthy volume prepared by Dr. Edward Young (1814–1909), chief of the United States Bureau of Statistics. Entitled *Labor in Europe and America; A Special Report on the Rates of Wages, the Cost of Subsistence, and the Conditions of the Working Classes, in Great Britain, France, Belgium, Germany, and Other Countries of Europe, Also in the United States and British America* (18), it began with a long discussion of the social and economic status of working people from early Biblical times.

Young had spent the years from 1852 to 1866 gathering data on American industry. In 1872, as the American delegate to the International Statistical Congress in St. Petersburg, he took the opportunity to gather statistical data on industry and labor in Great Britain, Belgium, Germany, and Russia. Although Young was not particularly careful in labeling the sources for the considerable statistical data he presented on wages and costs, the reader today cannot but admire the scope of his effort. It is indicative of the research of the period, as well as the unstable situation of unions, however, that the only references to trade-unions occur in sections on ancient Rome and the United Kingdom; no mention is made of any of the American unions of the time.

During the seventies there was a long depression and considerable social strife, resulting in a great many discussions of the causes and consequences of particular strikes and riots. J. A. Dacus, for instance, in his most readable *Annals of the Great Strikes in the United States* (3), carefully traced the source of violence in the railroad riots of 1877. His study was paralleled by an official investigation conducted by the Pennsylvania legislature (10). The federal government also sought factual descriptions of labor unrest. Other state governments were similarly interested in general developments. The Massachusetts bureau, for instance, made studies in 1877 and in 1881 of the development of "industrial arbitration," at that time a generic term for what is now included in "collective bargaining" (cf. 5). The repeated plea, however, was for more and better data.

In the mid-eighties, when the need for interpretive analyses rather than purely statistical data was demonstrated, the picture began to change. Congress, after considering the matter several times, finally passed a bill to establish a bureau of labor in the Department of the Interior. Four years later the Bureau of Labor became an independent agency, as the Department of Labor without executive rank. Its scope of operation approximated that of the present Bureau of Labor Statistics, and it should not be confused with the present Department of Labor, organized as the ninth executive department in 1913. Moreover, the social flux of the seventies had yielded to some organization, and the Knights of Labor, as well as the trade-unions affiliated with the Federation of Organized Trades and Labor Unions of the United States and Canada, were articulately present on the scene. Scientific socialism and Bakunin anarchism had appeared, and their adherents had succeeded in alarming, if not terrifying, much of the conservative element in the country. The time was ripe for some interpretive literature.

One semi-interpretive work that is particularly worthy of mention had appeared in 1879: *Nordamerikanische Arbeiterverhält-nisse* (15), by Arthur von Studnitz (1851–1927). Von Studnitz spent several months in 1876 visiting industrial cities in the New England and Middle Atlantic states, where he circulated questionnaires that with his observations served as the basis for his generalizations. Topics discussed in his book include wages, hours, living conditions, family budgets, clothing, lighting, heating, welfare organizations, and sanitary and health facilities as they affected working people.

In the period 1886–89, no less than five major sympathetic treatises appeared, with the avowed purpose of explaining the trade-union movement and of pointing out the distinctions between unions, on the one hand, and purely revolutionary and/or political organizations, on the other. There were others as well, especially T. Edwin Brown's *Studies in Modern Socialism and Labor Problems* (2), but the five to be discussed are most characteristic of the new thinking. Of the five, Richard T. Ely's *The Labor Movement in America* (4), probably the least ambitious, attracted the most attention, including a review in the *Nation* (9) seriously questioning the writer's place in a university. The book covered comprehensively co-operation, socialism, and the development of trade-unions. Its contents are analyzed in later chapters, where its effect on further university research is examined.

Another of these treatises was an extensive social history, *The Story of Manual Labor in All Lands and Ages* (14), written by John Cameron Simonds (d. 1896) in collaboration with a newspaper man, John T. McEnnis, and published in 1886. The book was divided into six parts: labor in the Orient, labor in antiquity, labor in the middle ages, labor in the modern (European and Near Eastern) world, labor in America, and an analytical survey of guilds and trade-unions. For his historical matter, Simonds drew on Ely's book as well as on Lujo Brentano's (1844–1931) epochal works, but went beyond Ely in detailing the events of 1886 itself. In addition, Simonds took care to point out the disastrous effect on American labor of competition with immigrants, who were paid low wages, and with convict labor. There is a twenty-page chapter on trade-unions in the United States, exclusive of the Knights of Labor, but it does little more than list the dates of establishment, the facts relating to contemporary membership, and certain of the outstanding policies of several active unions. In spite of a short reference to the Federation of Trades and Labor Assemblies (*sic*),[2] it is clear that Simonds considered the Knights of Labor to be historically the most significant labor movement of his time. "The Knights of Labor may fail," he wrote, "but whether the organization dies or lives, it has taught a lesson which will never be forgotten as long as man shall earn his bread by the sweat of his brow. It has demonstrated the overmastering power of a national combination among workingmen. If the Knights of Labor were to dissolve tomorrow, on the next day a new society would be formed to push on their work" (14, p. 649).

Simonds' primary intent was to present the gentle, almost Rousseauan, theme that the workers of the world were gradually demonstrating their inherent decency and discovering that they must depend upon their own co-ordinated efforts to find solutions to the economic and social problems they faced. He summarized this theme briefly in the last sentences of his 715-page work with an oblique criticism of the insidious results of govern-

---

[2] The Federation of Organized Trades and Labor Unions was the forerunner of the American Federation of Labor during the years 1881–86. It was made up largely of craft unions, and was organized primarily for the purpose of political lobbying.

ment: "One of the indications that the toilers of the world are awakening to the fact that they are very little interested in the broils of governments may be seen in the formation in the fall of 1885 of a district assembly of [the] Knights of Labor, composed of soldiers of the union and confederate armies. It is known as The Gray and the Blue, and its motto is: 'Capital Divided, Labor Unites Us'" (14, p. 670). Simonds also included two appendices. One deals with comparative statistics on national income; the other is a compendium of some of the salient features of state labor laws.

Another, more scholarly writer who was greatly impressed with the historical destiny of the Knights of Labor was the German, August Sartorius, Freiherr von Waltershausen (1852–1938), who spent part of two years traveling in North and Central America after his graduation from Göttingen University in 1880. In 1886 Sartorius, later a professor at Zurich and at Strasbourg, published a study in four parts, *Die nordamerikanischen Gewerkschaften unter dem Einfluss der fortschreitenden Productionstechnik,* on the problems of labor organization in America. Since the book was not translated, it received notice only in certain interested academic circles, but a review by E. R. A. Seligman (13) compared the work most favorably with Von Studnitz' *Nordamerikanische Arbeitverhältnisse.*

After a historical and then an analytical summary of American working people's early organizations, Sartorius stressed the Americans' distinct and peculiar intellectual isolation from European developments. He noted, for instance, that William A. Sylvis knew little of the Hegelian dialectic used by Marx and Lassalle. Nor did Sylvis share the typical European intellectual's hatred of the church and the clergy; he was instead a devout Christian who regularly attended the Methodist Church, enthusiastically taught Sunday School, and was an active worker in the temperance movement. Only in the last years of his life did he become aware of and interested in the international labor movement (12, pp. 35–36).

Although Sartorius associated the collapse of the National

Labor Union with the death of Sylvis, he explained this collapse by expounding a theory of the effect of the business cycle on unions. The political labor movement of the sixties, he wrote, fell apart in the beginning of the seventies because its underlying motivations had disappeared (12, pp. 48–49). The two years 1871–73 were years of great economic activity, when wages generally went up sufficiently to match rising prices. Skilled workers were thus satisfied and loath to turn to politics, since they were interested primarily in immediate benefits and not in long-run goals. Even Sylvis, Sartorius believed, would have been unable to retain general worker interest in political action.

With the advent of the long depression, political activity revived, as the Kearneyite and "soft-money" movements reveal. Sartorius, observing the closing frontier and the concentration of capital, predicted that wages in America would tend to fall and that working people would turn more and more to political agitation. As a consequence, trade-union activity, popular only during good years when strikes were short and usually successful, would decline. But Sartorius took care to point out that worker psychology was such that they would tend to favor, wherever possible, trade-union rather than political action.

On the whole, Sartorius was skeptical of the future of "pure and simple," or apolitical, unionism. Among the reasons for his skepticism were the problems of job competition presented by "greenhorns" (immigrants) and by women. Moreover, he believed that the days of the craftsman were numbered, and that large-scale industrial enterprise would destroy the effectiveness of trade-union (that is, craft-union) efforts (12, pp. 122–23). Unions, he noted, took four forms. Only one of these, of which the Knights of Labor was an example, had real elements of stability. The obsolete or inadequate types were local trades assemblies, craft locals, and general, or "one big union," organizations (cf. 12, pp. 134 ff., 141 ff., and 148 ff.). Only a composite structure like that of the Knights, with its modifications of the simple craft form of organization, gave the flexibility required by the American situation (12, pp. 153 ff.). Sartorius outlined the

history of the Knights, analyzing among other things its successful use of the boycott (12, pp. 257–62).

The third section of Sartorius' work, which dealt with strikes,
boycotts, and the practical program of union organizations, was
conceptually the best and presented him at his most sophisticated.
An example of the balance in his views was his weighing of a
distinct dislike of boycott action against the consequences of its
legal prohibition, and his conclusion that the "cure" was worse
than the original evil. It was in this section that he made his
most stimulating observations.

Sartorius' sanguineness about the Knights, as well as his consequent hesitation about the adaptive qualities of the craft unions,
showed poor judgment. But his understanding of the effect of
the business cycle on, and the complexities of political action by,
working people's organizations was good. By and large, it is
unfortunate that the book was not available to a larger public.

Another of the important treatises to appear during this period
was *The Labor Movement: The Problem of Today,* edited by
George E. McNeill (8), and published in 1887. It consisted of a
well-organized series of essays, written by almost a score of
officials and leaders of union organizations to give a balanced
view of labor's side of its many problems. The first three short
chapters, on historical developments abroad, were written by Dr.
Edmund J. James (1855–1925) of the University of Pennsylvania, later president of Northwestern University and the University of Illinois. These were followed by McNeill's own exposition of developments in American labor history, and by eight
chapters on specific industries and trades, each written by a leader
in the field. These include essays on the printers by John M.
Farquhar, the shoemakers by Frank Foster, the textile trades by
Robert Howard, the coal miners by John McBride, the ironworkers by John Jarrett, the railroad men by P. M. Arthur, and
the building trades by E. H. Rogers.[3]

[3] Farquhar was then a member of Congress, a former president of the printers' union, and later a member of the U.S. Industrial Commission; Foster was a
printer active in the Knights of Labor; Howard served terms in both houses of

These essays varied in quality and tended to emphasize the success of trade-union, as contrasted with political, action. Following them in the volume was an essay on the origins of the Knights of Labor, written by the six surviving founders. McNeill himself wrote a chapter on the theory behind the "Declaration of Principles." [4]

The final chapters of *The Labor Movement: The Problem of Today* were devoted to such specific issues as the threat of Chinese immigration, the hours of labor, arbitration, industrial education, unemployment, and the effect of new land settlement and taxation on wages. Contributions were made by specialists ranging from Henry George to the Reverend R. Heber Newton (1840–1914), the rector of All Souls Church, New York, and noted for the "radical liberality" of his religious views, and F. H. Giddings (1855–1931), a sociologist and newspaperman who later taught at Bryn Mawr College and Columbia University. The last chapter of the book, on unemployment, was written by Terence V. Powderly (1849–1924), at that time head of the Knights of Labor and associated with the U.S. Immigration Service. There is reason to believe that the chapter was not prepared for this book and that it was included without Powderly's consent (**11**, pp. 3–4, and **17**, p. 206). At the time Powderly, too, had wanted to publish an interpretation of the labor movement, and it is likely that he resented the premature disclosure of his ideas. In any event, Powderly subsequently took excessive pains to disassociate himself from McNeill's work.

The virtues of McNeill's book lay in the selection and diversity of the viewpoints expressed, the concentration on specific rather

---

the Massachusetts legislature; McBride was a former president of the miners' union, later president of the AFL, and active in Democratic politics in Ohio; Jarrett was active in the Sons of Vulcan and in the organization of the iron and steel workers; Arthur was an organizer and later president of the International Brotherhood of Locomotive Engineers, and a proponent of simple craft unionism.

[4] This was the preamble to the constitution of the Knights of Labor. It describes the social aggressiveness of capital and expresses the belief that unless checked, it "will inevitably lead to the pauperization and hopeless degradation of the toiling masses." It includes a general program designed to "check" the powers of capital and to aid the workers.

than general or abstract topics, and the pithiness of the language used. In retrospect, the amount of space given to the Knights of Labor seems unduly generous. Unlike the other labor studies appearing at the time, however, this one gave considerable attention to the achievements of the "limited-goals" unions. One can therefore say that McNeill's insight compares favorably with that of the other major writers on labor of the time.[5]

In 1889 Terence Powderly brought forth his long (almost 700-page) apologia with the massive title, *Thirty Years of Labor, 1859 to 1889, in Which the History of the Attempts to Form Organizations of Workingmen for the Discussion of Political, Social, and Economic Questions Is Traced. The National Labor Union of 1866, the Industrial Brotherhood of 1874, and Order of the Knights of Labor of America and the World, The Chief and Most Important Principles of the Knights of Labor Discussed and Explained, with Views of the Author on Land, Labor and Transportation.* Spread throughout the book are the author's views on the inevitability of the Knights' historical mission, on the necessity for the catholicity of the Knights' social interests, and on such topics as temperance, the ambition of others, the social structure, money, and cheap foreign labor. Powderly's bitterness toward the "pure and simple" trade-unions had by this time mounted (it may be recalled that he was maneuvered into open opposition to the AFL [**17**, pp. 191–242, 280–98]), and he took care to emphasize the selfish interests of the craft unionists, attributing to this selfishness the demise of earlier labor organizations. Conversely, in a detailed history of the development of the Knights, he pointed out the enlightened altruism that attended virtually every important decision they made. In many instances, Powderly revealed a clear understanding not only of social questions but also of the complexities of administrative problems. The chapter on labor bureaus, for example, contained some useful analysis of their development and of reasons why neither Powderly nor John Jarrett (of the iron and steel workers' union) was appointed to be commissioner of the federal Bureau of Labor

[5] For a view of McNeill's as well as Frank Foster's interpretations of unionism, see below, pp. 246, 251, 267–68.

Statistics. Powderly had a tendency, however, to gloss over if not actually to mislead about such issues as the eight-hour day strikes set for May 1, 1886, and the handling of matters before the general assemblies of the Knights.

The book is chiefly valuable as an example of Powderly's missionary zeal and as a broad explanation of his actions taken as Grand Master Workman of the Knights of Labor. Particularly useful are his detailed views of the administrative and structural problems faced by the Knights in the two decades of their existence. Powderly preferred to justify specific policies rather than, like McNeill or Sartorius, to analyze the general purposes served by working-class action. His book, in marked contrast to theirs, provides the careful reader with an insight into the administrative process of a labor "government." In this sense it has unequaled merit.

During the eighties other writers—among them journalists and editorialists—also took up the question of the labor movement. Their articles appear to have been very effective in focusing public attention on the growth of socialism and anarchism, as well as on the growth of unionism. Many of these labor articles were excellent: one need mention only the names of John Swinton (1829–1901), on the editorial staff of the *New York Sun* and founder of *John Swinton's Paper,* a four-page weekly, and Joseph Buchanan (1851–1924), editor of the Denver *Labor Enquirer,* the *Chicago Enquirer,* and successful engineer of several major railroad strikes in the eighties, to illustrate the high caliber of these writers. In 1886 William E. Barnes brought out a small volume entitled *The Labor Problem: Plain Questions and Practical Answers* (1), which originally appeared in *The Age of Steel,* a St. Louis newspaper publication. It was mainly a symposium on five questions relating to strikes and lockouts, arbitration, profit sharing, and producers' co-operatives.

But journalism is not well suited either to careful research or to meticulous theory; for this reason most of our attention is directed to other, more formal studies. We will not endeavor, therefore, to fill in the background of these important nonacademicians and social theorists. In the next chapter, however, we will round out the background of university research in the theories of unionism.

It may be well to repeat here that the quest for labor statistics, strong in the seventies, gave way in the next decade to a quest for interpretive data. This shift of interest, which was paralleled by the growth of the Knights of Labor and of the various trade-unions affiliated with the Federation of Organized Trades and Labor Unions (as well as some that were never affiliated with it), also reflected the growth of an anarchistic labor movement. These developments came to a head in 1886, the year of the "Great Upheaval." A national fondness for self-analysis, accentuated at the time by the extension of popular education, led several writers to consider a new area of social action. It is to a consideration of their efforts that we now turn.

References

1. Barnes, William E. (ed.), *The Labor Problem: Plain Questions and Practical Answers.* New York: Harper & Bros., 1886.

2. Brown, T. Edwin, *Studies in Modern Socialism and Labor Problems.* New York: D. Appleton & Co., 1886.

3. Dacus, Joseph A., *Annals of the Great Strikes in the United States.* Chicago: L. T. Palmer & Co.; Philadelphia: W. R. Thomas, 1877.

4. Ely, Richard T., *The Labor Movement in America.* New York: Thomas Y. Crowell Co., 1886.

5. Jensen, Vernon H., "Notes on the Beginnings of Collective Bargaining," *Industrial and Labor Relations Review,* IX (1956), 225–34.

6. Leiby, James R. W., "The Massachusetts Bureau of Statistics of Labor: Its History to 1886; Its Influence; Its Significance." Unpublished manuscript, private copy.

7. ———, "Statistics and the Labor Problem: A Biography of Carroll D. Wright." Unpublished Ph.D. dissertation, Harvard University, 1954.

8. McNeill, George E. (ed.), *The Labor Movement: The Problem of Today.* Boston: A. M. Bridgman & Co.; New York: M. W. Hazen Co., 1887.

9. Newcomb, Simon, review of Ely, *The Labor Movement in America,* in *Nation,* XLIII (1886), 293.

10. Pennsylvania General Assembly, *Report of the Joint Committee Appointed to Investigate the Railroad Riots in July 1877.* Legislative Document No. 29. Harrisburg, 1878.

11. Powderly, Terence V., *Thirty Years of Labor, 1859 to 1889, in Which the History of the Attempts to Form Organizations of Workingmen for the Discussion of Political, Social, and Economic Questions Is Traced. The National Labor Union of 1866, the Industrial Brotherhood of 1874, and Order of the Knights of Labor of America and the World, The Chief and Most Important Principles of the Knights of Labor Discussed and Explained, with Views of the Author on Land, Labor and Transportation.* Columbus, Ohio: Excelsior Publishing House, 1889.

12. Sartorius, August, *Die nordamerikanischen Gewerkschaften unter dem Einfluss der fortschreitenden Productionstechnik.* Berlin: Hermann Bahr, 1886.

13. Seligman, E. R. A., review of Sartorius, *Die nordamerikanischen Gewerkschaften . . . ,* in *Political Science Quarterly,* I (1886), 512–14.

14. Simonds, John C., and McEnnis, John T., *The Story of Manual Labor in All Lands and Ages.* Chicago: R. S. Peale & Co., 1886.

15. Studnitz, Arthur von, *Nordamerikanische Arbeiterverhältnisse.* Leipzig: Von Dunker & Humblot, 1879.

16. [Sylvis, William H.], *The Life, Speeches, Labors, and Essays of William H. Sylvis,* with an introductory essay by James C. Sylvis. Philadelphia: Claxton, Remsen, and Haffelfinger, 1872.

17. Ware, Norman J., *The Labor Movement in the United States, 1860–1895.* New York: D. Appleton & Co., 1929.

18. Young, Edward, *Labor in Europe and America: A Special Report on the Rates of Wages, the Cost of Subsistence, and the Conditions of the Working Classes, in Great Britain, France, Belgium, Germany and Other Countries of Europe, Also in the United States and British America.* Philadelphia: S. A. George Co., 1875.

TWO

Early Union Theory in the Universities

Having discussed early individual interpretations of the American labor movement, we now turn to the accomplishments of groups of university scholars in order to discover why they responded as they did to the problem of unionism. For it was at university centers that four of the five basic theories discussed in this book came to be developed. Each of these four theories is the result of a combination of the interests of individuals with their estimates of the problems of American society at large. In the history of the university research into trade-union problems one can, therefore, find the diverse influences of varying interpretations regarding the economic development of America, of the reorientation of scientific methodology and the curriculums in our universities, and of such Continental ideas as scientific socialism and the welfare state.

As we have seen, America went through a significant social and economic transformation in the seventies and eighties that resulted in a need for a new interpretation of social movements. It is not surprising to find that this need was reflected in certain university circles. The struggle during this period between traditional classical economists and a new group advocating the investigation of social problems reflected the prevailing dichotomy of intellectual thought. This new group felt that the traditional, time-honored analysis was inadequate for the questions of the hour.

The rise in the eighties of The Johns Hopkins University in Baltimore under the leadership of Daniel Coit Gilman (1831–1908) marks the period of change. President Gilman, who had previously served as president of the University of California, modeled his institution on the Second Reich type of German university, which reflected and incorporated the dynamic elements of contemporary German life and culture. The emphasis at Johns Hopkins on postgraduate research in taking up the empirical investigation of contemporary issues introduced a new element into American scholarship. Under President Gilman's administration, Johns Hopkins quickly achieved world-wide fame as a postgraduate research institution specializing in the biological, physical, and social sciences.

The academic procedures in German universities did far more, however, than merely suggest the possibility of advanced study of contemporary issues. In the social sciences, there was in German universities the methodological tradition of meticulous fact-gathering, examples of which are the two German historical schools in economics. Moreover, there was also a great concern with the *controlled* growth of society and a consequent dedication to state-inspired social welfarism. And, last of all, there was a certain interest in scientific socialism, the Marxian mutation of the Hegelian tradition. Each of these areas of interest had its effect in America, as one university after another modified its earlier pattern of concentration to include research on the new questions that arose with the growth and changes in the contemporary American society of the late nineteenth century.

This change in university procedures first became apparent when several leading American students were encouraged to go to Germany to complete their education. Most of these young men had previously been instructed in American colleges in the classical traditions of English economics, with its general commitment to explain, if not to justify, the concepts of market price and *laissez faire*. In Germany these students were impressed with the socially conscious aspects of the Bismarckian system of governmental responsibility, and with the application of empirical methods to social data by the leaders of the German historical school of political economy (20, pp. 582 ff.). Their intellectual experience resulted in an attempt, on their return to America, to reorient the study of basic economics. Their aims, they thought, could be accomplished in three ways: greater classroom emphasis on applied social problems instead of concentration on the analysis of economic value, an emphasis on empirical research concerning pressing social problems instead of on abstract economic models, and the organization of a professional association dedicated to the propagation and, if necessary, the defense of their "new economics." This organization, the American Economic Association, came on the scene as a "radical" institution. It was in time subdued; nonetheless its radical origin left an imprint on the discipline that is well worth consideration.

In the classroom the "new economics" prepared scores of students to scrutinize closely the development of new cultural patterns or social alignments. Observers were initially drawn to the "labor problem" because of compassion and, later, by the awakening of a more critical and dispassionate interest in the structure, philosophy, and effect of working-class organizations. In some schools, scholars considered Socialist theories first advocated in nonuniversity circles, examining them in the light of the history of American trade-unions. Their conclusion that American working people were not class conscious led them to develop alternate explanatory frameworks for unionism.

At other schools attention was focused on the effect of the machine process on the individual laborer. His organization into unions was viewed as a protest, expressing profound personal dissatisfactions. The examiners attempted to gain an insight into the psychology of industrial workers. Ultimately, their approach led to a statement of the principles of personnel administration, something certainly far removed from what had originally been the "new economics" of the period.

How the new thinking evolved from its start in humanitarian interest through several important academic approaches to the "labor question" has been discussed. We now examine the development of systematic academic thought relative to the moral approach to the unionism issue, the administrative and structural approach, the social-history approach, and two psychological approaches.

The Approach through Conscious Morality

In the eighties the two professors who stood out most clearly among those who were attempting to interest students in the social structure of workingmen's organizations were William Jewett Tucker (1839–1926), professor of sacred rhetoric at the Andover Theological Seminary from 1880 to 1892, and Richard T. Ely (1854–1943), associate professor of political economy at The Johns Hopkins University from 1881 to 1892 and professor of economics at the University of Wisconsin until 1926.

Tucker's interest in the labor problem grew out of his training in pastoral theology and his conviction that charity as the basis for economic relief was simply not enough.[1] In his opinion, the church had not assumed its proper responsibility toward the working classes; theology had to bring material help to the "vast army of unskilled labor" who, in rejecting charity as a solution to their economic problems, also rejected as callous the traditional answer of the church. Early in his professorship, he turned one of his classes to the examination of working-class organizations and aspirations and to the obstacles in their path. Arley B. Show, 1882 holder of the scholarship in pastoral theology, for example, was directed to spend six weeks investigating the religious convictions and social activities of workingmen in Boston, New Haven, and Pittsburgh. Show's fairly comprehensive report was summarized in the 1884–85 *Andover Seminary Bulletin*. He considered the protective features of trade-unions[2] as well as

[1] For the background of these views, see 51, pp. 62 and 172–73; 1, and 55.
[2] "The purpose of Trades-Unionism, as defined in its platforms, was set forth as *self-protection by combination*. The working-man's creed is this: Capital is organized against us; we must organize against capital. We must unite labor in self-protective movements; must enter into politics, and secure the legislation we need; must somehow hold our own against capital, or be pushed to the wall" (2, pp. 20–21).

certain devices such as strikes and boycotts. Show also analyzed alternatives to the established patterns of industrial relations, and discussed systems of producers' and consumers' co-operation and such concepts as "industrial arbitration and conciliation" and "industrial partnership." There is, unfortunately, little evidence that Show's work had any practical effect.

In his years at Andover, Tucker maintained broad social and religious interests and inspired others to emulate his humanitarian approach. In 1889 he summarized his attitude and the development of his thinking in a course on "The Social Evolution of Labor," subtitled "A Sympathetic Approach to the Study of the Labor Movement through the Proper Historical Perspective."

In addition to his classroom activities, Tucker and four Andover colleagues began publication in 1884 of the *Andover Review,* a monthly periodical devoted to "progressive orthodoxy." Intended as the voice of those "who believe that the safety of the Church and its power lie in the resolute advancement of Christian doctrine and its broadest application to the problems of society," the *Review,* for the nine and one-half years of its existence, spoke for those whose interest in the labor movement was colored by an interest in Christian reform and Christian socialism.

Tucker induced the seminary to establish in 1891 the Andover [settlement] House (later called "South End") in Boston, where the theological students were offered an opportunity to live and work with the laboring classes. Modeled directly after London's Toynbee Hall,[3] Andover House was considered a great success and came to typify a religio-intellectual attitude toward working people.

Throughout Tucker's association with the seminary, however, he labored under a cloud of suspected heresy. He and his editor colleagues were thought by some of the sects sponsoring the seminary to be far too radical. Thus in 1886 the Board of

---

[3] A settlement house established in East London by the friends of Arnold Toynbee (1852–83), where university men could live and mingle with poverty-ridden citizens. The intention was twofold: to show the better classes the mores of the poor, and to provide the poor with cultural and educational opportunities.

Visitors, representing the opposition, filed formal charges of religious disaffection, alleging that the five men were no longer actively subscribing to the Andover Creed, which was a contractual condition necessary for continued appointment. Four of the five, including Tucker, were ultimately acquitted by a tie vote among the trustees. (The fifth, although initially found guilty, was acquitted in 1892 after a retrial ordered by the Massachusetts Supreme Court.) Notwithstanding this limited vindication, bitterness toward Tucker and his confreres, exemplified by the legal proceedings, spelled the eventual end of his work at Andover. Shortly after the final resolution of the case, Tucker resigned his position at the seminary and accepted the presidency of Dartmouth College. With his departure from Andover the seminary's interest in the labor question waned. Almost immediately the faculty became immersed in administrative problems, a natural consequence of the years of litigation (51, pp. 233-47). Even the *Review* ceased publication in 1893.

The Andover experience is interesting because it shows how the conscience of intellectual Protestants was sharpened, much as the pronouncement of *Rerum Novarum* by Leo XIII gave rise to a similar response in the Roman Catholic Church.

Richard T. Ely was not the first secular scholar to examine the labor movement,[4] but it was his appointment at The Johns Hopkins University in 1881 that marked the beginning of the first systematic academic consideration of trade-unionism in America. Trained at Heidelberg under Karl Knies (1821-98), who was the cofounder with Roscher and Hildebrand of the elder German historical school of economics, Ely was particularly interested in studying "man in society in terms of its historical growth." In an important sense, Ely's dedication to this goal preceded his interlude of study in Germany, for his family tradition included

---

[4] Earlier, less empirical courses in the social sciences were offered at Williams in 1865 by Perry, at Pennsylvania in 1868 by the Rev. Mr. Thompson, at Yale in 1872 by Sumner, at Missouri in 1876 by Laws, and at Columbia in 1878 by Mayo Smith (cf. 22, p. 12).

an interest like W. J. Tucker's in doing something for the workingman (cf. **28**, p. 95). In Germany Ely witnessed the beginning of the Bismarckian social reforms. Visibly impressed with the meaning of state responsibility, within two years after coming to Johns Hopkins he wrote of his admiration for the German achievements (**27**, pp. 216 ff.). An experience that also had its effect on his thinking was a year of unemployment immediately after his return to America (**32**).

The social environment of Baltimore in the eighties, influenced by the progressivism of James Cardinal Gibbons (1834–1921), who played a significant role in the events that led to the papal enunciation of the encyclical *Rerum Novarum,* and by the spirit of scientific investigation at The Johns Hopkins University under Daniel Coit Gilman, was such as to reinforce Ely's personal interests. Moreover, the vague definition of Ely's academic duties permitted him to continue the study of socialism and the labor movement initiated in Germany. After publishing an essay in political theory, *Recent American Socialism* (**31**), in 1884 he undertook to assemble all the available empirical data on American trade-unions and co-operatives. These, combined with a summary of his own research on the political aspects of the Socialist movement, were presented in 1886 as *The Labor Movement in America* (**30**), and became a credo for American Christian Socialists (see below, Chap. 3). Ely's discussions of the elements of faith and political theory are more impressive than his knowledge of trade-union policies or structure, a weakness which Ely acknowledged, but the book was the initial academic work on trade-unionism in America.

The type of work that absorbed the interest of Ely and his colleagues attracted to Johns Hopkins many of America's most promising scholars intent on studying "man in society in terms of its historical growth." Among these, Ely numbered as his students young political economists like Edward W. Bemis (1860–1930), who after a brief academic career became an expert on municipally owned monopolies; John R. Commons (1862–1945), whom we will discuss later; Edward A. Ross (1866–1951), later a professor of sociology at Wisconsin and an advocate of legal restrictions to free immigration; Albert Shaw (1857-1947), educator and editor who established the *American Review of Reviews* and wrote extensively on American governmental problems; and Amos G. Warner (1861-1900), interested in organized charity work, who later became professor of applied economics at Stanford University; as well as such future political scientists as Woodrow Wilson and John H. Finley (1863-1940), who became in turn the editor of *Harper's Weekly,* a professor at Princeton, the president of City College of New York and of the University of the State of New York, and the editor of the *New York Times.*

Ely encouraged some of these men to make careful analyses of producers' co-operation—to his mind a major aspect of the labor question. Their essays, no doubt influenced by the explicit endorsement of producers' co-operation in the preamble to the constitution of the Knights of Labor, resulted in a series of monographs, of which three appeared in the earliest publications of the American Economic Association (49, 14, and 53). Ely rather proudly related that the demand for them did much to make the Association solvent in its early years (28, p. 106). These essays, with three others, were brought together in 1888 into a single volume, significant as the first effort to establish a program of trade-union and labor research in America on the university level (29). In it Ely added his own introduction, emphasizing the necessity for the profession to form the habit of relying on observation. He attacked "the undue ascendancy of deduction in [the] social sciences," and the overweening conceit of the traditional economists, "who, feeling that they have nothing to learn . . . become mere advocates."

Another of Ely's projects of this period shows the moral side of his interest in the labor movement. In a desire to increase interest in the field of economics, he and J. B. Clark, E. J. James, S. N. Patten, and E. R. A. Seligman [5] organized the American

[5] Clark (1847-1938) was best known for his *Philosophy of Wealth* and his contribution to the principles of marginal analysis; James (1855-1925) taught at

Economic Association in 1885, with Ely as the first secretary. The Association, as its founders envisioned, exercised a restraining influence on the contemporary doctrine of *laissez faire* by favoring greater state intervention. The subsequent history of the organization reveals the partial success of their effort to give a consciously moral and socially comprehensive meaning to the economic science. However, it must be noted that by 1894 the Association, considered radical at first, had made its peace with all but the most intransigent of the old stalwarts.

Ely's tenure at Johns Hopkins came to an abrupt end in 1892, when, dissatisfied with the promotional opportunities, he resigned to accept a chair at the University of Wisconsin. In his new position he directed the School of Economics, Political Science, and History and went to work to develop quickly a well-rounded curriculum.[6] His academic achievements and the recognition accorded his books on socialism and labor gave him considerable stature in Madison as an impressive addition to the university faculty and to the community as well (43). Nevertheless, in the summer of 1894 the maverick State Superintendent of Public Instruction, Oliver E. Wells, an *ex officio* member of the University Board of Regents, launched a violent attack on Ely's character and work and demanded his dismissal. Citing the emotionalism of *The Labor Movement in America* as an example of the type of teaching that not only undermined the faith of students in American institutions, but also turned them to socialism, the

---

the University of Pennsylvania and was later president of Northwestern University and the University of Illinois; Patten (1852–1922) was an ardent protectionist but otherwise a fairly conventional follower of marginal-utility economics; Seligman (1861–1939) was the scion of a wealthy banking family, whose catholic interests ranged from taxation to labor legislation and the history of economic thought.

[6] In 1892–93, for example, Ely lectured in a course, Economics 4, "Socialism," which was officially listed as a "historical account—its origin followed by a criticism of its nature, strength and weakness." The following year, 1893–94, Economics 4, taught by two instructors, was retitled "Practical Economic Questions: Socialism, Communism, Cooperation Profit Sharing, Labor Organizations, Factory Legislation, and Similar Topics." Phillip W. Ayres of Cincinnati gave a special lecture course on the "Labor Problems of the Poor in Great Cities."

gateway to anarchism, Wells charged: "Professor Ely is a socialist who teaches largely by inference and indirection. He either lacks the courage of his conviction or more probably deludes himself into the belief that he is a friendly judge and not an advocate. . . . Under . . . [his] tuition, respect for the orderly institutions which young men and women bring from quiet homes is insidiously undermined."

The regents, who were quite liberal, appointed a committee that held hearings and accepted depositions on Ely's character. Ely's associates and former students immediately rallied to his defense, and Carroll D. Wright, the United States Commissioner of Labor, wrote: "His influence upon the workingmen has been the influence of the pulpit. . . . I know from my personal knowledge that Dr. Ely's views would lead men away from strikes, away from violence, and to adopt a better mode of settling their difficulties." His list of supporters included such names as David Kinley (later president of the University of Illinois), Frederick Jackson Turner, E. A. Ross, Albion W. Small, and H. C. Adams (21, I, 508 ff.). Eventually, the regents exonerated him and concluded their report with the now famous Wisconsin Declaration on academic freedom.[7] The attack on Ely—one of several made in the period on "liberal" secular academicians [8]— served not only to strengthen Ely's academic position but to publicize the *moral* base of his views on labor.

Ely ultimately brought two former Johns Hopkins students, John R. Commons and Edward Alsworth Ross, to join him on the Wisconsin faculty. With his approval, Commons organized a

[7] ". . . In all lines of academic investigation it is of the utmost importance that the investigator should be absolutely free to follow the indications of the truth wherever they may lead. Whatever may be the limitations which trammel inquiry elsewhere we believe the great State University of Wisconsin should ever encourage that continual and fearless sifting and winnowing by which the truth can be found."

[8] Other notable cases involving academic freedom include those of E. Benjamin Andrews, president of Brown University, E. W. Bemis of the University of Chicago, and E. A. Ross of Stanford University (the latter two both Ely-trained academicians). See 24, p. 240; 23, pp. 368–89; and 36, pp. 420 ff.

research and teaching program which eventually resulted in the now famous "Wisconsin historical approach," but Ely himself did not participate actively in this program, and its development will be discussed in another section of this chapter.

During this period Ely became interested in land economics and, except for a recurrent interest in protective labor legislation, abandoned his research work in the general topic of trade-unionism. After World War I, Ely and Commons went their separate intellectual ways, and by the time of his retirement from Wisconsin in 1926 Ely was no longer part of the labor-research team. He died in 1943.

The "moral approach" that Ely had developed into a school of thought [9] was eventually replaced at Wisconsin by Commons' "historical approach," which now appears to have had far more recognition. But it would be a mistake to minimize the contributions of men like Tucker and Ely. Working in a climate actively hostile to the notion of unionism, they not only founded the moral school but paved the way for a study of labor problems from other points of view. The moral basis of their arguments was one that could be appreciated by men of good faith everywhere, and their inspiration, as well as their rallying of public support, made much of the later research possible.

The Administrative and Structural Approach

At Johns Hopkins interest in trade-unionism lagged for about a decade after Ely's departure. Except for some discussion of the Webbs' *Industrial Democracy* in the late spring of 1898, when Jacob Hollander reviewed the book for the Economic Seminary, there appears to have been no systematic examination of the trade-union movement and its implications for labor until 1902, when E. Dana Durand, later professor at the University of Minnesota and tariff expert, addressed the Economics Seminary on "Arbitration in the United States." Durand was one of the two men

[9] Ely's work is discussed in Chap. 3, pp. 49–55.

in charge of labor research for the United States Industrial Commission.[10] His visit and his intimate knowledge of unexplored aspects of the labor field possibly stimulated a latent interest. In any event, in the following fall the Department of Political Economy [11] adopted the subject of the methods and stratagems of unions as the primary area for specialized research.

The leaders in this renaissance at Johns Hopkins were Jacob Hollander (1871–1940), associate professor of political economy, who was to serve as umpire in the Maryland and Upper Potomac coal fields and as impartial chairman of the board of referees of the Cleveland garment industry, and George Ernest Barnett [12] (1873–1938), associate professor of political economy and later professor of statistics, both rigorous students of traditional economic theory. The studies which they themselves completed, as well as those studies supervised by them, were exhaustive and objective, but did not reveal any explicit interest in social philosophy (42). In this regard these two men differed from Ely and Commons, whose works on the American labor movement had their intellectual origins in the social and political movements of western Europe. Hollander, in the usual academic tradition, wrote of the necessity for impersonal scientific analysis that emphasized the close examination of extensive data. He felt that the influence of the German historical school, "emphasizing microscopics," but not (according to him) the integration of the material concerned, had left an undesirable imprint on economic research in America.

Bearing in mind the absolute importance of trade unionism in American industrial life, on the one hand, and the keen popular interest in its nature and activities, on the other hand, it is astonishing that no detailed description of American trade unionism and no adequate analysis of its operations have been forthcoming. . . . Nowhere has there been any comprehensive study of the history, structure, and functions of trade unionism as an actual part of the contem-

[10] See pp. 272, 276, 277–78.
[11] The Department of Political Economy was separated from those of history and political science in 1901.
[12] Barnett's work in the theory of trade-unionism is discussed in Chapter 6.

porary economic organism. Such an investigation as Sidney and Beatrice Webb have brilliantly achieved of trade unions in Great Britain finds no counterpart in the United States . . . [37, pp. 3–4].

In brief, Hollander and Barnett put the stress on methodology, rather than on ideology. Hollander's view was succinctly stated.

If the economic investigator—and, in particular, the economic investigator in the United States,—is to attain his highest scientific possibility, he must realize more fully than heretofore that there is no short-cut to economic knowledge. He must adopt a mode analogous to that employed by the physical scientist and described as extensive or experimental, rather than intensive or institutional. *He must derive his subject-matter not from history alone, nor from the present experience of restricted localities; but he must observe and collate the phenomena under consideration from an area practically co-extensive with their manifestations; he must interpret each group of facts in the light of conditions prevailing in the particular place; and he must test the uniformities revealed by reference, as tentative hypotheses, to conditions in still other localities* [37, p. 5; italics added].

Hollander also suggested that extensive research should, of necessity, be conducted on a group basis (cf. 54, pp. xxiii–xxxii), and he carefully elaborated a workable plan of organization.

. . . The successful conduct of economic investigation along empirical and extensive lines must involve the use of a group of workers, instead of the individual student, as the unit of research. Until such time as the number of independent investigators has greatly multiplied or the activity of appropriate government agencies has greatly enlarged, the well-equipped department of political economy in the American university may be expected to be the prime factor in economic research. Such an economic laboratory or seminary will include not only a directing and teaching staff and a body of students actually in residence, but affiliated workers in the field and associated beneficiaries of subventions desirous of operating from an established base. A particular body of contemporary economic phenomena will be selected for collective, rather than coöperative investigation; and specific aspects thereof will be assigned to individual workers for research in accordance with an organic plan. In regard to books and documents, the investigator must be in possession, in addition to ordinary library apparatus, of all primary documentary material relevant to his inquiry, whether it be as ephemeral as municipal reports and trade-union journals, or as unobtainable by formal request as trade agreements and corporation records. Finally, each investigator must be in command of funds sufficient to enable him to visit, and upon certain occasions, temporarily to reside in representative localities for the purpose of gathering additional evidence . . . [37, pp. 5–6].

This plan was carried into effect in the Economic Seminary jointly conducted by Hollander and Barnett. Considerable attention was given to standardizing reports and, in the course of the following years, to the reassignment of topics. The reports were delivered to the seminary as formal papers, précis of many of which were published (1903–10) in *The Johns Hopkins University Circular*.[13]

The seminary undertook an examination of trade-unionism in the United States, as we have already noted, in 1902. By the end of that academic year their research was summarized in the *Trial Bibliography of Trade-Union Publications,* which was initially published in 1904 and then expanded in 1907 (12, cf. 48). This publication, an example of the seminary's emphasis on methodology, was the first general contribution of the "second Johns Hopkins School" (so called to distinguish it from the earlier group under Ely).

A few years later the two professors edited a series of essays that had originally been presented to the seminary as papers, and Hollander wrote an introduction for them (37). These "Studies," even more than the *Trial Bibliography,* attracted attention to

---

[13] ". . . Hollander did not, in my time, supervise any labor dissertations, but he was a keen critic in the Seminary.

"The degree of 'supervision' by Barnett depended on the student. Barnett was there every day, practically all day, ready to give advice or to help with establishing contacts. I do not recall his 'reading over' proposed chapters in advance; the Seminary took care of proposed chapters. But Barnett did edit the brief papers that we published every year in 'The Johns Hopkins University Circular' in a report of the Economic Seminary for the academic year. . . . I have a distinct recollection that Barnett was a ruthless eliminator of 'dress up' style; 'printing costs money,' he would say" (42).

the meticulous character of the work being done on the structure and operation of trade-unions in America.

With the passage of time, the responsibility for supervision of research on trade-unions passed almost entirely to Barnett, who encouraged his students to submit their studies as doctoral dissertations. The approved dissertations were generally published in the "Johns Hopkins University Studies in Historical and Political Science" (42).

Barnett himself prepared and in 1909 published under the auspices of the American Economic Association a rigorous analysis of the International Typographical Union (10) that has come to be recognized as the classic contribution in the field of union administration. In addition, he wrote two extremely important essays, "National and District Systems of Collective Bargaining in the United States" (8) and "The Dominance of the National Union in American Labor Organization" (5), published in the *Quarterly Journal of Economics* in 1912 and 1913. A third study incorporated virtually all of his own research on trade-union administration and problems as well as the genesis of his and Leo Wolman's work on the measurement of union membership. This was prepared in 1914-15 by Barnett, Wolman, and others on the research staff of the United States Commission on Industrial Relations, but never published (7).[14] These three studies as well as two others—*Mediation, Investigation and Arbitration in Labor Disputes* (13) and *Chapters on Machinery and Labor* (4)—comprise the bulk, but not the entirety, of Barnett's own published work. Three further essays by Barnett, on the quantitative changes in trade-union membership, were published: "Growth of Labor Organization in the United States 1897-1914" (6), "The Present Position of American Trade Unionism" (9), and a note appended to his presidential address to the American Economic Association (3, pp. 9-15). All these works are discussed in Chapter 6, along with several papers given at AEA conventions.

During the twenties Barnett's personal interests reverted increasingly to the areas of banking and statistics and less toward la-

[14] Microfilm copies of all the papers may be purchased from National Archives and Records Service, General Services Administration, Washington 25, D.C.

bor union research. His dissertation, "State Banks since the National Bank Act," was published in the "Johns Hopkins University Studies in Historical and Political Science" (11). He continued his measurements of trade-union membership, however, and chose to speak on "American Trade Unionism and Social Insurance" in his presidential address before the American Economic Association in 1932 (3). The pessimism that pervaded that speech was a portent of later events.[15] Barnett was commissioned by the Carnegie Corporation to investigate the various arbitration systems in Australia, but returned to the United States almost as soon as he reached that country. He suffered extreme concern over a possible physical breakdown, and committed suicide on July 17, 1938.

Beloved by his students, of whom David A. McCabe and Leo Wolman are perhaps the best known, Barnett was in a major sense the master of a new, research-oriented school. Conscious of the necessity for precise methodology, he published comparatively little, but he was responsible for the initiation of much of the academic research on the structure and administration of trade-unions in America. His own view of unions, as will be shown in Chapter 6, was that at that time they represented the most economic means to attain better wages, hours, and working conditions. His preference for careful topical examinations is partly explained by his training in economic analysis, but may also have been partly due to an explicit agreement with Commons at Wisconsin.[16] Lloyd Ulman's *The Rise of the National Trade Union* (52) gives a synthesis of the work done on unions under Barnett and Hollander at Johns Hopkins, and is in many ways the *summa* Barnett never undertook.

As a "school" of labor union research, Johns Hopkins declined

[15] He had presented an unnecessarily glowing prediction of trade-union growths in 1921 (cf. 9).

[16] "The reason for concentration on topical studies, as contrasted with historical, was, I was told, a desire to avoid duplication of the work being done at Wisconsin on the historical side; indeed, there was an understanding, I believe, between Commons and the Hopkins pair [Hollander and Barnett] on this general division of labor" (42).

with Barnett's waning interest in the subject, but the university's development under Barnett and Hollander had indicated a new way for the expert academic economist to approach the question of trade-unionism. This new approach was encouraged by the contact of the university specialists with the McKinley [U.S.] Industrial Commission. The Johns Hopkins "Studies" were influenced by ideas gathered in this contact and ultimately matured in *academia*. And though these early "Studies" were at least equaled in significance by subsequent research, such as William Haber's *Industrial Relations in the Building Industry* (34) and Sumner Slichter's *Union Policies and Industrial Management* (50), it is to Barnett and Hollander that recognition must be given for their development of an important point of view.

The Social-History Approach

With the appointment of John Rogers Commons (1862–1945) to the Wisconsin faculty for the 1904–5 academic year, the socio-historical environment of the American labor movement received its first emphasis. The selection of Commons by Ely was probably one of the most successful gambles in recent academic history, since Commons up to that time lacked a continuous record of professional achievement. Whether in a professional meeting, a public gathering, or a routine interview with a college president, he had somehow managed to mishandle almost every opportunity.

Commons was a native of the Middle West and had been trained as a printer. He attended college at Oberlin, where he not only thwarted his mother's plans by refusing to become a minister but also became an ardent single taxer. Upon completion of his studies there, which took six years because of his ill health, he was given a loan by two of the college's trustees to continue his work under Ely at Johns Hopkins (15, p. 41). After failing to get a fellowship in 1890, he left Baltimore without a doctorate to replace Princeton-bound Woodrow Wilson at Wesleyan University. Within a year he was notified by President Raymond of

Wesleyan of his failure as a teacher, and moved on to Oberlin. Two semesters later he left to go to Indiana University as professor of economics and social science.

While at Indiana, Commons joined Ely in reorganizing the American Institute of Christian Sociology, a version of the European Christian Socialist movement (17). Ultimately, as he later claimed, he "became suspicious of Love as the basis of social reform" and even came to have doubts regarding Christian socialism and Christian sociology. As a result, the Institute's membership split and eventually dissolved. Nonetheless, Commons' relationship with Ely remained friendly.

The heterodoxy of Commons' views seems to have gotten him into some trouble (cf. 26 and 36, p. 421), and when in 1895 he carelessly mentioned to President Swain of Indiana that he had received an offer of a chair at Syracuse University, the inevitable occurred, and he was chagrined to be told to accept it. In a burst of confidence he told his new superior, Chancellor Day, that he was "a socialist, a single taxer, a free silverite, a greenbacker, a municipal-ownerist and a member of the Congregational Church." Day merely replied, however, that these intellectual affiliations meant nothing as long as Commons was not an "*obnoxious* socialist" (15, p. 53; italics added).

Nevertheless, after four years Commons' chair at Syracuse was abolished in 1899 when, rather unwisely, he chose to support publicly a decision by the Roman Catholic mayor to ignore the blue law against Sunday baseball. As a result, his name had become a liability in university fund collections. This led Commons, once again out of a job, to the wry conclusion that "it was not religion, it was capitalism, that governed Christian colleges" (15, p. 58).

Commons, now out of the academic environment, went to work for George H. Shibley, a money reformer. He was hired to construct a weekly wholesale price index, the first of its type. This index appeared initially in July, 1900, but came to a sudden end later that year during the Bryan-McKinley campaign, when it behaved in a significantly pro-Republican fashion. Since Shibley was economic advisor to the Democratic National Committee and a strong Bryan man, it is not surprising that Commons once again found himself unemployed.

At this point one of Commons' former Oberlin students, E. Dana Durand, secretary of the U.S. Industrial Commission, offered him the job of finishing a report on immigration.[17] It was this study that eventually led Commons to the fields of labor unionism and public administration. After completing this job, he stayed on to help write the final report of the commission and to help T. W. Phillips, sponsor of the commission, to write a bitter dissenting report on trusts.

After the commission's work was completed, Commons was engaged by William English Walling (1877–1936), the Socialist grandson of William English, to edit a one-volume summary of their findings. For technical reasons, however, the plan had to be abandoned, and Commons, though compensated in full by Walling, again sought a new job.

This turned out to be a position with Ralph Easley of the National Civic Federation, where he shifted into a study of labor conciliation. Commons was convinced, during this period, that the federation (then being damned by Socialists) was not stacked against labor. He recounts that the federation aided in the settlement of many streetcar strikes to the obvious advantage of the workers (**15**, pp. 84–86).

It was during the 1901 steel strike that Commons' experience led him to one of the conclusions destined to play a major role in his later work. President T. J. Shaffer of the Amalgamated Association of Iron, Steel, and Tin Workers had, Commons felt, been precipitated by his own oratory into the strike. Shaffer's antagonism to the National Civic Federation, which intervened to help settle the dispute, merely ensured the union's failure. "It was here," Commons noted much later, "that I first learned to distrust the 'intellectuals' as leaders in labor movements" (**15**, p. 87).

Commons remained with Easley until the end of 1903, when

[17] See below, pp. 272, 274.

he asked to be released to finish a project for Carroll D. Wright on the restriction of output by capital and labor. He included in this research Ethelbert Stewart's notable study on the working rules in the Illinois bituminous coal industry. This, Commons notes, was the first detailed analysis of the common rule ("working rule" is a term coined by Commons) in America (**15**, pp. 71 and 93).

In 1904 Ely established the American Bureau of Industrial Research with the aid of John Bates Clark and Albert Shaw. He brought Commons to Wisconsin in that year to help supervise the work of the bureau and to assist in the preparation of an exhaustive history of the American labor movement. Commons was given several assistants, among them John B. Andrews and Helen Sumner, both well-trained economists. Ulrich B. Phillips was hired to work on a history of the evolution of southern agricultural society. Andrews and Miss Sumner set out to locate and classify all existing materials on the American labor movement (**19**, I, 24–25). In this search they unearthed a great many documents and records of long-forgotten trials, as well as evidence of an attempt at a national labor federation in 1834–35. So comprehensive was their research that it exhausted most of the $30,000 that Ely had collected for the project, and additional funds were obtained under a grant from the Carnegie Institution for the actual writing of the labor history. About a quarter of the collected documents were published in a ten-volume series, *Documentary History of American Industrial Society* (**19**).

Several interpretive essays by Commons made up the core of this series. The most notable of these essays were on the history of the American shoemakers (**19**, III, 18–58), the role of idealism in American social history (**19**, VII, 19–44), and the effect of business cycles on the growth of the trade-union movement (**19**, IX, 19–51). Commons' insights and ideas became the foundation of a new philosophic approach to the subject of trade-unionism and the basis for what was termed the "Wisconsin School."

During 1904, Commons' first year of research, no labor-history course was offered at Wisconsin, though Commons and Ely had outlined an alternating two-year sequence of courses that fitted in with their research program. Instead, Commons lectured on "Race Elements in American Industry," using the material he had collected during the earliest phase of his employment with the U.S. Industrial Commission (cf. **16**). The following year, however, he was able to present his initial labor-history findings in a course entitled "History and Industrial Organization Prior to the Civil War." In 1906–7 the course consisted of a summary of succeeding research—"Labor and Industrial History: The Development of the Modern Labor Movement Including Political, Legislative, and Judicial Changes." Commons also taught in the field of comparative labor legislation and supervised the research of selected graduate students.

His approach to the study of labor unionism and industrial relations had many sides. Fundamentally, however, he applied the methods of the social historian to problems of political administration. His keen discernment and appraisal of relevant facts and his instinct for workable administrative arrangements found expression in his early years at Wisconsin not only in scholarly analysis, but also in his organization of and participation in the American Association for Labor Legislation, the Pittsburgh Survey, and, ultimately, the Wisconsin Industrial Commission. These were the "practical" aspects of the Wisconsin approach, which Commons insisted must transcend purely academic activity.

Commons' work with the Wisconsin Industrial Commission began in the classroom. With a student assistant, Francis H. Bird, he organized his 1910 class "into a miniature world-wide council of capital and labor for the investigation of labor administration in all countries, and then . . . [incorporated] what fitted the Wisconsin situation into [a quasi-judicial] industrial commission [factory] law for the State." Afterwards he worked with Charles McCarthy, director of the Wisconsin Legislative Reference Library, to frame the law in constitutional terms. By shifting the emphasis from "reasonableness of standards" to the prescription of conditions consistent with "the highest degree of safety, health, well-being of employees . . . that the nature of the industry or employment would reasonably permit," the pair were able to formulate a new principle of legal regulation that ultimately came to be adopted throughout the United States. Commons' truly pragmatic mind is revealed in his frequently expressed maxim, "reasonableness is idealism limited by practicality" (cf. 15, pp. 153–65). His part in the establishment and initial supervision of the commission illustrates vividly the operative side of Commons' work (41, Introduction and pp. 27 ff.).

In 1911 he accepted a two-year appointment as one of the first commissioners of the Wisconsin Industrial Commission. During this term, however, he continued his university association and supervised work on the analytical history of organized labor in the United States that he and Ely had originally planned. Once again he turned to his superior students and gave each a period in labor history to review. To David J. Saposs went the assignment of summarizing events before 1827; to Helen Sumner, the period of aggressive Jacksonianism, 1827–33; to Edward B. Mittleman, the period of the Jacksonian "depression," 1833–35; and to Henry Hoagland, the pre–Civil War period, 1840–60. John B. Andrews dealt with the Civil War and the decade immediately following, 1860–76, and Selig Perlman with the period of 1876–96. The completed study, published in 1918 after a lengthy editorial process, was entitled *History of Labour in the United States* (18); it is discussed in Chapter 8.

Commons, although stimulating and intellectually generous to able students, was not a good classroom lecturer. In 1922 he turned over his undergraduate teaching program to Selig Perlman. Perlman, Elizabeth Brandeis Raushenbush, Don D. Lescohier, and Philip Taft continued the work on the analytical history of the labor movement, and in 1935 published the final volumes (41 and 47).

Two Psychological Approaches

The work of two men who investigated trade-union philosophy from a psychological point of view had, for a brief interval, certain of the characteristics of a unique approach. These investigations were the independent but simultaneous research and teaching of Robert Franklin Hoxie (1868–1916) at the University of Chicago and Carleton Hubbell Parker (1878–1918) at Berkeley and Seattle. Each was interested in examining the American labor force and movement from a psychological point of view. Although both died young and neither wrote extensively, the theoretical work of each had tremendous influence. Hoxie was primarily interested in mass psychology and contributed a generally useful taxonomy of union types, while Parker concentrated on instinctive individual psychology.

Hoxie, born in Edmeston, New York, was educated at Cornell University and the University of Chicago. Though he was influenced by J. Laurence Laughlin (1850–1933), a traditionalist in matters of political economy, and Frank Fetter (1863–1949), who wrote on the psychological determinants of value, it was Thorstein Veblen and the pioneer American sociologist, Charles Horton Cooley (1864–1929), who predominated in shaping his intellectual development (33; 35). After teaching for short periods at Cornell College (Iowa), Washington University, and Washington and Lee University, Hoxie accepted an appointment as instructor in economics at Cornell University. He remained at Ithaca from 1903 to 1906, when he left to accept a similar appointment at the University of Chicago.

In Ithaca he greatly expanded the economics curriculum in the areas of trade-unionism and socialism. Before his arrival these fields had been cursorily treated in a single problem course, "The Modern Regime." Others at Cornell had, of course, evinced earlier interest in labor problems. H. C. Adams, for example, lectured on job rights as early as 1886, and in 1900 Professor Jeremiah Jenks, speaking for the university, formally thanked Samuel Gompers for an excellent series of four lectures on the American labor movement. In 1904–5 Hoxie offered a course of lectures on the "Problems of Organized Labor" in which he discussed "conditions of employment, methods of industrial bargaining and remuneration, the economic claims and legal status of labor," considered "mainly in connection with the growth, policies, and activities of labor unions." Given the same year was "Modern Socialism," a course intended to yield not only a summary knowledge of the theories involved, but also to stress the environmental causes of the "rapid growth of socialistic parties and upon the practical limit of government interference in production and distribution." The next year he went still further by adding "Labor Problems: American Labor Conditions," described in the catalogue as "an elementary descriptive course . . . the unemployed, wages, hours and conditions of employment in mining, manufacturing, transportation and trade; state protection of labor legislation by means of factory legislation and inspection and other restrictions on freedom of competition; plans and projects for the betterment of labor conditions by means of voluntary associations, workman's insurance, profit sharing, cooperation."

In 1906 Hoxie left Cornell for the University of Chicago, where his reputation was subsequently established. There he lectured with others on socialism and trade-unionism, in 1908, for example, covering the "modern" Socialist theorists, among them Kautsky and Bernstein. His course, "Trades-Unions," notes for which provided the nucleus of his posthumous volume, *Trade Unionism in the United States* (40), was offered, along with a related course, "The Labor Movement," taught by John Cummings (1868–1936), statistician and economist later associated with the Federal Reserve Board and United States Office of Education. (The 1908 Chicago catalogue also listed "Legal Status of Labor," given regularly by Sophonisba Porter Breckenridge although omitted that year.)

Hoxie's contributions as an investigator and as a teacher cannot be considered apart from Veblen's influence. He got from Veblen a passion for scientific research and a respect for the effect of environmental differences (40, p. 16) that markedly shaped his own work. It might be added that Veblen acknowledged an intellectual debt to Hoxie as well (25, p. 354).

It is also significant that Hoxie's posthumous work stressed the methodological problems of teaching. In two appendices, Hoxie covered fully not only his criticisms of historical exposition (which he said usually served to cloud the issue), but also his ideas on the application of scientific method to research in the social sciences (40, pp. 376–409). He went on to illustrate what he meant, explaining in detail how he had organized material on trade-unions for his own students and how he guided them in their research. In addition, several chapters of this general treatise included comprehensive suggested reading lists. So thoroughly was he conscious of questions of scholarly procedure that this interest must be recalled whenever his work is analyzed. It may also explain why his approach to labor problems has continued to be particularly appealing to contemporary scholars interested in developing a methodology for research in the social sciences.

Before his untimely death, Hoxie completed several important research projects. Most famous was the investigation of union opposition to scientific management that he undertook for the U.S. Commission on Industrial Relations (38).[18] He was, in addition, associate editor of the *Journal of Political Economy,* for which he wrote several articles on the psychological bases of socialism and the American Socialist movement. Shortly after his death the *Journal* published a "tentative bibliography" of his published works (39). He was succeeded in his labor courses at Chicago by Walton H. Hamilton (b. 1881), who left Chicago almost immediately, Harry A. Millis (1873–1948), later a member of the National Labor Board and chairman of the National Labor Relations Board, and Paul Douglas (b. 1892), professor at Chicago and subsequently U.S. senator from Illinois. Only Hamilton, however, continued Hoxie's extensive efforts to relate the disciplines of economics and psychology.

Carleton Parker was born March 31, 1878. Although he was awarded a California baccalaureate degree in 1904, it was not until 1909–10, when he went to Harvard to get a master's degree,

[18] This study was termed "a faulty investigation" by Charles W. Mixter (of Yale's Sheffield Scientific School) in an *American Economic Review* appraisal. Mixter criticized Hoxie's allegations that scientific management was far less scientific than it purported to be, and that collective bargaining was committed to economic leveling, while scientific management tended to emphasize differences in economic rewards (44).

that he became interested in academic research problems. While there he prepared an essay, "The Decline of Trade Union Membership" (46), which was his first formal work in the field. After two semesters he left Harvard to study in Germany (Leipzig, Berlin, and Heidelberg), and was awarded a doctorate at Heidelberg on December 5, 1912. By the rules of that university he was obliged to present his dissertation, "The Labor Policy of the American Trusts," by the end of a year. The study was not completed until the outbreak of war in 1914, however, and he never submitted it, destroying the existing copies.

In 1913 Parker returned to California as an assistant professor, lecturing on labor problems, a course that had been given earlier (from 1903 to 1909) by Wesley Clair Mitchell. During the following year he took a one-year appointment as executive secretary of the State Immigration Commission of California, and as a result was generally absent from the campus. This job, however, brought him into direct touch with depressed labor conditions and in particular with the Industrial Workers of the World.

During this period he made several special studies for the U.S. Commission on Industrial Relations, including the outline of a program for obtaining industrial peace in Phoenix, Arizona, where several strikes were then in progress. Parker was much impressed with the necessity for determining the psychological element in an understanding of human dissatisfactions on the job and for assessing the causes of such unhappiness. He therefore used his opportunities for firsthand observation to great advantage. The sordid conditions he observed, and his growing interest in the possibility of a relationship between the study of economics and the sciences of human behavior, led him, on his return to Berkeley, to direct the reading of his California seminar to such works as Keller's *Societal Evolution,* Holt's *Freudian Wish,* Veblen's *Instincts of Workmanship,* Wallas' *Great Society,* and G. H. Parker's *Biology and Social Problems.* With these books as a start, he began to fashion a theoretical teaching approach and a general social philosophy.

In the autumn of 1917 he went to the University of Washington at Seattle as head of the Department of Economics and Dean of the College of Commerce. There he gave the departmentally required economics course, "Man and His Economic Life," described as "An analysis of man's original nature, a description of the evolution of his economic environment and a statement of his problems of adjustment in modern life." He also lectured on "Work, The Efficiency and Welfare of Those Engaged in Economic Activity." It is evident that his belief in the importance of examining the psychological basis of society was put into practice as soon as he got control of a curriculum. He even used as his textbooks during the first semester McDougall's *Social Psychology* and Wallas' *Great Society*.

During this year in Seattle he prepared an essay on the IWW for the *Atlantic Monthly* and a paper, "Motives in Economic Life," which he presented to the American Economic Association convention in Philadelphia. These two pieces, plus several others, were collected by his wife and published posthumously as *The Casual Laborer and Other Essays* (45), with a dedication to Thorstein Veblen. In addition, Parker was actively concerned with community labor problems, particularly in the lumber and longshore industries, giving to them considerable time and energy. All these efforts proved too exhausting, and his health broke under the strain. After a short illness, he died of pneumonia on March 17, 1918.

It is evident that he did not succeed in founding a school of theory at California and that his stay in Seattle was far too brief for its inception. Unlike Hoxie, Parker left no direct intellectual heirs, and his written work was at most no more than a set of unrelated essays. Yet his posthumous influence was great. Perhaps this can be explained by the timing of his essays, which appeared during a period of growing popular conviction that the ills of industrial society were not the consequence of economic conditions so much as they were of psychological maladjustment in the factory and society. Others took up this theme of Parker's just as he had taken it from Veblen, and found in it new interpretations. These later writers usually acknowledged Parker's contribution, which explains the attribution to him of intellectual leadership. The work of both Hoxie and Parker was the forerunner of later interest in personnel administration. In brief, then, the two are the precursors of much of the research in industrial human relations carried out by industry and, very recently, by a number of university engineering and industrial relations centers.

References

1. Andover Theological Seminary, *The Andover Case: With an Introductory Historical Statement.* Boston: Stanley & Usher, 1887.

2. *Andover Theological Seminary Bulletin, 1884–85.* [Andover, Mass.: The Seminary Faculty, 1885.]

3. Barnett, George E., "American Trade Unionism and Social Insurance," *American Economic Review,* XXIII (March, 1933), 1–15.

4. ———, *Chapters on Machinery and Labor.* Cambridge, Mass.: Harvard University Press, 1926.

5. ———, "The Dominance of the National Union in American Labor Organization," *Quarterly Journal of Economics,* XXVII (1913), 455–81.

6. ———, "Growth of Labor Organization in the United States 1897–1914," *Quarterly Journal of Economics,* XXX (1916), 780–95.

7. ———, "Joint Agreements." Unpublished research paper of the United States Commission on Industrial Relations, Wisconsin Historical Society Library [n.d.].

8. ———, "National and District Systems of Collective Bargaining in the United States," *Quarterly Journal of Economics,* XXVI (1912), 425–43.

9. ———, "The Present Position of American Trade Unionism," *American Economic Review,* XII (Supplement) (1922), 44–55.

10. ———, *The Printers: A Study in American Trade Unionism.* "Publications of the American Economic Association," Ser. 3, Vol. X (October, 1909).

11. Barnett, George E., *State Banks since the National Bank Act.* "Johns Hopkins University Studies in Historical and Political Science," No. 20. Baltimore: The Johns Hopkins Press, 1902.

12. —— (ed.), *A Trial Bibliography of Trade-Union Publications* (2d ed.). "Johns Hopkins Studies in Historical and Political Science," No. 22. Baltimore: The Johns Hopkins Press, 1907.

13. ——, and McCabe, David A., *Mediation, Investigation and Arbitration in Industrial Disputes.* New York: D. Appleton & Co., 1916.

14. Bemis, Edward W., "Coöperation in New England," *Publications of the American Economic Association,* Ser. 1, I (1886–87), 334–464.

15. Commons, John R., *Myself.* New York: The Macmillan Co., 1934.

16. ——, *Races and Immigrants in America.* New York: The Macmillan Co., 1920.

17. ——, *Social Reform and the Church.* New York: Thomas Y. Crowell Co., 1894.

18. ——, and Associates, *History of Labour in the United States.* 2 vols. New York: The Macmillan Co., 1918.

19. ——, and Others, *Documentary History of American Industrial Society.* 10 vols. Cleveland: The Arthur H. Clark Co., 1910–11.

20. Curti, Merle, *The Growth of American Thought.* New York: Harper & Bros., 1943.

21. ——, and Cartensen, Vernon, *The University of Wisconsin: A History, 1848–1925.* Vol. I. Madison: University of Wisconsin Press, 1949.

22. Dombrowski, James, *The Early Days of Christian Socialism in America.* New York: Columbia University Press, 1936.

23. Donnan, Elizabeth, "A Nineteenth-Century Academic Cause Célèbre," *Bulletin of the American Association of University Professors,* XXXVIII (1952), 368–89.

24. Dorfman, Joseph, *The Economic Mind in American Civilization,* Vol. III, 1865–1918. New York: Viking Press, Inc., 1946–49.

25. ——, *Thorstein Veblen and His America.* New York: Viking Press, Inc., 1934.

26. Dorfman, Joseph, (ed.), "The Seligman Correspondence," *Political Science Quarterly,* LVI (1941), 107–24, 270–86, 392–419, 573–99.

27. Ely, Richard T., *French and German Socialism in Modern Times.* New York: Harper & Bros., 1883.

28. ———, *Ground under Our Feet.* New York: The Macmillan Co., 1938.

29. ———, "Introduction" in *History of Cooperation in the United States.* "Johns Hopkins Studies in Historical and Political Science," No. 6. Baltimore: The Johns Hopkins University, 1888.

30. ———, *The Labor Movement in America.* New York: Thomas Y. Crowell Co., 1886.

31. ———, *Recent American Socialism.* Baltimore: The Johns Hopkins University, 1884.

32. Fine, Sidney (ed.), "The Ely-Labadie Letters," *Michigan History,* XXXVI (1952), 1–32.

33. Goodrich, Carter, "Hoxie, Robert Franklin," in *Encyclopaedia of the Social Sciences,* VII, 524–25.

34. Haber, William, *Industrial Relations in the Building Industry.* Cambridge, Mass.: Harvard University Press, 1930.

35. Hamilton, Walton H., "The Development of Hoxie's Economics," *Journal of Political Economy,* XXIV (1916), 855–83.

36. Hofstadter, Richard, and Metzger, Walter P., *The Development of Academic Freedom in the United States.* New York: Columbia University Press, 1955.

37. Hollander, Jacob H., and Barnett, George E. (eds.), *Studies in American Trade Unionism.* New York: Henry Holt & Co., Inc., 1906.

38. Hoxie, Robert F., *Scientific Management and Labor.* New York: D. Appleton & Co., 1915.

39. [———], "A Tentative Bibliography of Robert F. Hoxie's Published Works," *Journal of Political Economy,* XXIV (1916), 894–96.

40. ———, *Trade Unionism in the United States.* New York: D. Appleton & Co., 1917.

41. Lescohier, Don D., and Brandeis, Elizabeth, *History of Labor in the United States,* Vol. III, *Working Conditions and Labor Legis-*

lation, 1896–1932, with an Introduction by John R. Commons. New York: The Macmillan Co., 1935.

42. McCabe, David A., private communication, Nov. 3, 1952.

43. *Madison* [Wisconsin] *Democrat,* February 15, 1892.

44. Mixter, Charles W., review of Hoxie, *Scientific Management and Labor,* in *American Economic Review,* VI (1916), 373–77.

45. Parker, Carleton H., *The Casual Laborer and Other Essays.* New York: Harcourt, Brace & Howe, 1920.

46. ———, "The Decline of Trade Union Membership," *Quarterly Journal of Economics,* XXIV (1909–10), 564–69.

47. Perlman, Selig, and Taft, Philip, *History of Labor in the United States,* Vol. IV, *Labor Movements, 1896–1932.* New York: The Macmillan Co., 1935.

48. Reynolds, Lloyd G., and Killingsworth, Charles C., *Trade Union Publications.* 3 vols. Baltimore: The Johns Hopkins Press, 1944–45.

49. Shaw, Albert, "Coöperation in a Western City," *Publications of the American Economic Association,* Ser. 1, I (1886–87), 127–228.

50. Slichter, Sumner H., *Union Policies and Industrial Management.* Washington, D.C.: The Brookings Institution, 1941.

51. Tucker, William J., *My Generation: An Autobiographical Interpretation.* Boston: Houghton Mifflin Co., 1919.

52. Ulman, Lloyd, *The Rise of the National Trade Union: The Development and Significance of Its Structure, Governing Institutions, and Economic Policies.* Cambridge, Mass.: Harvard University Press, 1955.

53. Warner, Amos G., "Three Phases of Coöperation in the West," *Publications of the American Economic Association,* Ser. 1, II (1888), 3–119.

54. Webb, Sidney, and Webb, Beatrice, *Industrial Democracy,* 1920 ed. London: Longmans, Green & Co., 1920.

55. Williams, Daniel D., *The Andover Liberals: A Study in American Theology.* New York: Kings Crown Press, 1941.

THREE

Unionism As a Moral Institution

The points in which Christian and Socialistic collectivism are at one are simple and fundamental. As, however, we must proceed carefully in this matter, we may state these points of resemblance under three heads.

(1) Both rise from the deeps of an emotion, the emotion of compassion for misfortune, as such. This is really a very important point. Collectivism is not an intellectual fad, even if erroneous, but a passionate protest and aspiration: it arises as a secret of the heart, a dream of the injured feeling, long before it shapes itself as a definite propaganda at all. The intellectual philosophies ally themselves with success and preach competition, but the human heart allies itself with misfortune and suggests communism.

(2) Both trace the evil state of society to 'covetousness,' the competitive desire to accumulate riches. Thus, both in one case and the other, the mere possession of wealth is in itself an offence against moral order, the absence of it in itself a recommendation and training for the higher life.

(3) Both propose to remedy the evil of competition by a system of 'bearing each other's burdens' in the literal sense, that is to say, of levelling, silencing and reducing one's own chances, for the chance of your weaker brethren. The desirability, they say, of a great or clever man acquiring fame is small compared with the desirability of a weak and broken man acquiring bread. The strong man is a man, and should modify or adapt himself to the hopes of his mates. He that would be first among you, let him be the servant of all.

These are the three fountains of collectivist passion. I have not considered it necessary to enter into elaborate proof of the presence of these three in the Gospels. That the main trend of Jesus' character was compassion for human ills, that he denounced not merely covetousness but riches again and again, and with an almost impatient emphasis, and that he insisted on his followers throwing up personal aims and sharing funds and fortune entirely, these are plain matters of evidence presented again and again, and, in fact, of common admission.

—G. K. Chesterton
"Notebooks," c. 1895 [1]

The philosophy of individualism is well rooted in America. Not only has its association with the Protestant ethic caused it to be identified with the American ideal, but it has been written into the basic law of the country. The pervasive influence of this philosophy was challenged by the industrial revolution, however, when an ever-increasing proportion of the population came under the impersonal influence and control of the factory system. Nonetheless, individualism, based on the rural republicanism of John Taylor and Thomas Jefferson, was only challenged—not abandoned. Man continued to be considered as an individual, rather than merely as a member of an organized economic community. The necessity for reconciling this traditional national philosophy based on conditions permitting *laissez faire* with the obviously inescapable miseries of industrial life thus became increasingly evident (cf. 3).

In England, where attention was first given to the problem, an attempt at reconciliation was made by a company of low-church religious moralists. These leaders, John Malcolm Forbes Ludlow (1821–1911), Frederick Denison Maurice (1805–72), and Charles Kingsley (1819–75), called for upper-class moral responsibility, education for all, encouragement of the producers' cooperative movement, and support of the program of the trade-union junta (2, pp. 290–301). These three men, it should be emphasized, were different from the contemporary utopian So-

[1] Quoted in 13, p. 150.

cialists because, far from being hostile to Christian dogma, they urged greater religious identification and based their reforms on religious precepts. Their movement, described as "Christian socialism," did not prescribe church affiliation, but did recognize the divine injunction regarding the brotherhood of man and the consequent development of mutual obligations.

The American Christian Socialist movement appears to have been more secular. Unlike the English movement, American "social Christianity" as it developed in the last two decades of the century, though not antireligious, had a decidedly atheological emphasis (14). Its leaders moved rapidly from consideration of moral betterment as the preparation for salvation to moral betterment as an aid to greater personal fulfillment in this life. Having made this shift in point of view, they advocated the improvement of society in general rather than the redemption of the individual. In their quest for reform they tended to herald every piecemeal improvement in working conditions and every new factory act as progressive steps toward the kingdom of God. Most characteristic of them was their belief in ethical improvement as the essence of the divine in man, with social reform as a similar manifestation of God in society.

Many small factions made up the American Christian Socialist movement. Some, such as the one associated with the Reverend R. Heber Newton of New York City, were greatly influenced by English Christian socialism, particularly by the writings of Maurice and Kingsley. One, led by the Reverend George D. Herron (1862–1925), a Socialist party member after 1899, was quite radical, eventually approaching "scientific" (Marxian) socialism. The great majority of American Christian Socialists, however, were concerned with the local scene and were in program liberal rather than radical.

Among the leading liberal figures in this general movement were Richard T. Ely, whose activity at The Johns Hopkins University and at the University of Wisconsin we have already noted, and Father John A. Ryan (1869–1945), a Catholic cleric and teacher whose thinking was shaped by papal encyclicals as well as Ely's influence. Both of them believed that the solutions to social and industrial relations might be found in an application of religious ethics, by keeping watch on the moral consequences of union policies. Both saw in the field of industrial relations an opportunity as well as a responsibility for organized churches.

Ely and Father Ryan in their time exerted great influence, but this discussion of their work will emphasize the development rather than the effect of their theories.

The Christian Socialism of Richard Ely

At The Johns Hopkins University Ely's first writings were in the field of socialism. In 1886, however, he published his *Labor Movement in America* (6), which comprised other material as well, and also in 1886 he wrote an introductory chapter for W. E. Barnes's *The Labor Problem* (1). In this piece he argued that producers' co-operativism had been oversold as a cure. He called for greater state control of industrial activity, stating that

glittering generalities will never solve any social problem, and this is a truth that the Church, in particular needs to bear in mind. It is all very well to say, be good, love your neighbor, obey your God, and these things must be repeated often, but they must also become incorporated in our institutions and must become an animating force in the State. . . . Cooperation is a good thing; arbitration is a good thing; profit sharing is a good thing; but let us remember amid all this discussion that every hope of a permanent reform in industrial and social life must be illusory unless it has a firm foundation in a lasting State reformation (1, pp. 14–16).

The Labor Movement in America presented some original historical summaries of the origins of American trade-unions and was popularly recognized for its philosophical outlook. Ely strongly advocated trade-unionism on ethical grounds, although he also expressed a tempered enthusiasm for producers' co-operativism as another remedy for the evils of the wage system. By and large, he was a moderate reformer and advocated gradual socialism rather than the more comprehensive Marxian or violent anarchist forms as a means toward change (see 7).

The first part of *The Labor Movement in America* was devoted to a general, over-all survey of certain early religious and trade-union organizations in America. It was not until the fourth chapter, "The Economic Value of Labor Organizations," that Ely revealed the lines of his own thinking. Here he asserted that workingmen lack the peculiar talents necessary for effective organization and that consequently Adam Smith, although his sympathy for workingmen was readily apparent, erred in thinking that the mere removal of the usual common-law checks on union organization would be advantageous to them. Ely held that the labor market differs from the usual product markets and that the individual laborer with a perishable service to sell becomes, in the absence of positive controls, completely dominated, body and soul, by the modern industrial (wage) system. Ely felt that the only ways to cure this evil were through (1) statutory protective legislation and (2) social encouragement of self-help efforts of workingmen's labor organizations. Actually, he favored the latter as more practicable, since adequate legislation was difficult to put through.

Unions, he noted, had definite economic patterns and were not at all the irresponsible or uninformed agencies which their detractors represented them to be. He observed, for instance, the tendency of American labor organizations to preserve wage rates in times of unemployment rather than to insist on the maintenance of certain aggregate hours of employment opportunity. The need to retake lost ground with the eventual return of prosperity was in this way obviated. He also pointed out that American unions, during prosperous times, occasionally deferred demands for wage increases in favor of more far-reaching concessions that would improve the security of their jobs. More, he noted that laboring men in their own associations soon developed responsibility in economic matters that greatly influenced their attitudes toward their jobs and their personal relationships.

"Trade-Unions," he concluded, [even] educate the laborers to prudence in marriage" (6, p. 117).

In his next chapter, "The Educational Value of Labor Organization," he posited that labor unions did much directly to counteract the evils of job specialization, and acted as "schools of political science." Unions, having led the fight for free public schooling, had become in his time "perhaps the chief power in this country for temperance." They taught "true politeness and . . . grace in manners." Best of all, the labor movement advocated international peace and pacifism, or as he phrased it, "The labor movement, as the facts would indicate, is the strongest force outside the Christian Church making for the practical recognition of human brotherhood" (6, p. 138).

While generally in favor of a policy of arbitration for trade-unions, Ely did not condemn strikes when they were necessary. He felt that industrial peace was possible only when labor organizations were strong enough to gain the attention and respect of employers, whose frequently intransigent attitude toward unions was due to "ancient prejudice," violent partisanship, or ignorance. He assured his readers that, whether employers liked it or not, "labor organizations are with us, and will remain with us. There never will be peace until they receive full recognition. Employers who really mean well should seek, as many of them are doing, to work through them and to develop everything that is good in them" (6, p. 162).

Ely recognized the possible existence of demagoguery in trade-unions. He also noted that the ablest trade-union leaders were often tempted by offers of high pay to desert their trade-union posts for management jobs. He deplored some of the anticompetitive practices of trade-unions and their use of the boycott. But all these weaknesses he associated not so much with the institution of unionism itself as with evils in the contemporary industrial system.

Ely went on to consider co-operation as a possible solution to modern social ills. Much of his material had been assembled and partially analyzed by his graduate students; it included discussions of such examples of distributive co-operation as the Work-ingmen's Protective Union (1845-60) and the Patrons of Hus-bandry, or Grangers, which reached its zenith in 1876, as well as the Knights of Labor. Although Ely concluded that the Ameri-can experience with distributive co-operation was not an unqual-ified success, he remarked that it had been a good schooling institution. Ely's emphasis on the value of personal educational experience, a characteristic emphasis of Christian Socialist doc-trine, was typical of his conclusions.

He then turned to the topic of producers' co-operation and reviewed several historic attempts at (1) "industrial partnership or profit sharing," (2) "pure co-operation," which abolished the single employer or "captain of industry," and (3) a union of producers, in which the actual workers were also stockholders and managers. He acknowledged the successful experiments by President William H. Sylvis of the molders' union to organize co-operative foundries, and pointed out some Knights of Labor efforts of the same type. The penultimate section of Ely's résumé dealt with profit sharing, co-operative insurance plans (assess-ment companies in which the "reserve" was privately held until needed), and co-operative credit organizations (mainly building and loan societies).

Particularly evident in the works of his students, and to a lesser degree in his own book, is the conclusion that co-operatives were not a panacea for labor problems. Both Ely and his stu-dents, in analyzing the causes of failure of co-operatives, decried the lack of conscious altruism in the labor movement. They also noted the need for additional legislation to facilitate group fi-nancial responsibility. Pointing to the tendency for managers of any marked ability to leave working-class co-operative ventures, they explained that the excessively narrow margin of profit and small volume of business made it difficult to pay sufficiently attractive salaries to keep good men. Inferior management there-fore reduced the already negligible rate of profit still further. Then, too, there was the opposition from private enterprises and the destructive hostility of company-store owners, as, for example, in the mine fields. "Venality and corruption among the masses have often ruined cooperative enterprises," Ely wrote, "and there was, most tragic of all, little or no integration between different individual cooperatives." This, despite such significant achievements as those of the Minneapolis coopers and the Amana (Iowa) colony, "[where] crime is absolutely unknown" (5, pp. 240 and 359). But although Ely had little faith in the immediate usefulness of co-operatives, he sought to publicize a few successful efforts because ". . . while waiting for a more fortunate basis on which to operate, it is well to encourage every attempt of working people and of others to cooperate. It is a training, a sowing of the seed. . . . We must not . . . despise the day of small things" (6, p. 208).

In Ely's discussion of socialism and the German influence on the Socialist movement in the United States, he favored the "Socialistic [*sic*] Labor party" (the "Blues"), which was at that time the most conservative of the three Socialist factions. But he discussed the other parties as well, and noted features common to all; none were "levelers," and none really wished to abolish capital; all were internationalistic and in favor of economic efficiency. In addition, each party claimed to possess an understanding of the historical process. Ely was strongly critical of the anarchistic International Working People's Association (the "Black International") because it advocated violent direct action and, particularly, because it attacked such bulwarks of civilization as the family unit and religion. In his words, ". . . [it] wages war against all that we consider most sacred . . ." (6, p. 242). Ely's attitude toward the International Workmen's Association (the "Reds") was somewhat less hostile, since the "Reds" made a point of favoring the education of the working classes rather than immediate violence, but he was unequivocally against their goal of open revolution. He felt that in time they would see the errors of their immediate conclusions (6, p. 287).

With the aims of the Socialist Labor party, which did not seek to abolish the state but "believe[d] in peaceful agitation and lawful means in behalf of their principles until their enemies force[d] the struggle upon them . . . ," Ely expressed complete sympathy. This party was "far more decent than the [Black] International" and it did not regard "the present state as so utterly bad that it [was] not worth while to advocate specific reforms at once . . ." (6, pp. 272, 275). Yet he placed little faith in the future of the party. He believed instead that trade-unionism, rather than co-operativism or socialism, offered the most direct solution to labor problems.

In the final section of his book Ely considered the ways in which unions and public policy might be improved. He renewed his arguments against unqualified physical force and repression, and, even though unsympathetic toward union-directed boycotts, opposed their abolition by law. He wrote of the necessity for greater equality before the law. He also attacked the heartless and extravagant display of wealth by some employers, which he considered to be a significant cause of social unrest. Ely ended his book with a plea to the church to assume its rightful place in the forefront of the movement for social reform.

Ely's understanding of the actual trade-union movement was limited to the little he had learned of the Knights of Labor. Though he lacked a detailed knowledge of the day-to-day policies of the Knights, he could approve heartily of the general reform program, given in the "Triad of First Principles"—union of all trades, education, and producers' co-operation. He liked its advocacy of reasonableness and of governmental responsibility for social development. On the whole, his only major criticism of the Knights related to the secrecy that continued to shroud some of its operations (8, p. 18). However, Ely's assessment of the Knights was imperfect, since, as time was shortly to show, the key to the survival of labor unions lay not in the general reform program of the Knights, but in the detailed programs of the craft unions, which did not greatly interest him.

Ely was aware (8, p. 30) of the factual shortcomings of *The Labor Movement in America* that are in essence our major criticism of the book; his decision to sponsor Commons' work at Wisconsin is ample evidence of this point. He was also later to regret the exhortative tone of the book, though he never repudi-, ated its argument.[2] Indeed, there is no reason why he should have desired to disassociate himself from it: the book went through three editions and had a profound effect on the thinking of the time, even though the reviewers were not particularly kind (see especially 15). It was the pioneer effort in the field, and attracted a great number of able, socially conscious students to the study of economics. In point of fact, it is probably this book, written by a leading professional economist, that explains why the history of American unionism became associated initially with economics rather than with political science or history.

The Economic Democracy of John Ryan

THE INFLUENCE OF ELY

The obvious bridge between the intellectual convictions of Richard T. Ely, the Protestant Christian Socialist, and Father (later Monsignor) John Augustine Ryan was the explicit influence of Ely's thinking on Ryan's doctoral dissertation (20). Not only was Ely cited in the personal dedication as the one ". . . through whose Writings the Author first became interested in the Study of Economic Problems," but Ely wrote the introduction and arranged for the publication of the dissertation. In addition to these academic ties, the "student" had a second and no less significant source of inspiration in the canons and encyclicals of the Roman Catholic Church.[3] Particularly important in this regard was the encyclical *Rerum Novarum* (1891).

Father Ryan, who was professor of moral theology at Catholic University for most of his active life, made the propagation of

---

[2] In later years Ely was to recount with a little embarrassment his earlier enthusiasm for the "mission," but as he himself noted, he could not disavow this first effort: "After all, it is my child, and there it stands and will stand indefinitely" (4, p. 72).

[3] R. F. Hoxie commented on this point in his review of *A Living Wage*. "As a whole the work appears to be scholarly. The organization of the material used is excellent. On the main point, however,—the validity of the author's ethical theory and judgment—the economic student cannot, of course, pass judgment" (11).

his ideas on economic democracy and self-government in industry his life's work. Going far beyond Ely's in their advocacy of certain specific types of reform, Ryan's ideas undoubtedly had a much greater effect on the country as a whole. His advanced social views were adopted for a time even by his ecclesiastical superiors, as well as by some of the architects of the Roosevelt New Deal. But it was the papal encyclical *Quadragesimo Anno* that climaxed his career, for it incorporated much, if not most, of his thinking. "Well," Bishop Shahan of Catholic University is reported to have said in 1931, when the encyclical was issued, "this is a great vindication for John Ryan" (23, p. 242).

THE DEVELOPMENT OF HIS VIEWS

In the course of his forty-year career, Ryan's views on trade-unionism moved away from Ely's, until in the end he came to favor a modified syndicalism. It is important, however, not to forget that he shared certain fundamental commitments with Ely at all times. These were their mutual commitments to moral judgments and reform and to co-operativism and education, and they were at the heart of Ryan's thinking. It is in this sense that the bond with Ely remains unsevered and the work of the two has a common denominator.

Father Ryan's intellectual development may be divided into four periods (cf. 10). Ely's influence was most readily seen in the first, when Ryan supported increased state supervision of working conditions. In *A Living Wage* he stressed the need for minimum-wage legislation; for laws guaranteeing the right of organization; for publicly supported employment agencies and social security against unemployment, sickness, and old age; for public housing projects and public ownership of public utilities; and for regulation of monopolies in exchange markets. Secondary to these demands for governmental responsibility, as Ryan saw it, was his advocacy of the cause of trade-unionism.

Acknowledging that "the effectiveness of organization is naturally greatest where it is least needed, in the higher [paid] groups" (20, p. 293), Father Ryan nonetheless insisted that organization could "add *something* to the resisting power of the individuals who enter [a union]." Because of the intensity of his concern for the economically underprivileged, he naturally favored the industrial type of unionism, which, in his words, afforded "a splendid opportunity to the workers to create a real brotherhood of labor in which the strong will help to bear the burdens of the weak." Unionism, he acknowledged in this phase of his development, "will not by itself obtain a Living Wage for all the underpaid, but . . . will accomplish more in this direction than all other efforts that the laborer can make, put together" (**20**, pp. 291–96). Yet during this period Ryan generally favored state intervention, and his endorsement of unions, although by no means hesitant, was only incidental to a more important consideration.

His gradual recognition of the critical importance of unions is revealed in a major article, "Moral Aspects of Labour Unions," prepared by him in 1910 for the *Catholic Encyclopedia* (**21**). Arguing that a moral judgment of labor unions must be based on their constitutions, their aims, the results achieved, and the means employed by them, he examined each point in succession. His examination was based on the belief that morality involves a simultaneous consideration of the ends and of the means used to attain these ends. He concluded that the constitutions of the sample group of unions were morally satisfactory. He also approved such union aims as were encompassed in plans for mutual insurance and the procurement of better conditions of employment. "Inasmuch as these benefits rarely exceed, and probably in the majority of instances still fall below, the amount to which labour is entitled in justice," he wrote, "this, the chief aim of the union, is morally justified. The morality of the insurance feature is obvious" (**21**, p. 724).

Father Ryan argued that a union was ethically justified in making only those demands which were in accord with "the law of right," and that wrong was done when the power of organization was used to extort more. He further explained that ". . . although the evil effects of the union are frequent, and sometimes very serious, they seem to be, on the whole, morally outweighed by its good effects," and that ". . . the good results obtained by organization are considerably enhanced by the fact that they could not have been secured in any other way. . . ." He concluded, ". . . the presumption, therefore, is that the labour union in general will in the future be justified from the viewpoint of its results, and that it may claim the allegiance of conscientious men . . ." (21, p. 724).

The greatest part of his article, "Moral Aspects of Labour Unions," was, however, devoted to a discussion of the morality of four major devices used by unions—strikes, boycotts, closed or union shops, and limitation of output. Father Ryan endorsed recourse to the strike only when four specific conditions existed: (1) the presence of an equitable claim, (2) the failure of all peaceful attempts at settlement, (3) the comparative greater evil of the grievance over the immediate harmful effects of the strike, and (4) the relative likelihood of successful strike action. Strikers were not, in any case, willfully to destroy property, because a strike is never the moral equivalent of war. Were strikebreakers to appear, it was immoral to harm them *if they needed the work*. (He did not discuss the action to be taken if the strikebreakers did not need a job.) Although Father Ryan believed that refusal to cross picket lines could, under certain conditions, be considered thoroughly moral, he did add a cautionary note regarding one other type of "morally legitimate" union activity: "While we cannot be certain that a general strike is never justified, we can safely say that there is against it an overwhelming presumption."

His discussion of the boycott reflected his fundamental belief that the morality of means bears some relationship to the ends served: "When the cause and the need are sufficiently grave, the [primary] boycott may be employed with due moderation against any unreasonable conduct that inflicts harm, material, moral, or religious, upon a section of the community. Witness the boycotting of perverse newspapers and theatres." He suggested that the "innocent" third party of a secondary boycott could often choose to avoid economic injury with little added inconvenience to himself, as in the case of the merchant who buys sweatshop goods. Once again, Father Ryan argued that morality was associated with the relation between ends and means. "Whatever may be the legal aspect of the matter, a threat is not morally wrong *per se*. Its morality depends upon what is threatened, and how, and why."

The closed or the union shop was justified if essential to effective organization or to the protection of the union members' right to jobs. In any event, if a choice had to be made between no union or the closed shop, the latter was preferable. Any argument concerned with a possible infringement of individual freedom as a result of compulsory union affiliation Ryan countered with the assertion that, while no one can be denied the basic God-given right to work, there is no inherent right to a job under any or all conditions: the nonunionist's right is not superior to the unionist's. If unionism is necessary for securing decent conditions, then the unionist enjoys a superior right, even at the price of the closed-shop policy so offensive to nonunionists.

Father Ryan's attitude toward limitation of output was that the unequal distribution of abilities often encouraged superior workmen callously to destroy the opportunity for less gifted workmen to earn a decent income. In such instances, the less gifted workmen were justified in protecting their job rights and insisting that strict union rules be observed. Moreover, Ryan appeared to think that there was little real danger that these regulations would seriously restrict production.

Although Father Ryan was concerned, both explicitly and implicitly, with the destructive aspects of economic competition in contemporary society, he affirmed his faith that there is a place for labor unions in a truly Christian society. In such a society "the union would still be desirable, indeed, just as organization is desirable for every class of men whose interests are common; but a far greater proportion of its activities could be devoted to mutual help, especially in the form of insurance, and a much smaller proportion to the struggle against the imposition of unfair terms, and to economic warfare generally." Ryan concluded that *"In that better, though still remote, day most of the extreme methods of the union, such as the strike, the boycott, and the closed shop, could be discarded in favour of milder practices, such as collective bargaining, insurance, and education"* (21, p. 728; italics added).

By 1914 Father Ryan had shifted his emphasis away from limited state ownership as a panacea to an emphasis on self-organization by workingmen. Of the two literary efforts most characteristic of his views in this second stage of development, his serialized debate with Morris Hillquit is the better known; it was published in book form (24) after appearing in seven consecutive issues of *Everybody's* magazine.[4] In this colloquy Ryan described the greatest social defects as being (1) insufficient wages, (2) excessively high profits, and (3) too narrow a distribution of capital ownership.

The obvious and eventual cure for insufficient wages was a legal minimum wage; in the meantime, legislative provisions against the hazards of sickness, accidents, unemployment, old age, and inadequate housing could serve as palliatives (24, pp. 39 ff.). For the other evils, trade-unions seemed to be the only reasonable cure. Ryan explicitly criticized Hillquit's Marxian view of history, claiming that it was an unnecessarily "apocalyptic" theory of the future of capital-labor relations (24, p. 135). Moreover, he attacked the notion that the key to progress lay in Marxism. "The truth that the progress of the working-class depends mainly on their own united efforts," he argued,

was not discovered by Karl Marx. As the history of trade-unionism attests, it was fairly well known to the labouring people even before the rise of modern capitalism. In England and the United States the trade-unions have done far more to diffuse this knowledge than have the Socialists. The influence of the latter in educating the labouring people need not be denied, but over against it must be set the fact that Marx and his followers have exaggerated the power of the work-

---

[4] The less well known work of this period was "Social Reform on Catholic Lines," written in 1913 and reprinted in *The Church and Socialism and Other Essays* (17, pp. 37 ff.).

ers, minimized the assistance obtained and obtainable from other classes, and led the wage-earners whom they captured into a blind alley [24, p. 111].

Father Ryan's views on unionism fitted nicely with his religious faith. It is possible that his espousal of unionism also served to point out to many Americans the relatively "progressive" attitude of the Roman Catholics on the subject (cf. 12 and 9, pp. 27 ff.). Most significant, however, was the pinpointing of differences in emphasis between his Catholic economic views and those held by the Socialists, for, unlike them, he now was prescribing collective bargaining, a measure significantly different from the expropriation and nationalization of industry. Yet his endorsement of collective bargaining, strong as it was, did not cause him to lose sight of his real aim—universal economic justice for the underprivileged. Unionism and collective bargaining were merely preferable, although admittedly imperfect, means to that end. The actual attainment of justice required something more —probably the establishment of a religious hegemony on earth.

It would therefore be fallacious to conclude that Ryan regarded unionism as a cure-all, for at the time that he was stressing the achievements of labor organizations in public debate with Hillquit, he still argued that unionism had touched too small a portion of the working population, and that those it helped were not from the "unskilled and underpaid classes, who stand most in need of organization" (19, p. 417). He attacked the social callousness inherent in craft unionism, but though he pointedly endorsed industrial unionism as an alternative, he acknowledged the existence in the skilled craft unions of much opposition to structural changes, saying, "the most that can be expected is that the various occupational unions within each industry should become federated in a more compact and effective way . . . , thus conserving the main advantages of the local and craft association, while assuring to the unskilled . . . some of the benefits of the industrial union" (19, p. 420). From this point of view it was entirely reasonable for him to continue advocating state responsibility for the protection of the underpaid while arguing the merits of unionism. Despite some traditional labor protests to the contrary, he saw no incompatibility between collective bargaining and legislative enactment (**19**, p. 423).

Moreover, he continued his support of producers' co-operation, even though he admitted that many investigators considered it a practical failure. He listed the following as its obvious advantages: (1) it makes for a better distribution of wealth; (2) it helps to educate society in ways of using the energies and resources of its weaker members; and (3) it stimulates and fosters "initiative, self-confidence, self-restraint, self-government, and the capacity for democracy. In other words, it vastly increases the development and efficiency of the individual" (**19**, p. 420).

By 1919 Ryan had entered the third phase of his intellectual development. His views, incorporated in the 1919 "Bishops' Program" of the Administrative Committee (which included all the American Roman Catholic archbishops) of the National Catholic War Council, included two proposals to expand worker participation in the duties and rewards of management. The failure of unionism to cope successfully with the employers' open-shop drives in the twenties led him to suggest that the best thing labor could hope for would be a joint-shop committee system like that of the Baltimore and Ohio Railroad Plan. By showing reasonableness and conservativism in its relations with management, labor could thus secure an attainable reform, and at the same time acquire experience valuable for the future.

Ryan also sketched out a newly defined ultimate goal for unions:

. . . education of the workers in self-respect, in the conviction that they are fitted to be something more than mere instruments of production, and in the capacity to take a gradually and indefinitely increasing share in the management and operation of industry. *Through this process of training the wage earners will in due time be able to demand a share in the surplus profits and a share in determining all the policies of the industrial concern, and will become fitted to carry on cooperative industries and to sit on the directing boards of publicly owned and democratically managed industrial enterprises* [18, pp. 218 ff.; italics added].

He concluded this new argument by decrying the tendency of wage earners to be dependent and class conscious. Pointing to labor unions as the obvious means for thwarting such submissive tendencies, he suggested that "the first step in the process [of salvation] is to establish the practice of labor sharing in management" (18, pp. 21–22).

With the promulgation of the papal encyclical *Quadragesimo Anno* in 1931, Ryan reached the fourth and final stage in the development of his ideas about industrial democracy. Before this, he had limited his proposals for worker-management co-operation to plants or firms. Since Pope Pius XI recommended the application of this principle to whole industries (16, pars. 99–103),[5] Father Ryan, for whom the encyclical was, as already noted, a vindication before his many Catholic critics, naturally amended his own position accordingly. When within two years the American government adopted the National Industrial Recovery Act, with its industrial codes and administering authorities, it appeared that the temporal authorities, too, had caught up with him. Even the NRA debacle did not discourage him, and he was eventually to write, as the culmination of his views,

. . . If employees had been represented [adequately, of course] in the associations which drew up the NRA industrial codes and in the "authorities" which administered the code provisions, the NRA and its institutions would have been fairly comparable with the proposed occupational groups. Had the NRA been permitted to continue, it could readily have developed into the kind of industrial order recommended by the Holy Father [22, p. 309].

IN SUMMARY

It is only fair to point out that Father Ryan, like Ely, never intended to provide a complete philosophy of trade-unionism. As a moralist and a theologian, he was interested in the development of an increasingly moral society. Only as a means to that

[5] The Pope's caveat related to state domination of these industrial councils.

end was he intrigued with the self-governing features of trade-unions. Moreover, though he enthusiastically endorsed union pressure for raising the real wages of low-paid personnel, he was forced to admit that this union policy was ineffective where it was most needed.

As a competent Roman cleric, Father Ryan's "authorities" and his intellectual guides were canonical decisions, interpretations, and epistles. From these sources he derived the justification for his programs and moral campaigns. And it was to the preparation of these pronouncements that he directed much, if not most, of his creative effort. Thus his ideas on unionism were essentially a small part of his life's work. It was merely fortuitous that unions and the problems treated by them were among the religious matters upon which he had focused his attention.

References

1. Barnes, William E. (ed.), *The Labor Problem: Plain Questions and Practical Answers.* With an introductory chapter by Richard T. Ely. New York: Harper & Bros., 1886.

2. Cole, G. D. H., *Socialist Thought: The Fore-runners, 1789–1850.* London: Macmillan & Co., Ltd., 1953.

3. Dombrowski, James, *The Early Days of Christian Socialism in America.* New York: Columbia University Press, 1936.

4. Ely, Richard T., *Ground under Our Feet.* New York: The Macmillan Co., 1938.

5. ———, "Introduction" in *History of Cooperation in the United States,* "Johns Hopkins Studies in Historical and Political Science," No. 6. Baltimore: The Johns Hopkins University, 1888.

6. ———, *The Labor Movement in America.* New York: Thomas Y. Crowell Co., 1886.

7. Fine, Sidney, "Richard T. Ely: Forerunner of Progressivism, 1880–1901," *Mississippi Valley Historical Review,* XXXVII (1951), 599–624.

8. ——— (ed.), "The Ely-Labadie Letters," *Michigan History,* XXXVI (1952), 1–32.

9. Fox, Mary Harrita, *Peter E. Dietz, Labor Priest*. South Bend, Ind.: University of Notre Dame Press, 1953.

10. Gearty, Patrick W., *The Economic Thought of Monsignor John A. Ryan*. Washington, D.C.: Catholic University of America Press, 1953.

11. Hoxie, Robert F., review of Ryan, *A Living Wage*, in *Journal of Political Economy*, XV (1907), 641–42.

12. Karson, Marc, "The Catholic Church and the Political Development of American Trade Unionism (1900–1918)," *Industrial and Labor Relations Review*, IV (July, 1951), 527–42.

13. Longmate, Norman, *A Socialist Anthology and the Men Who Made It*. London: Phoenix House, 1953.

14. McKelvey, Blake, "Walter Rauschenbusch's Rochester," *Rochester History*, Vol. XIV, No. 4 (October, 1952), pp. 1–27.

15. Newcomb, Simon, review of Ely, *The Labor Movement in America*, in *Nation*, XLIII (1886), 293.

16. Pius XI, Pope, *Quadragesimo Anno: The Reconstruction of the Social Order*. . . . Papal encyclical promulgated May 15, 1931.

17. Ryan, John A., *The Church and Socialism, and Other Essays*. Washington, D.C.: The University Press, 1919.

18. ———, *Declining Liberty and Other Papers*. New York: The Macmillan Co., 1927.

19. ———, *Distributive Justice*. New York: The Macmillan Co., 1916.

20. ———, *A Living Wage; Its Ethical and Economic Aspects*. New York: The Macmillan Co., 1906.

21. ———, "Moral Aspects of Labour Unions," *Catholic Encyclopedia*, VIII (1910), 724–28.

22. ———, *Seven Troubled Years, 1930–1936*. Ann Arbor, Mich.: Edwards Bros., Inc., 1937.

23. ———, *Social Doctrine in Action*. New York: Harper & Bros., 1941.

24. ———, and Hillquit, Morris, *Socialism: Promise or Menace?* New York: The Macmillan Co., 1914.

25. Ware, Norman J., *The Labor Movement in the United States, 1860–1895*. New York: D. Appleton & Co., 1929.

FOUR

Unionism As a Revolutionary Institution

All the groups that developed theories of trade-unionism believed that unions shaped society, directly or indirectly, but only one group believed that unionism had an active and important role to play in the abandonment of the system of private capitalism. This was the Marxian group.

The Background of Marxism in America [1]

Scientific socialism was dominated by three concepts: the concept of the class structure of society, the concept of historical materialism, and the labor theory of value. Implicit in the first was the idea that social structure has an economic basis; in the second, the nature of social conflict; and, in the third, that the ultimate victory of the working class was economically, and thereby morally, justified. In more general terms, this meant that labor in industrialized society was the most productive economic class, since it alone created surplus value. Labor was exploited by the *bourgeoisie,* who, driven by forces of economic competition, expropriated this surplus. This bourgeois pressure had to be resisted by the workers lest they be starved to death. The resulting conflict affected not only the distribution of material goods and services but also the very nature of social

[1] For an alternative treatment see David J. Saposs, *Left Wing Unionism: A Study of Radical Policies and Tactics* (24).

values. Ultimately labor would, according to the Marxists, triumph over its exploiters, the *bourgeoisie,* and the latter's weapon, the government. Then labor would run society for the benefit of itself, that is, for the productive workers.

All scientific socialists believed in this general goal; the varying factional interpretations stemmed mostly from differing estimates of what were the most desirable and economic means of achievement. For example, one faction, influenced by Ferdinand Lassalle (1825–64), held that political action was absolutely necessary as the first step to a classless society and that workers' economic organizations, such as trade-unions, impeded rather than helped the success of the class struggle. This view was particularly popular in New York during the economically depressed seventies, but with the revival of business activity at the end of that decade Lassalleanism virtually disappeared in the United States.

Marxian Socialists, on the other hand, accepted the necessity of trade-unionism in bourgeois-controlled society. Within this Marxian group there were numerous "sectarian" divisions. One "sect" believed that the Socialist virus could be successfully introduced into the American Federation of Labor by a process that amounted to "boring from within." A second and opposing sect despaired of success by infiltration and advocated the establishment of an alternative, truly Socialist federation to replace the AFL. This "smashing from without" would, they believed, result in the universal development of industrial unionism, a desirable step in the development and expression of class-consciousness.

Both these sects were opposed to the "pure and simple" (wage-conscious) unionism advocated by Samuel Gompers (1850–1924), who accepted capitalism as a system. Comparing Gompers to a Judas goat, whose function it is in abattoirs to lead cattle to slaughter, they believed that the rank and file of American workers could be shown the historical as well as the perfidious errors in his position. The two sects were divided, however, by their conflicting estimates of Gompers' strength. Among the "borers from within" were Max Hayes (1866–1945), Victor Berger

(1860–1929), and Job Harriman (1861–1925), who refused to abandon hope of the eventual conversion of the AFL. The partisans of dual unionism or "smashing from without," such as Daniel De Leon (1852–1914), Eugene Debs (1855–1926), and William Z. Foster (b. 1881), had either been expelled from the AFL or, despairing of successful conversion, had left the organization to try their luck elsewhere.

Unfortunately, minor ideological differences and the tendency of its members toward vituperation make the tracing of the American Socialist movement somewhat difficult. In the 1870's, however, there existed several identifiable segments of the Socialist movement. These were integrated at a unity convention in July, 1876, when the Workingmen's Party of the United States was formed. That year the party eschewed politics in favor of trade-union action, but in 1877 they reconsidered and repudiated this decision. At their second convention in December, 1877, under the leadership of Philip Van Patten, Thomas J. Morgan, and Albert Parsons, they adopted a new name, the "Socialist Labor Party," and resolved to enter into political campaigns, a policy pursued for several succeeding decades (3, II, 279 ff.).

During the eighties the party scored some local political successes, but at the same time suffered from severe internal dissension. Those of its members who, like the Anarchist Albert Parsons (1850–87), were discontented with the slow progress of the movement wished to speed success by a direct attack on economic and political evils. There were, on the other hand, members like Joseph R. Buchanan (1851–1924), labor newspaper editor and active member of the Knights of Labor, who sought to reconcile the moderate programs of trade- and labor unions with the plans of the more politically minded Socialists. Both these groups had to contend with the nonsocialist, purely wage-minded trade-unionists, led by Gompers and Strasser (the latter was many times president of the cigar makers' union and mentor of Gompers), as well as with some of the less definitely committed officers of the Knights of Labor.

The results of the 1886 Haymarket explosion were, of course, disastrous to all factions of the labor movement, from those most politically minded to those in right-wing trade-unions concerned essentially with wages. Adversity appears to have stimulated anew a desire for compromise, however, and after a short interlude the Socialists modified their earlier stand on political activity to one more closely corresponding to that of the trade-unions. In fact, so cordial was the general atmosphere that except in New York City there remained no friction between the American Federation of Labor and the Socialist Labor party (3, II, 514 ff.).

Gompers, however, in preventing the representative of the New York City Central Labor Federation (a fusion of some party regulars with some dissidents from the Central Labor Union in that city) from being seated at the Detroit convention of the AFL in 1890, precipitated what eventually became the great split between the Socialist party and the main body of American unions. One of the leaders of the Socialist party group, and a major critic of Gompers, was Daniel De Leon, who came to the United States in 1872, studied law at Columbia, and joined the Knights in 1888 and the Socialist Labor party in 1890. In 1892 he took over the editorship of the official English-language weekly newspaper, *The People*. De Leon's inflexible judgments grated on many nerves and his vituperative editorials did much subsequently to create dissension in the party's ranks.

De Leon first attacked the AFL by attempting to capture the remnants of the New York Knights of Labor organization, which he immediately hailed as truly representative of the ideal Socialist trade-union. That attempt at dethroning the Gompers group proved abortive and De Leon was summarily expelled from the Knights, so he organized a new federation, which was intended to rival and ultimately to replace both the AFL and the Knights. The new organization, the Socialist Trade and Labor Alliance, included the New York City Central Labor Federation, District Assembly 49 (of the Knights of Labor), the United Hebrew Trades, and some smaller groups. It was never very successful, and in 1905 De Leon, whose control of it was absolute, carried it with him into the Industrial Workers of the World.

Notwithstanding its relative ineffectiveness, it was endorsed by implication at the 1896 Socialist Labor party convention and was frequently cited by De Leon as the very model of a trade-union.

None of the factions making up the Socialist Labor party was ever entirely satisfied with De Leon's autocratic fundamentalism. In 1896 the official German-language paper of the party even made so bold as to attack De Leon's hegemony. The paper particularly criticized trade-union dualism, the heart of his policies.[2] He considered this attack to be *lèse-majesté*, and in his rage brought about a permanent split in the Socialist Labor party. So bitter did he become that he actually resorted to a suit in the "capitalist" courts, where his faction was given possession of the party name and the publishing machinery of *The People*.

Several of the leading dissenters from the De Leon line, including N. I. Stone (b. 1873) and Morris Hillquit (1869–1933), then met at Rochester, New York, in March, 1900, for a "unity convention" at which they recounted their differences with De Leon and his followers. Stone, an immigrant from Russia in 1891, studied economics and earned a doctorate at Columbia, worked with John R. Commons at the Bureau of Economic Research, was later an economist with the U.S. Tariff Commission, and served as chief statistician of the Wage Scale Board of the Dress and Waist Industry. Hillquit emigrated from Latvia in 1886, became a lawyer in 1893, joined the Socialist Labor party in 1888 and was repeatedly a delegate to national conventions, and had been a Socialist candidate for mayor of New York. The convention nominated for the presidency of the United States Job Harriman (1861–1925), who was a California lawyer and the Socialist Labor party candidate for governor of California in 1898 as well as a 1911 mayoral candidate in Los Angeles, and for the vice-presidency Max Hayes (1866–1945), a Cleveland union printer and founder of the *Cleveland Citizen*,[3] who was

[2] "Dualism" was the term used to describe the policies of those who set up rival unions in order to smash the established (AFL) unions from without.

[3] The *Cleveland Citizen* was so successful a newspaper that Gompers was forced to bring out the *American Federationist*, lest the leading voice of organized labor be that of Socialists.

prominent in the AFL. They also made plans to seek a *rapprochement* with the midwestern (Wisconsin and Missouri) "Social Democracy," or German factions of the Socialist movement.

The midwestern group, long subjected to the particular scorn of De Leon, were Social Democrats of the Eduard Bernstein stamp. Bernstein (1850–1932), a German and a leading Marxian revisionist, believed that Marx's prediction of class polarization was extreme. He advocated "possibilist" reforms, and remained a pacifist even after 1914. Led by Victor Berger (1860–1929) of Milwaukee, the first Socialist elected to Congress, the group counted as their prize convert Eugene Debs (1855–1926), who had been exposed to socialism during his jail term following the Pullman strike. The first attempts at cordial relations between the Rochester and the midwestern groups were futile. Much hostility had accumulated between them, and the Berger group, though calling themselves Marxian, were really revisionists of the most pragmatic variety. The reluctance of the Berger and Debs clique to unite with the Rochester group then caused a split in the latter camp. But eventually all the Socialist groups except De Leon's decided to endorse the same nominees in the 1900 election: Debs for president and Job Harriman for vice-president. To their great pleasure—and even amazement—these nominees got almost one hundred thousand votes, more than the unified Socialist Labor party had ever polled.

This success encouraged the moderate groups to unify, and in 1901 they formed the Socialist Party of America. In spite of some nominal successes, this party, with a revisionist-populist-pragmatic amalgam for a philosophy, suffered continually from internal tensions and never quite succeeded in cementing itself together. (See 25 for a general history of the party.) At its 1904 convention, for instance, there was a lengthy and heated debate on the party plank concerning trade-unions (see 27, 1904, pp. 175–215). The right wing, including Victor Berger, Max Hayes, and the Socialist writer John Spargo (b. 1876), objected to all proposals reflecting criticism of the AFL. Others tried to condemn the National Civic Federation, as well as the unionists (notably

Gompers) affiliated with it. Left-wing dissenters sought to endorse only industrial unionism—that is, organization of all workers, regardless of their crafts, into the same local unions—rather than craft unionism. One delegate even made a derogatory comparison between all trade-unions and "a little crutch," which could weaken but not materially help the worker. Ultimately, however, the views of the right wingers prevailed, 107 votes to 52. Yet this division revealed the significant strength of the dissenters.

At the Socialist party convention of 1908 the same divergent opinions were again evident. After a sharp exchange of views, the delegates, influenced by Morris Hillquit and John Spargo, voted 93 to 92 against sending a telegram extending support and fraternal greetings to the Western Federation of Miners (27, 1908, pp. 23–24). The convention then turned its attention to the desirability of including a trade-union plank. The right wingers once more prevailed, managing not only to defeat attempts to eliminate the plank, but also to tone down any hostile references to the AFL. In its final statement the party declared that, although the Socialists did not want to give the impression of dictating to the trade-unions, they did hope that the recent Moyer-Haywood experience would lead to greater solidarity.[4] The party then pledged its support to the workers in their economic struggles and urged them to make efficacious use of the ballot. The left-wing opposition was defeated, 138 to 48, in its attempt to amend the plank (27, 1908, pp. 93–102).

At the next convention, in 1912, there was every reason to expect the schism to reappear. The contentious trade-union resolution was so ably and ambiguously worded, however, that immediate harmony reigned and adoption of the resolution was unanimous (27, 1912, pp. 98–101). The party noted with satisfaction the progress being made toward industrial unionism, and, though it reiterated a fancied hesitancy about interfering in union matters, it took the liberty of pointing out the continuing neces-

[4] Moyer and Haywood were tried and acquitted for the murder of former Governor Steunenberg of Idaho. See below, p. 83.

sity for organizing immigrants and the unskilled. The party pledged its support to trade-unions in their struggles and urged all Socialists to join the unions with jurisdiction in their occupations (27, 1912, p. 195).

But the left wing was not to be deprived of its issue, for almost immediately an acrimonious debate commenced on Article II, Section 6, of the party constitution. This section called for the expulsion from the party of any member who "oppose[d] political action or advocate[d] crime, sabotage, or other methods of violence. . . ." The left wingers, seeing in this clause not only a denunciation of the Industrial Workers of the World, but also their own future nemesis, fought back with all their force. As might have been expected, the bitterness of the dispute met the expectations of those who had been disappointed by the peaceful resolution of the trade-union issue. Max Hayes, a spokesman of the right, probably summed up their attitude correctly when, in the course of his remarks, he said,

. . . apparently there is a new spirit . . . which attempts to draw the political organization in behind the economic organizations. In some parts of the country this spirit is rapidly developing to the anarchistic point where if men [like] Johann Most [1846–1910] [5] were still on earth, they would undoubtedly make application to join. I want you comrades and particularly those of you who have not [sic] practical experience in the every day struggles in the industrial field to go slow, and I refer particularly to some of our so-called parlor variety of Socialists. Some of the intellectuals who have never been in the labor movement but sit in their parlors and theorize and write books that tell the industrial workers what to do. The point I wish to make is simply this: You yesterday adopted a declaration regarding the matter of organization on the industrial field, which certainly ought to be satisfying to every right-thinking, honest-minded man and woman in the Socialist movement. Let us stand by that. Keep your hands off the American Federation of Labor . . . [and] the Industrial Workers of the World. . . . As far as the American Federation of Labor is concerned, no resolution that you would adopt here

[5] A German-born anarchist who served time in English and American jails for glorifying or advocating assassination of heads of state.

would be sufficient to drive me to join the Industrial Workers of the World if I didn't see fit to do so. We can take care of our own affairs on the industrial field. We do not want you to butt in. Leave the industrial field to the unions [27, 1912, p. 124].

Eventually, the antiunionists and other critics of the AFL sought to strike out all reference to sabotage, but the clause, somewhat reworded, was retained by a vote of 191 to 90. There were teeth in the decision. William Haywood was recalled from the National Executive Committee for advocating sabotage. As a result, more bitterness developed and some young "intellectuals," such as Walter Lippmann, drew away from the party. A by-product of the discussion, however, was the emergence of strong "possibilist" sentiment among such men as Hillquit, Hayes, Berger, and Spargo. These men, essentially pragmatic in outlook, controlled the convention, although they could not dominate all the views in the party, much less those of their nominee, Eugene Debs.[6]

During World War I the Socialist party split in two. One group, anti-War in outlook, clustered around Victor Berger, Morris Hillquit, Job Harriman, and several members of the left wing. John Spargo was the key figure in the other group, which supported the war effort though initially opposed to conscription. The war marked the end of the most successful phase of the party's activities, and such harmony as there had been was never again re-established.

The left-wing De Leon-controlled Socialist Labor party had been centered in the non-English-speaking metropolitan manufacturing areas in the East. In 1905 De Leon combined forces with the western industrial unionists—most of whom were violent and radical believers in political action—and with a few radically inclined "right-wing" Socialists to form the Industrial

[6] "Possibilism" refers to a conviction that the party should concentrate on practical rather than utopian programs; "pragmatic socialism" was analyzed later in William English Walling's *The Larger Aspects of Socialism* (34), but the trade-union aspect is best reflected in the speeches of Stone, Hayes, and Harriman.

Workers of the World. Originally this *entente* was loosely controlled, permitting diverse points of view ranging from a belief in pragmatic industrial unionism to belief in revolutionary political unionism. A year later, after the incumbent president, William Sherman, was expelled, the delegation of the more pragmatically inclined Western Federation of Miners withdrew, thus virtually ending all hope of any significant union secessions from the hated AFL. Two years later, in 1908, some of the coarse and unmannered westerners offended De Leon's sense of revolutionary propriety, and, what is more, outmaneuvered him parliamentarily. After a showdown, De Leon was expelled. Eventually the Industrial Workers of the World, abandoning all notions of political action, purported to be the spokesman of all American unskilled, migrant labor. Such philosophy as the group advanced was expounded by William E. Trautmann (1869– ?), onetime editor of the *Brauer Zeitung,* William Haywood (1869–1928), and Vincent St. John (d. 1929), among others. De Leon, true to form, set up a rival Industrial Workers of the World organization in Detroit, the Workers' International Industrial Union, to which Trautmann switched in 1917 (**1,** pp. 219–20) before he abandoned his extreme radicalism after World War I. Thus the original "dual" union itself came to have a rival.

Once the main body of the Industrial Workers of the World had simultaneously abandoned De Leonism and political action, it endorsed a crude version of syndicalism. Interestingly enough, from a historical viewpoint, one of the men who evolved this unpolished syndicalism was William Z. Foster, then an organizer for the Brotherhood of Railroad Carmen.

This abbreviated history of the Marxian radical movements in America provides the framework for a discussion of several theories of unionism. These will be presented here in two major groups: those of the relative "left" and those of the relative "right." We shall first turn to the theorists of the left, discussing in turn Daniel De Leon, William E. Trautmann, William D. Haywood, and William Z. Foster.

The Left Wing: Four IWW Extremists

DANIEL DE LEON

Daniel De Leon (1852–1914), the stormy petrel of the American labor movement, was paradoxically both the clearest and the vaguest expositor of Marxian trade-union philosophy in America. He dealt largely in the realm of ideas and only to a limited degree in concrete realities, so that his prescriptions for successful working-class action have a beguiling intellectual neatness but are difficult to translate into positive institutional terms. Lenin was quoted as having declared that De Leon was "the only one who has added anything to Socialist thought since Marx" (**1**, pp. 241–42). De Leon's association with the labor movement dated from 1888, when, while an instructor at Columbia University, he left his desk to participate in a Knights of Labor demonstration (**10**). Within two years he was one of the leaders in the Knights' District Assembly 49 and the New York City Central Labor Federation, a body that Samuel Gompers would not allow in the American Federation of Labor as long as it was associated with the Socialist Labor party. By 1892 De Leon was taking an active part in Socialist Labor party politics. Having become convinced that any *rapprochement* with the AFL was unlikely, he appears to have resolved in 1895 to set up a rival, "truly socialistic" federation, the Socialist Trade and Labor Alliance (cf. **28**). Although unsuccessful as a union organization, the Alliance served as a demonstrative instrument for De Leon, who directed it from his position as editor of *The People,* then the official organ of the Socialist Labor party. And it was with the founding of the Alliance that De Leon's philosophy began to take shape.

His ideas centered in a program of class-conscious industrial unionism, with honest and open revolutionary action. He particularly stressed co-ordination between the economic and political branches of the labor movement. In 1896 he was inclined to think of unions as an essentially protective device ("a shield") and of the party as an aggressive instrument ("the sword") (**26**).

Eventually, he reversed these roles, assigning to unions the more aggressive one. His resultant strong insistence on the importance of political action made him unpopular, and he was expelled from the Industrial Workers of the World, which he had helped to establish (1, pp. 222–23).

Most persistent in all De Leon's thinking was a deep and fundamental distrust of palliatives, stopgap reforms, and non-revolutionary labor leaders. In several of his major speeches between 1896 and 1902 he carried this theme to the point of irksome repetition. Hurling invective at those whom he thought were betraying the proletarian revolution because of personal corruption or insufficient revolutionary ardor, he repeatedly marveled at what he felt to be the stupidity of settling for "half a loaf." Two lectures delivered in 1902 compared contemporary developments with the collapse of morality in republican Rome. Comparing the participation of Gompers, Mitchell, and ten others in the National Civic Federation (allegedly a tool of big business) with the seduction of the Roman tribunes of the plebs by the patrician class,[7] De Leon decried in the first lecture the apparent willingness of the AFL leaders to break bread with Mark Hanna (the United States senator from Ohio who directed the McKinley presidential campaigns and who symbolized big business and the trusts), and his rich associates. This willingness was, in De Leon's eyes, the crassest type of betrayal of the proletarian revolution. "As the Plebs Leader of old was a strategic post of peculiar strength for the patriciate and of mischief for the proletariat," he cried out,

so and for like reasons is the Labor Leader of today nothing but a masked battery, from behind which the Capitalist Class can encompass what it could not without—the work of enslaving and slowly degrading the Working Class, and, along with that, the work of debasing and ruining the country [10, p. 54].

[7] It was argued that the patrician class quieted the legitimate demands of the plebs by giving them representation, that is, tribunes, but that the patricians then corrupted these tribunes so that the material situation was not changed. In brief, the reform amounted to no significant change.

De Leon was also convinced that mere reforms were not sufficient guaranty against retrogression or reaction. In the second
1902 lecture he pointed to the historic failure of the attempts of
the Gracchi to mitigate the economic and social evils of Rome
in 134–21 B.C. (12).[8] He felt that their failure showed the errors
inherent in moderate steps or compromises, and that the plebs
should have been incited to bring about a new social order. He
listed in this same speech ten somewhat redundant principles
for revolutionary action: (1) abhorrence of "stopgap" reforms
(cf. 21), (2) trust in a relentlessly logical program, (3) the avoidance of palliatives, (4) the adoption of new and revolutionary
social values, (5) the complete destruction of all the old bourgeois mores, (6) dependence upon other revolutionary leaders
only, never on those on the outside, (7) avoidance of all sops
(a palliative was a mere portion of what was due; a sop was a
substitute), (8) distrust of rhetoric, (9) open rather than secre-
tive proceedings so that the mission will not become hidden and
thereby lost, and (10) an unfailing faith in the proletariat and
the righteousness of the revolutionary cause, regardless of short-
run perfidy on the part of the workers.[9]

These two essays synthesize particularly well De Leon's basic
theory. But, like many theorists, he concentrated so strongly on
strategic rather than tactical considerations that he was often
quite easily led into anomalous tactical situations. Occasionally
he was found supporting scab movements which he would justify
by claiming that the strikers had not sufficiently considered the
"strategic revolutionary implications" of their actions. In such
cases he argued that it was really the strikers who were the scabs
and that the ill-advised action, taken at the suggestion of a false
leader or "labor faker," actually impeded the true progress of the
working-class movement toward revolution.

[8] The brothers Tiberius and Gaius Gracchus were nephews of Cornelius Scipio
Amelianus. Each tried to limit the powers of the Senate (representing the patricians) and each, though initially successful, was eventually deserted by his supporters, largely plebs. Each was assassinated, Tiberius in 133 B.C., Gaius in 121 B.C.

[9] Gaius Gracchus, at the hour of his betrayal, asked the gods to curse the
Romans for their "base ingratitude."

In his view, the criteria for judging trade-union action were simple. As for strategy,

In the first place, the trades union has a supreme mission. That mission is nothing short of organizing by uniting, and uniting by organizing, the whole working class industrially—not merely those for whom there are jobs, accordingly, not only those who can pay dues. This unification or organization is essential in order to save the eventual and possible victory from bankruptcy, by enabling the working class to assume and conduct production the moment the guns of the public power fall into its hands—or before, if need be, if capitalist political chicanery pollutes the ballot box [9, p. 34].

It was in the area of tactics, however, that the difficult problems lay.

In the second place, the trades union has an immediate mission. The supreme mission of trades unionism is ultimate. That day is not yet. The road thither may be long or short, but it is arduous. At any rate, we are not yet there. Steps in the right direction, so-called "immediate demands," are among the most precarious. They are precarious because they are subject and prone to the lure of the "sop" or the "palliative" that the foes of Labor's redemption are ever ready to dangle before the eyes of the working class, and at which, aided by the labor lieutenants of the capitalist class, the unwary are apt to snap—and be hooked. But there is a test by which the bait can be distinguished from the sound step, by which the trap can be detected and avoided, and yet the right step forward taken. That test is this: DOES THE CONTEMPLATED STEP SQUARE WITH THE ULTIMATE AIM? If it does, then the step is sound and safe; if it does not, then the step is a trap and disastrous. The "immediate step" that acts like a brake on the decline of wages belongs to the former category, provided only the nature of the brake is not such that it inevitably invites a future decline, that requires a further brake and which brake only invites some later decline, and so on, towards a catastrophe or towards final cooliedom. We have seen that the pure and simple trades union belongs to the latter category, the category of "traps," and we have seen the reason why—it is merely a jobs-securing machine, consequently it inevitably rends the working class in twain, and, on the whole, has the love and affection of the capitalist exploiter [9, pp. 34–35; cf. also 13].

Since he was convinced that in a Socialist society unions were ultimately to control production, and that prior to that day unions were to strive to "take and hold" the machinery of production, De Leon felt obliged to justify his insistence on political action. This he did by arguing that the shift to a proletarian society required the orderly pruning of the machinery of social administration, a task that involved co-ordinated planning as well as moral resolution. This "destructive" function was best performed politically, since this made possible a relatively nonviolent transition from the bourgeois to the proletarian society.

The Preamble of the Industrial Workers of the World poses well both the political and the economic Movement of Labor, and it places them in their proper relation towards each other.

Inestimable is the value, dignified the posture of the political Movement. It affords the Labor Movement the opportunity to ventilate its purposes, its aspirations and its methods free [sic] over and above board, in the noon-day light of the sun, whereas otherwise, its agitation would be consigned to the circumscribed sphere of the rat-hole. The political Movement renders the masses accessible to the propaganda of Labor; it raises the Labor Movement above the category of a "conspiracy"; it places the Movement in line with the Spirit of the Age, which, on the one hand, denies the power of "conspiracy" in matters that not only affect the masses, but in which the masses must themselves be intelligent actors, and, on the other hand, demands the freest of utterance. In short and in fine, the political Movement bows to the methods of civilized discussion: IT GIVES A CHANCE TO THE PEACEFUL SOLUTION OF THE GREAT QUESTION AT ISSUE. By proclaiming the urgency of political as well as of industrial unity, the Preamble amply and sufficiently proclaims the affinity of the economic with the political Movement. At the same time, by expressly proclaiming that the "taking and holding" is an act that falls wholly within the province of the economic organization, the Preamble locked a dangerous switch, a switch into which to run [sic] there is grave danger, the danger of rendering the Socialist, which means the Labor Movement, illusory, and a roosting place for the "intellectual" riff-raff of bourgeois society [11, pp. 39–40].

Thus it appears that by 1905 De Leon had developed a unique theory of Socialist organization based on class-conscious, industrially organized unionism. Tactical considerations were subordinated to the strategic end of proletarian revolution, which is an approach contrary to the usual one of most military leaders, who prefer to put tactical needs ahead of strategic advantages. And, after all, De Leon believed in political action as a necessary part of the revolutionary movement because it educated the masses and facilitated as orderly a transition of power as possible.

In the years after 1905 De Leon made few changes in his theory. The Industrial Workers of the World's abandonment of political action and the ballot in 1908 seemed to him to be both theoretically erroneous and personally repugnant. Moreover, he was outraged by the conspiratorial, vulgar nature of the unskilled western members of the Industrial Workers of the World as well as by their ridicule of intellectuals. Until his death in 1914 he continued to edit the Socialist Labor party organ, the *Weekly People*, and to fulminate against syndicalists, right-wing trade-union leaders, and Socialists who dissented from his views.

WILLIAM TRAUTMANN

The leadership of the Industrial Workers of the World changed hands several times. We have already mentioned two expulsions, the first in 1906 of its president, William Sherman of the Western Federation of Miners, and the second in 1908 of Daniel De Leon. The key figure in each instance was William E. Trautmann (1869– ?), who in 1904 was one of the six men instrumental in organizing the Industrial Workers of the World. Although he renounced radicalism in later years, Trautmann was originally a leading proponent of its most extreme form—sabotage and industrial violence.

His little brochure, *Industrial Union Methods* (**31**; see also **30** and **32**), summarized succinctly the rationale of destruction.

The industrial unionist . . . holds that there can be no agreement with the employers of labor which the workers have to consider sacred and inviolable.

The worker, if he agrees to the terms of a contract insisted upon by an employer as condition of employment, does so under duress; he is neither legally nor morally bound to respect such an agreement as a sacred pact; moreover such contracts are used . . . as instruments to keep the workers divided. . . .

Industrial unionists will therefore sign any pledge, and renounce even their organization if necessary, at times when they are not well prepared to give battle, or when market conditions render it advisable to lay [*sic*] low; but they will do just the reverse of what they had to agree to under duress, when occasion arises to gain advantages for the workers [31, p. 16].

Trautmann also made much of the differences between his philosophy and that of the wage-conscious craft unionist.

The theory advanced by the craft unionists for their particular methods applied in strikes and lockouts is that the leaving and staying out of the workshops until the union's demands are acceded to, or a sort of compromise made, curtails the opportunities of the capitalists to exploit labor for profit.

But the employers, knowing the weakness of the craft unions and their methods, are always prepared, and they have, when necessary, enough workers available to continue the operation of the establishments. In long-drawn-out conflicts the workers alone pay the costs of conflict; "slave-bleeding," the term used by industrial unionists, implies that the resources of the striking craft unionists are exhausted by such protracted strikes; and they are then at the mercy of the employers of labor.

The theory of the industrial unionist is that the heavy burden of the class conflict should fall as much as possible upon the manufacturers, and all methods of warfare should be governed accordingly.

The industrial unionist, as demonstrated in hundreds of cases, recognizes the fact that by leaving the workshop the same is absolutely left in control of the employer, and he is at liberty to engage new hands if he cares to. The industrial unionist may leave the factory, mill or mine, and return to work, only apparently defeated, when he realizes that the points contended for cannot be gained at the initial move; yet, by maintaining the organization, can be ready at any time to institute well-directed actions at times and places selected by the working class organizations when chances for success are more promising [31, p. 14 ff.].

Trautmann's position in the Industrial Workers of the World remained strong only as long as he worked closely with Vincent St. John and William Haywood, but by 1912 that *entente* had collapsed and Trautmann withdrew to join the Detroit, or De Leon, version of the Industrial Workers of the World, the W.I.I.U. (cf. 1, pp. 219, 266, and 293). His place as nominal leader was taken by Haywood and St. John.

By 1923 Trautmann appears to have become an advocate of works councils and workers' education, although he retained his old hatred for craft unions and business agents. He argued that Haywood was the cause of most of the grief of the Industrial Workers of the World. Endorsing Walther Rathenau's *New Society* and Woodrow Wilson's concept of democracy in the shop, he was also vigorously critical of John Spargo (see **29**).

WILLIAM HAYWOOD

William D. Haywood (1869–1928), spokesman for western American syndicalism, came originally from the mining country of Utah, Nevada, and Idaho. In 1896 he became one of the most active members of the Western Federation of Miners and commenced the career that ultimately led him to power, notoriety, and death in exile.

In 1899 he was elected to the Executive Board of the federation; the following year he became its secretary-treasurer. An advocate of the most aggressive type of unionism, he was largely responsible for the militant nature of industrial relations in the mining fields. Because he had a reputation for fomenting violence, he was arrested in Denver in early 1906 and charged with conspiring to assassinate Frank R. Steunenberg, former governor of Idaho. Extradition papers were secretly signed and Haywood and two others (Charles H. Moyer, president of the WFM, and George A. Pettibone, a Denver merchant) were spirited across the state line for trial in Idaho. The irregularity of the proceedings, coupled with something of a widespread admiration of the WFM as a "non-capitalist militant defender of workingmen's rights" led to a nationwide expression of sympathy for the accused. The defense became a *cause célèbre,* and a large fund was collected for it. Before the trial Haywood was even nominated on the Socialist ticket for the governorship of Colorado, and managed to poll 16,000 votes. After his trial and acquittal in 1907, soon followed by the trial and acquittal of the other two men, Haywood's personal relations with Moyer and the Executive Board of the WFM rapidly deteriorated. On April 8, 1908, fairly soon after his career had reached its peak, the Western Federation of Miners formally fired him and repudiated him as a representative. Five years later, after the adoption of the antisabotage plank, he was also dismissed from the Executive Board of the Socialist party because of his reputation for espousing violence and "direct action." He remained, however, in the Industrial Workers of the World, where he had played a leading role from the time of its inception.

Haywood joined Vincent St. John and William Trautmann to gain clear control of the Industrial Workers of the World, which they then used as an instrument for their violent, antipolitics views. In 1911, prior to his expulsion from the Socialist party, these views were synthesized by Haywood and a collaborator (Frank Bohn, a former aide to De Leon), in a 64-page pamphlet entitled *Industrial Socialism* (20).

In this pamphlet they advocated control of society by a large industrial union that would have several subdivisions working in and controlling each of the major industries. (De Leon, on the other hand, argued in favor of a modified type of craft unionism, where all the workers in each industry would have their own district union.) Co-ordination was to be achieved by some undefined type of central direction. The workers were to assert this hegemony by employing the general strike. When hegemony had been achieved, then, and only then, would socialism be possible.

The Socialist Party and the labor union will come closer and closer together. The labor union will come to stand for Socialism. The Socialist Party will thus become a mere phase of the labor movement. The union and the party together make war upon the enemy, the capitalist class. This fight is, first of all, a shop fight. It takes place at the point of production where the workers are at present enslaved. Until this is understood there can be no real understanding of Socialism. To understand the world and the world's struggle at the present time we must look at it through shop windows. That is why college professors, preachers, authors and business men must take the working class point of view before they can understand Socialism. They must understand the struggle in the shop. Then only can they understand the needs of the workers and the power of the workers [20, p. 50].

Nationalization (government ownership) was not what these syndicalists sought, and their antipolitical bias was evident.

Government ownership can never lead to Socialism. It is not a step toward Socialism. It has nothing Socialistic about it, because all political government is administration from the top. At the present time the employes of the United States Postoffice are treated worse than many employes of private capitalists. The railway mail clerks are less protected and work for less wages than most of the other trainmen. Wherever the capitalists are being driven by the Socialist Movement they are crying out for "government ownership" to save them. The railroad thieves in the United States will soon want nothing so much as to turn over their watered stocks to the National Government. They would then draw their profits as interest on government bonds. No profits in the world could be safer. The government would then have to rob the railroad workers and turn over the stolen money to the idle government railroad bondholders [20, pp. 50–51; cf. 33, II, 1558].

There would have to be co-ordination, however, if complete chaos were to be avoided. These American syndicalists were somewhat less anarchistic in this way than their European counterparts.

In the shop there must be government. In the school there must be government. In the conduct of the great public services there must be government. We have shown that Socialism will make government throughout democratic. The basis of this freedom will be the freedom of the individual to develop his powers. People will be educated in freedom. They will work in freedom. They will live in freedom. Most of the diseases which now afflict humanity will be unknown because their causes will have been removed. Where there is plenty for all, none will be driven to swindle, to steal or to take profits. Higher education will be within the reach of everyone. Science and the arts will flourish.

Socialism will establish democracy in the shop. Democracy in the shop will free the working class. The working class, through securing freedom for itself, will liberate the race. Socialism will free not only the slave but the slave-driver and the slave-owner. Socialism today makes war upon the enemies of the working class. When it is victorious, the enemies of the working class will embrace it. Peace and brotherhood will come with freedom [20, pp. 63–64].

Whether these opinions actually represented the official doctrine of the Industrial Workers of the World is difficult to determine because of the organization's turbulent history. Paul Brissenden, the leading interpreter of the Industrial Workers of the World movement, notes that (1) the Industrial Workers of the World adopted the Knights of Labor policy of organizing the unskilled with the skilled, while it repudiated the middle-class ideology of the Knights in favor of Socialist policy; (2) the Industrial Workers of the World took from De Leon's Socialist Trade and Labor Alliance the idea of using union organization to overthrow capitalism, but it substituted one big industrial union for the separate industry-by-industry unions in the Alliance; (3) the antipolitical bias of the Industrial Workers of the World had an important effect on their thinking; and (4) the Industrial Workers of the World differed from one of its logical sources, European syndicalism, when it emphasized centralized control and planning (1, pp. 27–56).

On the basis of his reasoning in *Industrial Socialism,* Haywood can be considered as a representative theorist. It was he, rather than Vincent St. John or William Trautmann, who stood out as the distinctive figure in the Industrial Workers of the World (2).

During World War I, Haywood, along with more than one hundred other Industrial Workers of the World members, was indicted for sedition. While appealing his conviction and twenty-year sentence, he jumped bail and accepted the invitation of the revolutionary Russian government to live in Moscow. There he held several minor jobs until his death in 1928.

WILLIAM FOSTER

In the course of his intellectual development William Z. Foster set what might be considered a record for sampling policies in opposition to each other. By his own reckoning, he first joined the right-wing Socialist party in 1901 (16, pp. 23 ff.). From 1904 until 1907, according to his claim, he read avidly in the Socialist classics and moved to the left wing of the party. In 1909 his faction was expelled from the party, although he was given an opportunity to rejoin it as an individual. Disgusted with the way the Socialists played politics and with the ineffectiveness of all Socialist factions, he concluded that "political action in general was fruitless and that the way to working-class emancipation was through militant trade union action, culminating in the general strike." Thus he decided to devote his energies to the Industrial Workers of the World and the propagation of syndicalism. Later he was to recant this decision and to regret the "many years [necessary] to correct this basic mistake" (16, pp. 47–48).

This decision was fortified by observations Foster made on a six-month trip to France in 1910, where he also became convinced that it was possible for a militant minority to gain control of an organization by boring from within. He returned to the United States in 1911 intent upon winning the Industrial Workers of the World over to the policy of infiltration. At the sixth IWW convention he proposed that "the Industrial Workers of the World shall give up its attempt to create a new labor movement, turn itself into a propaganda league, get into the organized labor movement and, by building better fighting machines within the old unions than those possessed by our reactionary enemies, revolutionize these unions" (16, pp. 55–56). Needless to say, this proposal was rejected by most of the IWW leadership, although Foster was able to persuade several delegates to his belief.

One of these, Earl C. Ford, became coauthor with him of a

pamphlet on the philosophical tenets of American syndicalism (**14**, pp. 61–63; cf. **16**). To perpetuate the faith Foster and his colleagues founded the Syndicalist League of North America, an educational organization defined as "possibilist . . . with a practical program."

The S.L. of N.A. is a possibilist organization with a practical program. It considers the utopian policy of a universal dual organization a most pernicious one because it at once introduces disastrous jurisdictional wars in the labor movement and destroys the efficiency of the militant minority. Its first principle is unity in the labor movement. It is based on the demonstrated fact that the labor movement will become revolutionary in the measure that the individuals composing it become educated. It is, therefore, seeking to bring about this education by the exploitation of the militant minority. Consequently, it seizes every opportunity to introduce betterments, great or small, into the labor movement. Though in existence but a few months, it has already achieved remarkable success. It is responsible for the removal of a number of abuses from, and the introduction of a number of improvements into several international unions. It is also a potent factor in the various localities where it has branch leagues established [**14**, p. 47].

The league was strongly antiparliamentary as well as anarchistic. In fact, the leaders considered that they had inherited the mantle of the Haymarket martyrs, and Lucy Parsons, whose husband Albert had been one of the martyrs, permitted them to use her home in Chicago as the league's mailing address.

Later, Foster assessed the achievements of the Syndicalist League rather skeptically. Though he lauded it for being antisectarian when sectarianism was "the general besetting sin of the American left-wing," he added that its syndicalist outlook, "which it had inherited from the Industrial Workers of the World and the left-wing of the Socialist Party," eliminated it as an effective instrument. Moreover, it failed of major accomplishment and died out in 1914.

In 1915 a new organization appeared with Foster as secretary. The International Trade Union Educational League, as this organization was called, was an autonomous, decentralized body without dues (to preclude its development as a dual union); its program included the policy of "boring from within." Its other doctrines were less syndicalistic than those of the SL of NA, although insistence upon the hard core of trade-unionism remained. Foster emphasized in the ITUEL policy statement, which he wrote, an economic rather than a political basis for social reorganization. Thus he still emphasized unionism rather than political action as the prime method for the labor movement.

Trade Unionism secures its great end through organization. It substitutes a beneficent co-operation between the workers for their primitive dog-eat-dog competition. Just as a rope maker twists a multitude of delicate fibers into an unbreakable cable, so Trade Unionism binds together the hosts of individually helpless workers into one mighty organization.

Trade Unionism is based upon two indisputable truths: First, that all workers have common economic interests; and second, that in union there is strength. Hence, its method is to unite in fraternal and loyal brotherhood all the workers in a given shop, trade or industry, and then to present their collective demands to the employer. If necessary it backs up these demands with a strike of all the workers involved [18, p. 11].

Foster admitted that the trade-union movement appeared to be less than radical in its aims, but argued that this was merely a tactical feint.

. . . In their everyday war the Trade Unions seize upon every betterment they have the strength to take. The degree of their conquests is limited only by their power. This unchangeable policy assures them a golden future of achievement, for, so far, they have developed only a small portion of their inevitable power. What they have accomplished up to date, important though it may be, is only a hint of what is yet to come [18, p. 19].

He made clear his new position regarding governmental action. "Under the new order," he wrote, government, such as we know it, would gradually disappear. In an era of science and justice, this makeshift institution, having lost its usefulness, would shrivel and die.

. . . .

With war, crime, class antagonisms and property squabbles obliterated, and the management of industry taken from its care, little or no excuse would exist for government. What few extraordinary occasions arose requiring legislative action to arrive at some sort of solution could be handled by the Trade Unions, which would still contrive to have many uses [18, pp. 24–25].

The ITUEL did not catch on, and by the time the United States entered World War I it had foundered. Foster attributed this failure to an underestimation of the capitalist power of resistance.

During the war Foster worked for the AFL, first among the railroad workers in Chicago, where he was for a time business agent of the railway carmen's union, and later among the packing-house workers, where he directed a membership campaign for a combination of unions and actually organized about two hundred thousand Chicago packing-house employees. This success inspired Foster to undertake the organization of the steel industry. After a short period of preparation, Foster called a nation-wide steel strike, which ultimately proved completely unsuccessful. Foster, as might have been expected, found himself black-listed. He then turned on Gompers and blamed the failure on him, although Gompers, who distrusted Foster, had been dubious about the management of the strike from the start.

Undaunted by his failures, Foster organized in 1920 a new left-wing organization, the Trade Union Educational League, that was to bore from within the AFL. This TUEL received the endorsement of the Moscow Red International of Labor Unions (RILU), at whose convention Foster appeared as an American delegate in 1921. While in Moscow Foster also became officially a Communist.

The TUEL position was a repudiation of the wage consciousness of the Gompers group. It endorsed boring-from-within tactics, the amalgamation of existing craft unions into large, aggressive industrial unions, the establishment of a labor party, and a positive program of support for an extension of the Russian revolutionary movement to America (15). Of these, Foster certainly felt most strongly about the "decadence" of the AFL, particularly of its leaders, and the delusive ideal of dual unionism.

Notwithstanding his dislike of dual unionism, he and his Communist followers were gradually forced out of one AFL union after another, especially in the garment, textile, and mining industries, and Foster found himself the leader of what was actually a dual federation. The TUEL, too, appeared to have been unsuccessful.

Eventually even the Executive Committee of the Communist International in Moscow took cognizance of Foster's inability to capture the American Federation of Labor from within, and directed that a new organization—this time an avowedly separate federation—be established. The Trade Union Unity League was then set up in Cleveland in September, 1929. It was composed of unions (union factions) that had been expelled from the AFL and of some marrano cadres still within AFL unions. Foster did not like the TUUL, but as a disciplined party member did not protest the directive from Russia, which was read to the American "backsliders" by A. Losovsky, general secretary of the RILU, in 1928. Instead, Foster took care to voice an "understanding" of the necessity for and inevitability of "independent" (a word he preferred to "dual") unions.

When unorganized workers undertake to organize the fight, they cannot use the A.F. of L. The A.F. of L., consisting only of about 2,500,000 workers out of 25,000,000, and these mostly skilled workers —has shown throughout its history that it will not and cannot organize the unorganized. . . .

Likewise in the A.F. of L. unions themselves, the determination of the workers to struggle leads surely to the formation of independent unions. The A.F. of L. leaders refuse to fight the bosses and they also resist bitterly all attempts to use the unions as instruments of real struggle. The control of the unions cannot be captured from these leaders by the workers through democratic means. Trade union democracy is almost completely suppressed in the A.F. of L. The reactionary leaders control the unions by gangsterism, the blacklist, and by police and Tammany methods.

. . . .

The T.U.U.L. works inside the old unions. It is the organizer of the discontented masses in the A.F. of L. unions, now rising against their misleaders and bosses. It puts no trust in the A.F. of L. leaders and carries out a policy of independent leadership by the militant workers themselves. But the T.U.U.L. clearly recognizes and understands that the inevitable tendency of the struggle in the A.F. of L. unions, for reasons stated, leads in the direction of the formation of new unions [**17**, pp. 5–6].

Foster condemned those who continued to believe in the policy of boring from within that he himself had formerly advocated.

The so-called progressives of the Conference for Progressive Labor Action, of which A. J. Muste [b. 1885; a moderate left-wing reformer] is the head, disagree with the whole foregoing T.U.U.L. analysis and program. Their proposals, boiled down, are, 1—that the T.U.U.L. policy of class struggle is wrong and must be supplanted by class collaboration. 2—That the A.F. of L. can be used as a base for organization of struggle of the working class. 3—That the T.U.U.L. should be liquidated.

The C.P.L.A. comes forward with a whole program of measures to revive the A.F. of L. unions. Among these are industrial unionism, amalgamation, labor party, organization of the unorganized, etc. But the substance of all this, as we shall see, is merely the acceptance of the reactionary line of the A.F. of L. bureaucracy under the cover of a smoke-screen of "left" phrases. The heart of Musteism is radical talk and reactionary action [**17**, p. 8].

Foster's assessment of the TUUL experience is of value, if for no other reason than that it shows his preference for using the established labor unions if he could.

In the earlier stages of its work, the T.U.U.L. developed a number of sectarian weaknesses which injured its general efficiency. The first was a tendency, under the fierce attacks from its many enemies, to develop its union programs upon a too advanced revolutionary basis and to identify the organizations too closely with the Communist Party. This, of course, had the effect of checking the growth of the organization by making difficult its contacts with the more conservative workers and by narrowing down the T.U.U.L. united front with the left Progressives. It was a departure from the original plan for the independent unions, which called for programs not so sharply revolutionary, but more of a broad united front character.

The second serious weakness of the T.U.U.L. in this period was the beginning of a tendency in the direction of dual unionism, the traditional weakness of the American left wing. The basis of this was the deplorable situation in the A.F. of L.; its lassitude in the face of the employers' attacks and its rapid decline in strength and influence. This tended to make the T.U.U.L. neglect the work in the old unions, to concentrate on the new unions, and to establish new unions in some cases when it would have been more practical to have worked inside the A.F. of L. The left Socialists, Musteites, Trotskyites and Lovestoneites, who now criticize this weakness of the T.U.U.L., also were at the time actively engaged in organizing the Illinois miners' P.M.A. and other non-A.F. of L. independent unions [16, p. 278].

Foster's attitude toward political party action was never as clearly defined as his attitude, with all of its many variations, toward trade-union action. By World War I he had obviously abandoned his faith in unqualified syndicalism, and his acceptance of Communist party discipline indicates a willingness to subordinate union activity to political needs. It is probably fair to conclude that, given his choice, Foster was most comfortable with a program that involved the conspiratorial infiltration of existing craft and industrial unions (cf. 19, pp. 25–26).

Like De Leon a prolific writer and pamphleteer, Foster differed from the older man in ideas and expression as well as in his fundamental *Weltanschauung*. Whereas De Leon was a theoretician with a preference for political arrangements (Foster believed that De Leon was too bourgeois to get away from the core of nineteenth-century politics [cf. 16, pp. 33–34; cf. 22]), Foster was a revolutionary trade-unionist really at ease only when plotting an administrative coup (which rarely came off) within a trade-union unit. Foster was the more pragmatic of the two—although, to be sure, his own lack of success would have led him to avoid such a classification. In his criticism of De Leon one can see the gist of Foster's own views.

. . . De Leon looked upon the old craft unions as a sort of conspiracy of the capitalists and conservative labor leaders against the working class. With this sectarian conception, De Leon vigorously led several secessions of revolutionary elements from the A.F. of L. . . . the only substantial effects of De Leon's dual unionism being to disastrously weaken the A.F. of L. left wing and thus to leave the Gompersites more firmly in control of the trade unions.

The essentially syndicalistic character of De Leon's whole outlook is clear. In his theories the basic organs of the working class are the labor unions. As for the Party, its rôle is only a secondary one, instead of one of central, decisive leadership. The whole revolutionary struggle is reduced practically to a trade union question.
. . . .

De Leonism leads not to the revolution, but away from it. Its end-product, the present-day S.L.P., is a counter-revolutionary group, the very worst expression of the American sectarianism that Marx and Engels noted long ago. It is an enemy of the Soviet Union and of everything vital and revolutionary in the labor movement. It is the most isolated, sterile and futile national party ever produced by the American working class; a pitiful monument indeed to the sincere and courageous fighter, De Leon [16, pp. 35–36].

In summary, Foster's theory of unionism, like De Leon's, was based on the subordination of union tactics to the strategy of revolutionary leaders. Unlike De Leon, however, Foster believed in the stealthy capture of labor unions by disciplined minority groups within the unions. Like De Leon, but unlike Haywood and Trautmann, he favored industrial and amalgamated craft unionism. Unlike all of them he abhorred dualism except when circumstances forced him to tolerate it. His was, in essence, not really a theory of union origins, goals, or beliefs so much as it was a theory of general social revolution, permitting any use of unions that achieved its ultimate goal.

The radical views of Trautmann and Haywood, when compared with those of De Leon and Foster, were little more than cravings for a perverse social justice and for moral realization. De Leon and Foster had a theory, if not a program, but the other two had no more than a grudge or, at most, a grievance. Taken together, however, the four are fairly representative of the left flank of American unionism.

The Right Wing: Two Socialist Views

EUGENE DEBS

Eugene Debs (1855–1926) stands in the popular mind as the pre-eminent figure of moderate socialism and industrial unionism in America. Strangely enough, he took up socialism fairly late in life, and his actual participation in union affairs was largely in the capacity of a bureaucrat in a craft union.

Debs worked on the Terre Haute and Indianapolis Railway for fourteen years, during the last four of which he was a locomotive fireman. In 1878 he became associated with the Brotherhood of Locomotive Firemen. In 1880 he was appointed (and later in the same year elected) national secretary and treasurer of the Brotherhood, as well as editor of its magazine. He served the Brotherhood in these jobs for ten years, occasionally adding to them the duties of city clerk of Terre Haute.

In 1892 Debs served as a Democrat in the Indiana legislature. He resigned his union posts during his term, but was unanimously re-elected to them. The following year, in addition to his commitments to the Brotherhood of Locomotive Firemen, he took the leading part in forming the American Railway Union, an industrial rather than a craft organization. He was immediately chosen as its president.

After several successful strikes, notably one against the Great Northern Railroad, the new union appeared to be well established. Against Debs's personal advice, however, it decided to stage a sympathetic strike against the Pullman Company in June, 1894. The rest of the story is well known. President Cleveland overrode the protests of Governor Altgeld and put troops on all trains "to protect the mails." Two federal judges issued sweeping injunctions against the strikers, which led eventually to the indictment and prosecution of Debs and six others, who were sentenced to spend half a year in the McHenry County jail in Woodstock, Illinois. Six months later (November 22, 1895), having been converted to socialism through his reading of material given him by Victor Berger, Eugene Debs emerged as a hero and a man of public stature. It was at this point that his views, rather than his actions alone, began to attract popular notice.

Throughout the remainder of his life Debs espoused two causes, socialism and industrial unionism. As he used the latter term, it referred to the organization of all the workers in a plant into one union, regardless of their crafts. Beyond that, it implied class consciousness among all in the working class. Because Debs was an orator and not a theorist, it is misleading to associate his importance solely with the weight of his ideas. It is certainly apparent that they lacked De Leon's "bite" or even Foster's didacticism.

Politically, Debs's affiliation with Victor Berger, the Milwaukee Bernstein revisionist, and with the Social Democratic party, which was the Milwaukee faction at the time of the breakup of the Socialist Labor party in 1900, exposed him to the abusive enmity of De Leon, but was nonetheless a godsend. In Berger, Debs had an example of considerable revisionist success: the model city of Milwaukee. This gave him material for his undoubted oratorical powers.

Between 1900 and 1920 Debs was several times nominated as the Socialist candidate for the presidency of the United States. In 1912, the high-water mark of the Socialist movement in this country, Debs polled almost nine hundred thousand votes. In 1920, when he next ran—and while he was serving a sentence in the federal penitentiary in Atlanta for sedition—he managed to get almost one million votes.

It is with his labor union ideas that we are directly concerned, however. The defeat of the Pullman strike not only turned him to socialism but, what is more, convinced him that there was no hope for social progress within the American Federation of Labor (he felt that Gompers' withholding of support had not only doomed the strike, but had spelled the end of the American Railway Union). Furthermore, Debs was certain that there had to be political action if the "new society" was to be achieved. Thus he took the remnants of the American Railway Union with him into a new, short-lived federation, the American Labor Union, which included the Western Federation of Miners and several other western unions. The American Labor Union endorsed socialism, but as a concession to its western constituents it flouted the idea of the brotherhood of man by advocating that Orientals be excluded. The union did not do well; it participated in one strike in Haverhill, Massachusetts, where, out of its element and away from the steadying influence of the Western Federation of Miners, it failed. Eventually it became part of the Industrial Workers of the World.

Debs's anti-AFL dualism found felicitous expression in articles and speeches. In an article dated November, 1902, he summarized his position.

I am the friend, not the enemy of the American Federation of Labor. I would conserve, not destroy it. I am opposed, not to the organization or its members, many of whom are personal friends, but to those who are restraining its evolution and preventing it from fulfilling its true mission.

I would not convert it into a political organization, but simply bring it up to date and have it, as it must become if it is to survive, a class-conscious industrial union, its members recognizing the Socialist ballot as the weapon of their class and using it accordingly, thus escaping the incongruities and self-contradictions of the present "pure and simple" union, whose members strike against and boycott the effects of the capitalist system while voting industriously to perpetuate the system [8, p. 264].

His views on the function of trade-unions as contrasted with those of the Socialist party were quite succinct.

The trades-union is an economic organization with distinct economic functions and as such is a part, a necessary part, but a part only of the Labor Movement; it has its own sphere of activity, its own program and is its own master within its economic limitations.

But the labor movement has also its political side and the trades-unionist must be educated to realize its importance and to understand that the political side of the movement must be *unionized* as well as the economic side; and that he is not in fact a union man at all who, although a member of the union on the economic side, is a non-unionist on the political side; and while striking for, votes against the working class [7, p. 24].

Socialism, on the other hand, was to be more catholic than unionism.

. . . While the trades-union is confined to the trade, the Socialist Party embraces the entire working class, and while the union is limited to bettering conditions under the wage system, the party is organized to conquer the political power of the nation, wipe out the wage system and make the workers themselves the masters of the earth.

In this program, the trades-union and the Socialist Party, the economic and political wings of the labor movement, should not only not be in conflict, but act together in perfect harmony in every struggle whether it be on the one field or the other, in the strike or at the ballot box. The main thing is that in every such struggle the workers shall be united, shall in fact be unionists and no more be guilty of scabbing on their party than on their union, no more think of voting a capitalist ticket on election day and turning the working class over to capitalist robbery and misrule than they would think of voting in the union to turn it over to the capitalists and have it run in the interest of the capitalist class [7, p. 26].

But Debs insisted that the union movement be "progressive," by which he meant that it should be evolutionary and abandon outmoded economic forms.

At the very threshold of this discussion I aver that the old form of trade unionism no longer meets the demands of the working class. I aver that the old trade union has not only fulfilled its mission and outlived its usefulness, but that it is now positively reactionary, and is maintained, not in the interests of the workers who support it, but in the interests of the capitalist class who exploit the workers who support it . . . [4, p. 171].

. . . .

. . . The form of the union must correspond to the mode of industry. In other words, the union, like the trade, is subject to the inexorable laws of evolution. We want a union today that expresses all the various subdivisions of labor now engaged in a [manufacturing] establishment. Suppose there are 500 such employees in a plant. We organize them all, and they are assigned to their various departments; and if one of them has a grievance it becomes the concern of every worker in that establishment [4, p. 180].

The goal to be achieved was an industrial unionism in which one craft could not be played against another.

How is it now? Certain departments are organized in craft unions, meet with the officials and make an agreement or contract. They do not care what becomes of the rest, if only they can get what they are after for themselves. After they are thus tied up, the employees in some other department present a grievance and are turned down and out. They go out on strike. Those tied fast in an agreement say: "We would like to help you, we are in sympathy with you, but you see we have an agreement, and that agreement is sacred; it must be preserved inviolate; and while we are in sympathy with you and hate to see you defeated and lose your jobs, we cannot go back on our agreement." And in this way one union is used to crush another, labor is defeated and scabs are made by thousands [4, p. 180].

The industrial organization that Debs envisaged was to be socialistic in character. It was not to be merely an elimination of the possibility of divisions among working groups. Quite the contrary, it was actively to foster class consciousness and promote the revolutionary ideal. Later, in an address to an IWW audience in New York City, Debs discussed his ultimate goal. At the time he still favored and was favored by the Industrial Workers of the World, although the days of cordial relations between them were numbered.

The Industrial Workers declares [*sic*] that the workers must make themselves the masters of the tools with which they work; and so a very important function of this new union is to teach the workers, or, rather, have them teach themselves the necessity of fitting themselves to take charge of the industries in which they are employed when they are wrested, as they will be, from their capitalist masters.
. . . .

The old unionism would have you contented. We Industrial Workers are doing what we can to increase your discontent. We would have you rise in revolt against wage-slavery. The working man who is contented to-day is truly a pitiable object [5, p. 11].

Debs left the Industrial Workers of the World in 1906 and, as time went on, became appalled at the Haywood-inspired tactics of sabotage.

Its tactics alone have prevented the growth of the Industrial Workers of the World. Its principles of industrial unionism are sound, but its tactics are not. Sabotage repels the American worker. He is ready for the industrial union, but he is opposed to the "propaganda of the deed," and as long as the I.W.W. adheres to its present tactics and ignores political action, or treats it with contempt by advising the workers to "strike at the ballot box with an axe," they will regard it as an anarchist organization and it will never be more than a small fraction of the labor movement [6, p. 483].

More than that, his view of the new society allowed plenty of room for education, teachers, "intellectuals," and free discussion.

The sound education of the workers and their thorough organization, both economic and political, on the basis of the class struggle, must precede their emancipation. Without such education and organization they can make no substantial progress, and they will be robbed of the fruits of any temporary victory they may achieve, as they have been through all the centuries of the past.
. . . .

Another matter of party concern is the treatment of so-called "intellectuals" in the Socialist movement. Why the term "intellectual" should be one of reproach in the Socialist party is hard to understand, and yet there are many Socialists who sneer at a man of intellect as if he were an interloper and out of place among Socialists. For my-

self I am always glad to see a man of brains, of intellect, join the movement. If he comes to us in good faith he is a distinct acquisition and
is entitled to all the consideration due to any other comrade.

. . . .

An organization of intellectuals would not be officered and represented by wage-earners; neither should an organization of wage-
earners be officered and represented by intellectuals.

There is plenty of useful work for the intellectuals to do without
holding office, and the more intellectual they are the greater can their
service be to the movement. Lecturers, debaters, authors, writers,
artists, cartoonists, statisticians, etc., are in demand without number,
and the intellectuals can serve to far better advantage in those capacities than in official positions [6, pp. 483-84].

Finally, it should be realized that Debs was fundamentally neither an advanced theorist nor a dedicated labor unionist. His
lack of real interest in Marxian theory and even greater lack of
interest in its implications were matched only by his studied refusal to see the actual consequences of the dual unionism he advocated. His espousal of industrial unionism, like so much of
his thinking, was instinctive rather than rational. Much of what
he urged was already present in the AFL, yet his dislike of
Gompers' leadership was so strong that it blinded him to the
virtues that existed in the United Mine Workers as well as in
many other broadly defined "craft" unions. Debs, the "Bryan of
the American labor movement," was a man with a humanitarian
conscience rather than the executive organizer of a new society.
Even his dual unionism was the inchoate expression of a mind
that did not grasp the complexities of administrative logic. Certainly his dual unionism had none of the focused bitterness of
De Leon's, nor any of the conspiratorial quality that Foster's
many organizations had.

In brief, Debs spoke out in allegedly Marxian language for a
utopian socialism and for the brotherhood of men. These were
in some way to be organized along industrial lines.

The Pragmatists

Earlier we reviewed briefly the history of the Socialist Party
of America, noting how it grew out of the unity convention at

Rochester in 1901 and the Social Democracy movement in Milwaukee. Our intent now is to sketch the attitudes toward the
"trade-union problem" of several of the leading figures prominent in the party's right flank, and to show the essentially non-
doctrinaire position that they took toward the AFL, which they,
unlike those on the left, did not consider to be a lost cause.

At the Rochester convention of the Socialist party, N. I. Stone
delivered the major address on "trade-union problems," which
he believed had been created by the machinations of Daniel De
Leon.

The trade union movement is viewed in a different light by different Socialists. To the enthusiast who has just caught a glimpse of the
grand panorama of the Socialist vision without having yet thoroughly
digested the Socialist philosophy or comprehended its bearings on
events and conditions around him, trade unions will appear in one
light. To the narrow fanatic who conceives his Socialism as a panacea
evolved out of the fertile brain for his master, who sees nothing but
his "fixed idea" before him and is deaf and blind to life and its reality;
who neither consults with nor cares for actual conditions, but believes
that everything which does not suit his measure, must be either
chopped off or stamped out—to him trade unions will appear in another light. To the Socialist who has gone through the various prepara-
tory stages and has finally grasped the true spirit of Socialism, who
knows that our movement has become a power only since it has
shaken off all that was utopian and visionary and learned to conduct
its negative and positive work—the work of combating the old and
of building up the new—in conformity with actual conditions—to
him trade unionism will appear again in another light [28, p. 1].

Stone reviewed the history of socialism within the AFL, citing the list of its failures in the nineties in the repeated chal-
lenges to Gompers' leadership. He went on to describe how De
Leon's Socialist Trade and Labor Alliance came into being, taking considerable care to emphasize the unilaterality of De Leon's
original action and the highhandedness of his administrative
methods. He then analyzed De Leon's policies, and it is here
that he clearly reveals his distaste for all forms of dual unionism,

including the De Leon variant. Stone ended his address by endorsing wholeheartedly the party's decision to work with the AFL (cf. 28, pp. 18–19).

Stone was not actively associated with any particular union. Thus his views, though respected, could not be regarded as more than the opinion of an informed theorist or commentator. Fortunately, the Socialists did have at least two key figures who were personally engaged in union matters: Max Hayes and Victor L. Berger. Of the two, Hayes was the more active unionist, since Berger's union achievements involved the shaping of AFL policy in the Wisconsin State Federation rather than in any affiliated international union, and in the AFL the political units, city centrals and state federations, were relatively unimportant; the power was vested in the internationals.

Max Hayes was the pre-eminent representative of established trade-unionism in the councils of the Socialist Party of America. By profession Hayes was editor of the *Cleveland Citizen,* oldest of the currently published labor papers. By affiliation he was a leading member of the International Typographical Union and a key delegate to the AFL and the Socialist party conventions. By persuasion he was a moderate reformer, and several times was a candidate for high political and union office. At the same time, he was a pragmatist intent upon minimizing friction between workingmen's institutions.

Hayes founded the *Cleveland Citizen* in 1891, taking over its editorship when it was acquired the next year by the Cleveland Central Labor Union. In 1896 he joined the Socialist Labor party, even though he did not share De Leon's enthusiasm for dual unions. As one of the "Kangaroos" [10] who met early in 1900 at the Rochester unity convention, he received the group's endorsement as vice-presidential candidate, but later withdrew in favor of Harriman.

A clear statement of Hayes's attitude toward unions and socialism was made at the party convention in 1904, when he an-

[10] This term, apparently first used by Victor Berger, was applied to the group which opposed De Leon in the 1900 breakup of the Socialist Labor party.

swered several left-wing delegates who were openly intolerant of the "slowness" of trade-unions.

. . . I say to you that the trades union movement will survive all of the criticisms and denunciations that may be heaped upon it by the capitalists on one side or the traitors in labor's ranks upon the other side. . . . We of the trades union movement, those of us who belong to organized labor, are constantly in the forefront of the great battle that is waging [*sic*] in this country. Our battle does not last one day, or one week, or one month, or one year, but it goes on and on until one side or the other wins. . . . If we surrendered our trades unions and placed our dependence solely upon the casting of a ballot once or twice a year, the working class of this country would be in deeper misery than it is to-day . . . and it is only because of the resisting power . . . of the workers in the industrial field that we have secured some concessions, slight as they may be. All in fact that the workers have secured has not been gained by political movements, has not been gained through the old parties, but has been won despite the opposition of the old parties, and consequently, it is our duty to bring the trades unionists in line with the Socialist Party and attempt to accomplish politically what we are aiming to do now industrially [**27**, 1904, p. 184].

Another excellent example of Hayes's feeling that there was a harmony of interests between the AFL and the Socialist party can be found in his testimony before the United States Commission on Industrial Relations.

. . . the aims and objects of the American Federation of Labor, so far as its political and social demands are concerned, are quite similar; in fact, are about the same as those of the Socialist Party in the immediate demands of the platform on which the latter organization is based. Holding a sort of dual position in the two organizations, having attended the conventions of the American Federation of Labor during the last 15 years as a delegate, I have followed the trend quite closely, and naturally have gained some convictions relative to the principles upon which both organizations are founded. . . . In my capacity as a delegate to the American Federation of Labor and as a member of the Socialist Party, as editor of the Citizen for the last 25 years, as a member of the trade-union movements for 30 years, and about 19 years of the Socialist Party or the Socialist movement, I have come to the conclusion that the American Federation of Labor is the logical economic organization for this country [33, II, 1558].

Hayes emphasized not only his faith in the economic efficacy of trade-unions, but also his aspirations for a better society. It was because of these aspirations that he chose socialism.

I am a member of the trade-union movement because it is the bread-and-butter organization—the movement that meets the problems on the industrial fields. It has been stated by President Gompers that the matter of reducing the hours of labor, raising wages, gaining more decent working conditions in shops, mines, and on the railroads in the country is an absolute necessity and in that I fully agree. But I recognize the limitations of the trade-union movement, and hence I have come to the conclusion that it is absolutely necessary also to give a political expression to the wants and desires of the working class in order to place ourselves in a position of equality in waging the contest for these improvements with the capitalists, who are not only organized industrially but politically, and are in control politically and industrially.

. . . .

They would make no political effort whatever except to petition and make a demand here and there for some immediate relief where there was a possibility of obtaining it. But there has been a steady evolution even among those conservatives to the extent that they now operate through what they call a labor representation committee, adopting the name of the Labor Representation Committee of Great Britain [33, II, 1560].

Hayes's ideas were succinctly summarized at the end of his testimony:

MR. THOMPSON: Now, in regard to the concrete or present industrial situation, the Socialist Party believes in letting that field lie in the hands of the American Federation of Labor to adjust the present-day working hours, wages, and conditions?

MR. HAYES: Yes, sir.

MR. THOMPSON: Whereas they look forward to a program which

deals more particularly with the philosophy or theory of what society should be industrially?

MR. HAYES: In a political sense; yes.

MR. THOMPSON: That is correct?

MR. HAYES: Yes [33, II, 1561].

In the ensuing years Hayes was active both in politics and in trade-union affairs. He and Victor Berger were among those who refused an invitation to the Chicago meeting at which the Industrial Workers of the World was formed. In 1911 he helped prepare for the state of Ohio a workmen's compensation law, which was introduced by William Green, then a senator. In 1912 he ran against Gompers for the presidency of the AFL and scored a surprisingly high number of votes—27 per cent of those cast.

Since Hayes was an orthodox unionist whose socialism was idealistic rather than militant, what was his difference with Gompers? Essentially, it arose from the difference in their personalities as well as from disagreement about questions of administrative organization. Gompers, distrustful of the effect on union organization of all activity removed from the central job issues, sought to prevent "outsiders" from bringing their own causes into AFL councils for debate. He was convinced that both Hayes and his confrere, Victor Berger, were unknowingly playing into the hands of those outsiders. As a result, he willingly let them express their personal views, but refused to permit them to gain in the organization an administrative foothold that would make it possible for them to focus administrative attention on extraneous issues.

The reluctance of Hayes and Berger to secede from the AFL, in spite of their continual frustration, is evidence of their fundamental acceptance of unionism in which the job issue was paramount. That they did not at the same time despair of socialism shows how firmly they believed in the fundamental truth of their dream. Their belief in these somewhat conflicting theories is a strong indication of the breadth of their thinking. They could advocate the revolutionary cause in which they believed and at the same time admit some of the points scored by their adversary, Gompers. In the tradition of Mill's *On Representative Government,* they were true liberals; in the same tradition, Gompers was a true conservative (23, Chap. 2).

Norman Ware: Hindsight with a Purpose

Consideration of the work of Norman J. Ware (1886–1949), a professor of sociology at the University of Louisville and later a professor of economics at Wesleyan University, is useful in providing a sympathetic assessment of the right-wing Socialists' interpretation of American unionism.

By birth a Canadian, Ware emigrated to the United States, where he received a doctorate in economics at the University of Chicago in 1913. However, his first major work on the labor movement, *The Industrial Worker, 1840–1860: The Reaction of American Industrial Society to the Advance of the Industrial Revolution* (36), did not appear until 1924, after it had been awarded the 1922 Hart, Schaffner, and Marx prize for excellence in drawing "the attention of American youth to the study of economic and commercial subjects."

In this book Ware analyzed the nature and consequences of the profound social and ideological changes occurring during the two pre–Civil War decades as a result of American industrialization. He pointed out that previous to the depression of 1837–40, American workingmen frequently owned their own homes, and those who rented often raised much of their meat and vegetables. He concluded that they had a certain degree of independence of the job market and enjoyed a consequent, although limited, modicum of social status and voice in community affairs (36, pp. 27, 39, 65, and 68).

Much of this was changed in the forties, when the development of factories, which involved great amounts of capital investment and the installation of machines and job specialization, altered first the economic position and later the social status of workers. Where previously a chronic labor shortage had allowed skilled workingmen to demand and obtain relatively high wages, the new situation worked to the economic advantage of those who owned the machines and factories. Competition for jobs forced down wage rates and the workers' share of the national dividend fell (36, p. xii). Once semi-independent and self-reliant artisans were driven to cringing dependence; where earlier they had sold their wares, after the change wrought by the industrial revolution they were driven to selling their bodies by the hour.

Two passages from the introduction to this work serve to illustrate Ware's conviction that the changes in modes of production and the power of ownership of machines were the critical features of the period.

There were two aspects of the Industrial Revolution closely related and supporting each other, but of quite different texture and meaning. One of these—the obvious, new, dramatic aspect—was the application of water and steam-driven machinery to production, and its concomitant, the modern factory system. The other, not necessarily dependent upon machinery and not less revolutionary, though less regarded, was the social revolution in which sovereignty in economic affairs passed from the community as a whole into the keeping of a special class. It was this social revolution that primarily affected the industrial worker in this period and against which his protests were made . . . [36, p. xi].

[The] transition from the earlier to the later status was reflected in the terms of the labor contract. The old term for the remuneration of the mechanic was 'price.' It referred to his product rather than to his labor, for it was his product that he sold. When the producer, whether master or journeyman, sold his product, he retained his person. But when he came to sell his labor, he sold himself. The term 'wage' that displaced 'price' as the Industrial Revolution advanced had formerly applied only to day labor, and the extension of the term to the skilled worker was regarded by him as a symbol of a deeper change . . . [36, p. xiv].

Ware believed that the labor programs of the forties, involving phalanxes, co-operatives, and homesteads, were not essentially revolutionary in nature. Quite the contrary, he saw them as anticapitalistic impossibilist "struggles to return to a pre-machine past that had gone." In Ware's view, the reformers who advocated these programs gave ample evidence, by talking of the economic opportunities offered by the frontier, that they had little comprehension of the true difficulty or the avenues leading to its solution. Led by blind leaders, "unseeing" labor got nowhere and, in his words, "the labor movement in America finished the period 1840–60 as it had begun—practically in nothingness" (36, p. 240). Actually unable to shed "community consciousness," pre–Civil War labor failed to understand the basic implications of the new technology. After two decades labor found itself in a less advantageous position than before.

In his second book, *The Labor Movement in the United States, 1860–1895* (38), Ware discussed the Knights of Labor, which he described as "[in 1886] the most imposing labor organization this country has ever known." He interpreted the organization of the Knights as having grown out of the workingmen's twofold disillusionment with politics and "simple trade unionism." The central theme of the Knights, solidarity—"An injury to one is the concern of all"—was the logical result, representing an important aspect of the workers' state of mind at the time, as well as an entirely noble sentiment.

In ideological opposition to the Knights, in which Ware agreed noble solidarity had "ended in chaos," was the American Federation of Labor. Led by Gompers and McGuire, the AFL was, according to Ware, an uninspired aggregation where "exclusiveness reached something like sterility" (38, p. xiv). His argument consisted of four elements: (1) that the Knights, rather than the AFL trade-unions, appreciated the lesson of the industrial revolution—namely, that the machine age had wiped out craft distinctions and the protection they offered to artisans; (2) that worker solidarity, not industrial particularism, offered the only true hope to American wage earners in the struggle against "huge consolidations of capital with [almost overwhelming] economic and political authority"; (3) that the life of the Knights was shaped and eventually curtailed by an inane reliance upon "a windbag whose place was on the street corner rousing the rabble to concert pitch and providing emotional compensation for dull lives," to wit, Terence V. Powderly (38, p. xvi); and (4) that the establishment of the AFL was to a significant, if not a preponderant, degree the result of the personal ambitions and in the long run socially undesirable cravings of Samuel Gompers. These themes are quite consistent, incidentally, with the positions taken by Victor Berger and Max Hayes, although Ware had the advantage of hindsight, which the two Socialist unionists had perforce lacked in their earlier appraisal.

Class solidarity, which Ware believed was the core of the Knights' philosophy, was the outgrowth of the changes in the methods of production brought about by the industrial revolution. And class solidarity, by definition and implied purpose, had to eliminate parochial and particularistic divisions among the masses of wage earners. Yet having discovered these truths, how could the Knights have failed?

Ware's answers had the beauty of simplicity. The Knights foundered on the poor judgments of Powderly and his colleagues, who after 1886–88 failed to call a necessary retreat *pour mieux sauter.* Gompers, however, recognized the situation and responded intelligently, but then instead of launching a new attack, continued to fall back while preaching the allegedly pernicious doctrines of exclusive jurisdiction, *sauve qui peut,* and nominal acceptance of the wage system. Thus the AFL betrayed American wage earners generally, while entrenching specific groups of them behind the temporary barricades of opportunism. In truth, Ware saw Gompers as the quintessence of the misleader of labor and the Gompers policies as shortsighted betrayals of the labor movement.

The past rottenness, and implicit therein the possible future Messianic features, of leadership is an important refrain throughout the Ware analysis. According to his view, it is the leader who must correctly analyze the basic truths and then conceive, adapt, and execute appropriate policies. In other words, the justification of unionism lies in the benefits it provides for the whole working class; the policies of unionism selected to achieve that purpose are the primary responsibility of an enlightened leader who must convince the rank and file of their validity or himself go down in the attempt. Evidently Ware did not feel it right for a leader to sacrifice principle for "survival," for he seems uniformly to have condemned Gompers' policies, yet he did not criticize unionists for having endorsed by acceptance those same policies. To the original Marxian assumption of long-run economic determinism, Ware appended an analysis of the critical consequences of heroic leadership. As a historian he had some reservations regarding the previous existence of real class consciousness in America, although he expressed a qualified belief that it might develop in time (38, p. 335). "The Order," Ware wrote,

tried to teach the American wage-earner that he was a wage-earner first and a bricklayer, carpenter, miner, shoemaker, after; that he was a wage-earner first and a Catholic, Protestant, Jew, white, black, Democrat, Republican, after. This meant that the Order was teaching something that was not so in the hope that sometime it would be. It failed, and its failure was perhaps a part of . . . the general failure of democracy—or is it humanity? [38, p. xviii.]

Ware's third major work, *Labor in Modern Industrial Society* (37) appeared in 1935. It was intended to be the synthesis of his judgments, historical and analytical, of the American labor movement, and was primarily concerned with two issues: the characteristics and quality of leadership in American unions and the level of class-conscious idealism among the members.

Ware asserted that there were three types of union leaders—the intellectual, the executive, and the agitator. The intellectual type has generally been unsuccessful on the American scene because of the common-sense or practical temperament of the workers, because most of the intellectuals have been strange or foreign to workers, and because workers' sentiments have been turned by Samuel Gompers' fulminations against intellectuals. In part, the intellectuals too were responsible for their own failures, because of their doctrinaire rigidity. In any event, this type of leader was not conspicuous for his practical success, even though he was often honestly and intelligently motivated.

Ware had a complex attitude toward the executive type of union leader. While partially agreeing with the usual charges that a particular leader might be (1) interested only in his own craft, (2) interested only in "lining his own pocket," (3) interested too much in co-operating with employers, or (4) a racketeer, Ware argued that often the truth in these charges also reflected in part the same or similar failings in the rank-and-file membership. This was particularly true with respect to the first charge. He also emphasized that the temptations to become a deadwood bureaucrat, safe in his berth, were regrettably great in moribund unions.

It was the third charge, involving class collaboration—the particular dread of the Socialists—that Ware handled most analytically. He first rephrased the question, arguing that the charge of class collaboration, leveled at the union leaders, implies the existence of class-conscious workers and is therefore a misnomer when applied to the activities and relationships of most union officials in the United States, since neither they nor the members of their organizations are class conscious. " 'Union-management' coöperation is a better way of expressing the idea, and it leaves open the question of the legitimacy of the practice. . . . An established union and its leaders have to collaborate with management. . . . It becomes wrong only when it serves not the interest of the workers but the private fortunes of the leaders" (37, p. 39). Three planes of union-management relationship could be isolated: antagonism, co-operation with an eye toward mutually advantageous conditions for the workers and the industry, and conspiracy "between union officials [*sic*] and management for the private gain of each at the expense of both the workers and the industry—a form of racketeering."

The nature of the leadership function appears to depend on the maturity of the union-management relationship, on the level of rank-and-file interest, and to a significant degree upon the personality of the particular leader. Initially most leaders operate only as spokesmen for the workers. Later an entrenched leader finds that he himself develops a program which he sells first to the employer and then to the union members. Ultimately the leader may tire of having to argue with the members and may incline to arrangements and policies that minimize the possibility of his being challenged by them. This latter phase is conducive to racketeering, a situation which Ware felt was all too frequently found in the "senile" unions of the AFL, though no more frequently there than in comparable business circles.

Racketeering among union officials is simply a new name for an old graft [he wrote]. It is a cancerous growth on industry, labor, and government in the interest of the private fortunes of officials. It is found chiefly in those industries where small contractors are financially weak or, because of a time factor in their contracts or in the conditions of the trade, cannot afford stoppage of work [37, p. 41].

The third type of leader, the agitator, on the whole scored most of his success among alien (nonacculturated) workers in America. Ware expressed a limited admiration for the energy of these leaders, but he had a lesser regard for their intelligence. He considered his *bête noire,* Samuel Gompers, to be a shrewd combination of agitator and executive—in other words, a successful opportunist. "The authority of Samuel Gompers," he argued,

. . . was of two sorts: personal and machine. His personal authority was very great over both the rank and file and the national officers. His control of the annual conventions was almost complete after 1895 and was little disputed. His machine, consisting of a group of general organizers appointed by himself all over the country and not under the authority of the officers of the national unions, kept him in close touch with what was going on and in control of conventions. The Executive Council of the A.F. of L. became a part of the Gompers machine and, though some changes were made in its personnel, the nucleus at his death was that of the early years when the organization was in the process of building.

Outside the organization Gompers was practically the sole recognized spokesman of organized labor for a quarter of a century. And yet he really did not speak for labor, if by "labor" is meant the mass of American wage-earners. He spoke for the small section of wage-earners organized in national unions, in city centrals, and in state federations. These are generally called the "skilled workers," but the term is somewhat misleading. There is skill in all manual and mechanical operations, and some of the most skilled mechanics are not organized while some of the least skilled are. What Gompers really spoke for was trade union officialdom. His whole philosophy, if it can be called that, was built around the official point of view. The term "voluntarism" which came to sum up his outlook finds its roots in the smallest local agent and his followers afraid of losing one iota of their power, and it runs all through the hierarchy of officers of national and international unions. His distrust of "ideas" was that of the professional agent of the local whose business it is to get "more, more, now" not only in wages, and conditions of work, but in dues. Gompers found the trade union official as he was and so interpreted him to the country. Having done this he erected a wall around this official point of view and kept out all others. He surrounded himself with second- and third-rate men and women, and his organization went through the World War without learning, and without caring to learn, anything [37, pp. 496–97].

In all, Ware believed that three groups of factors influenced unionism: economic considerations, ideology and ideological motivation, and the personalities of the leaders. Noting that the first two could be the most important in the long run, he suggested nonetheless that they "seemed to have had little effect on trade union structure and policy [in the AFL] while . . . leadership has been of unusual significance."

One chapter of *Labor in Modern Industrial Society* contains an explicit discussion of labor philosophies, which were "basically of two sorts: (a) those in which the wages-profits system is itself repudiated, and (b) those in which the wages-profits system is accepted as a condition within which the worker must act to promote his interests" (37, Chap. 18, p. 378). Ware, unlike others whose ideas we have analyzed, was too conscious of the historical perspective to conclude that the former type of theory had ever been successfully adaptable to the American environment. At the same time, however, he was resolved that the second type not be oversold. ". . . The [Socialist] intellectual," he insisted, "is helpless without the wage-earner and some entente has to be reached between these two philosophies, methods, and forms of organization. The history of the relations of the Socialist party and the trade unions is a confused one but underneath the confusion lies this simple fact, *that a socialist without a labor following is impotent and a trade union movement without something larger than a wages philosophy tends to become sterile*" (37, p. 379; italics added).

At the time, Ware could not help but conclude that the explicit, historic mission of socialism had failed. Nevertheless, it is fair to surmise that he felt that part of its historic mission remained, albeit, perhaps, under the direction of a different political party. Ware was not a "vulgar" economic determinist; he recognized the roles of individuals and ideology in shaping history. But he emphasized that it was through their influence on economic relationships that history was, more or less violently, shaped. In this sense Ware's judgment again coincided closely with that of the right-wing Socialist revisionists. In the conclusion of the book Ware summarized his views:

Neither employers nor employees, singly or collectively, are in a position freely to decide what form industrial relations will take in the immediate future or in the long run. It is more than a matter of good or bad will or intentions. There are conditioning factors over which we have little control. But conditioning factors are affected in turn by human wills and choices and if this were not so it would be quite useless to discuss human affairs.

Among the factors, social and economic, which condition labor relations at this time the following are of importance:

(1) The balance of competition and monopoly in the industry considered.

(2) The rate of technical change and the distribution of the product.

(3) The stage of capitalist evolution.

(4) The characteristics of the wage-earning and employer groups.

(5) The attitude of government.

Under "normal" economic conditions the first of these is the most important. The last two are derivative and the third may be the determining factor in the future [37, p. 539].

"Many employers," he judged at the end of the study,

conscientiously believe themselves to be the best judges of what the workers need and frequently of what they want. And they may be right. But it is their business primarily to look after the interest of the owners or of those who control both owners and themselves, so that it is impossible for them, even when they know what the workers want, to give it to them.

Therefore, the following conclusions seem warranted:

(1) This attitude at least in industries where competition is severe is unwise in that it rejects in organized labor an important instrument for the enforcement of fair practices in that field—the labor bargain— in which employers are at least capable of such enforcement.

(2) This attitude is contrary to the spirit and practice of democracy in that it refuses adequate representation to a major interest in our economic life and substitutes either paternalistic or feudal practices. In view of the present unhappy status of democracy the world over this may not appear to be a significant point, but the alternative to democracy is dictatorship and there is no guarantee that a dictatorship will be more favorable to business interests than democracy.

(3) This attitude offers no solution of the problems which industry faces today and in especial [sic] of the problem of the distribution of the national income so as to maintain a market for the continuous operation of mass production industries under conditions of accelerated technical change.

(4) This attitude is an invitation to further government control of industry, for in the last analysis the government is not primarily interested in employers or employees but in the citizen and his contentment. It cannot allow, if it can prevent it, the public peace to be constantly disturbed by warring parties either of employers intrenched behind barbed wire entanglements or workers throwing cobble stones and overturning trucks.

(5) Finally, this attitude is an invitation to mass action of a revolutionary nature, and is the only significant incentive of this sort now

found in the United States. It is not the communists we have to fear, if we have to fear anything, but hunger, insecurity, and suffering [37, pp. 546–47].

Ware also wrote a fourth monograph, "The History of Labor Interaction" (35), which was not published until 1937.

As a synthesis of Ware's ideas, the foregoing discussion is illustrative of the right-wing revisionist view brought up to date (as of 1935). For this reason his work has been included in this chapter as a backdrop to the Socialist prescription.

References

1. Brissenden, Paul F., *History of the Industrial Workers of the World*. New York: Columbia University Press, 1919.

2. ———, "Industrial Workers of the World," in *Encyclopaedia of the Social Sciences,* VIII, 13–18.

3. Commons, John R., and Associates, *History of Labour in the United States*. 2 vols. New York: The Macmillan Co., 1918.

4. Debs, Eugene V., "Craft Unionism" (speech given at South Chicago, November 24, 1905), in *Writings and Speeches of Eugene V. Debs,* with an introduction by Arthur M. Schlesinger, Jr. New York: Hermitage Press, 1948.

5. ———, *Industrial Unionism, an Address Delivered at Grand Central Palace, New York, Sunday, December 10, 1905.* New York: New York Labor News Co., 1911.

6. ———, "Sound Socialist Tactics," *International Socialist Review,* XII (February, 1912), 481–86.

7. ———, *Unionism and Socialism: A Plea for Both.* Terre Haute, Ind.: [privately printed?], 1904.

8. ———, "The Western Labor Movement," *International Socialist Review,* III (November, 1902), 257–65.

9. De Leon, Daniel, *The Burning Question of Trades Unionism: A Lecture at Newark, N.J., on April 21, 1904.* New York: Socialist Labor Party, 1919.

10. ———, "Pleb Leaders and Labor Leaders," in *Two Pages from Roman History.* New York: New York Labor News Co., 1903.

11. De Leon, Daniel, *The Preamble of the Industrial Workers of the World: Address Delivered by Daniel De Leon at Union Temple, Minneapolis, Minnesota, July 10, 1905.* New York: New York Labor News Co. [1905?].

12. ———, "The Warning of the Gracchi," in *Two Pages from Roman History.* New York: New York Labor News Co., 1903.

13. ———, and Harriman, Job, *A Debate on the Tactics of the S.T.L.A. toward Trade Unions* [November 25, 1900, New Haven, Conn.]. [Privately published by Job Harriman, 1900.]

14. Ford, Earl C., and Foster, William Z., *Syndicalism.* Chicago: [n.d.].

15. Foster, William Z., *The Bankruptcy of the American Labor Movement.* Chicago: Trade Union Educational League, 1922. Reprinted from *T.U.E.L. Program and Principles* (February, 1922).

16. ———, *From Bryan to Stalin.* [New York]: International Publishers, 1937.

17. ———, *Little Brothers of the Big Labor Fakers.* New York: Trade Union Unity League, 1931.

18. ———, *Trade Unionism: The Road to Freedom.* Chicago: International Trade Union Educational League, [1921?].

19. ———, *What Means A Strike in Steel.* New York: Workers Library Publishers, Inc., 1937.

20. Haywood, William, and Bohn, Frank, *Industrial Socialism.* Chicago: C. H. Kerr, [1911?].

21. Lenin, V. I., *State and Revolution.* New ed. New York: International Publishers, 1932.

22. ———, *What Is To Be Done? Burning Questions of Our Movement.* London: Martin Lawrence, Ltd., [1929?].

23. Mill, John Stuart, *Considerations on Representative Government.* New York: Henry Holt & Co., Inc., 1875.

24. Saposs, David J., *Left Wing Unionism: A Study of Radical Policies and Tactics.* New York: International Publishers, 1926.

25. Shannon, David A., *The Socialist Party of America: A History.* New York: The Macmillan Co., 1955.

26. Socialist Labor Party, Ninth National Convention, 1896, *Proceedings.*

27. Socialist Party of America, *Convention Proceedings.* Chicago: The Socialist Party.

28. Stone, N. I., *The Attitude of the Socialists toward the Trade Unions: An Address Given at the Rochester Unity Convention, March 28, 1900.* New York: Volkszeitung Library, 1900.

29. Trautmann, William E., *America's Dilemma, by a Factory Worker.* Chicago: J. N. Bornholft, [1922?].

30. ———, *Direct Action and Sabotage.* Pittsburgh: Socialist News Co., 1912.

31. ———, *Industrial Union Methods.* Chicago: C. H. Kerr, [n.d.].

32. ———, *One Big Union: An Outline of a Possible Industrial Organization of the Working Class, with Chart.* Chicago: C. H. Kerr, [1911?].

33. United States Commission on Industrial Relations, *Final Report and Testimony.* 11 vols. Washington, D.C.: U.S. Government Printing Office, 1916.

34. Walling, William E., *The Larger Aspects of Socialism.* New York: The Macmillan Co., 1913.

35. Ware, Norman J., "The History of Labor Interaction," Part I of H. A. Innis (ed.), *Labor in Canadian-American Relations.* Toronto: Ryerson Press, 1937.

36. ———, *The Industrial Worker, 1840–1860: The Reaction of American Industrial Society to the Advance of the Industrial Revolution.* Boston: Houghton Mifflin Co., 1924.

37. ———, *Labor in Modern Industrial Society.* Boston: D. C. Heath & Co., 1935.

38. ———, *The Labor Movement in the United States, 1860–1895; A Study in Democracy.* New York: D. Appleton & Co., 1929.

FIVE

Unionism As a Psychological Reaction

In considering the work of the theorists who viewed the growth of unionism as part of the workers' conscious protest against the effects of industrialization on society, we must touch on several of the ideas of three academicians, Robert F. Hoxie (1868–1916), Carleton H. Parker (1878–1918), and Frank Tannenbaum (b. 1893). Their ideas, formulated in the first two decades of the twentieth century, were obvious attempts to explain the growth of unionism largely as a result of changing living and working conditions. In a discussion of these writers as a unit, it is useful to turn first to the theories of Thorstein Veblen (1857–1929).[1] Both Hoxie and Parker acknowledged the usefulness of Veblen's economic theory in the evolution of their own thinking.

Veblen's Ideas and Influence

Veblen's basic analysis appeared in several of his early works (16; cf. also 1) and comprised observations on man's instinctive psychology and an explanation of an alleged dichotomy in contemporary social-value schemes. Veblen considered that man had four fundamental instincts: the *parental,* which leads to concern with the welfare of the race; the *acquisitive,* from which self-interest arises; the instinct of *workmanship,* the source of efficiency

[1] For an excellent discussion of the life and ideas of Veblen, see Joseph Dorfman, *Thorstein Veblen and His America* (3).

in production; and the instinct of *idle curiosity,* which is behind man's drive to acquire knowledge. According to Veblen, the precise meanings and effective consequences of these instincts were shaped by the interaction between the individual and external economic institutions. The most critical, though not the only, external economic institutional influence, to his way of thinking, was the state of development of machine technology. He held that the social behavior of individuals and groups was determined by the interrelationship between man (vaguely guided by his instincts) and institutional values (partly shaped by physical techniques of production).

Veblen believed that the system of social values, termed "social institutions," was itself influenced by two conflicting sets of forces. One of these pulled it toward a pecuniary or "contract" society, based on individualism and the philosophy of individual natural rights, and the other toward a social order based on post–eighteenth-century technological changes wrought by the industrial revolution. The latter system of social values was pragmatic in nature, and emphasized problems of physical production and mechanical function. It defined each individual's place in terms of his role in the industrial process.

The pecuniary value system, Veblen explained, made several demands on the labor force. The major social effect of these demands was the development of a high degree of worker mobility, which, in turn, depreciated the value placed on the holding of real property. Without fixed social roots and without the usual socially condoned outlet of real-property ownership, workmen tended to spend their incomes on goods and services that were of doubtful functional use but reflected their pecuniary status. This "conspicuous consumption," as Veblen called it, symbolized for him the waste of contemporary industrial society.

Veblen argued that most economic thinking rested largely on the conservative customs associated with the pecuniary value system. On their jobs, however, workers encountered another and newer set of mores that were the by-products of the nonanimistic functioning of the machine process. As a result, a conflict of values became apparent. In his view, job specialization, an integral part of the modern industrial process frequently decried by reformers, did not rob the worker of significant skills nor did it numb his intelligence; it merely steered him away from what were once the traditional attributes of learning, but which now grossly overemphasized outmoded, nonscientific processes. When sentimentalists endorsed the individualistic values of the old pecuniary system, they demonstrated their inability to understand the modern worker. The worker, at least, appreciated the importance of the "cause-and-effect sequence" of modern scientific production.

Thus the picture became clear. On the one hand, the worker's inherent instinct of workmanship was gratified in the shop, where he saw finished products flowing from his place in the manufacturing process. On the other, his pride, set by outmoded customs and the misplaced efforts of sentimentalists, was hurt. Moreover, there existed a large trading class oriented to pecuniary value standards, that was no longer necessary from the point of view of efficiency and that made a fetish of the right to possess property whether that property was productively employed or not. Veblen felt that workers would ultimately revolt against the pecuniary tradition and turn to socialism, which, he argued, carried none of the redundant intellectual impedimenta of property rights and also eliminated the now "useless" functions performed by middlemen and other mere money-makers.

Veblen explained the adoption of unionism as the transition to the "new" society: "a concomitant of industry organized after the manner of a machine process." The major characteristic of the trade-union mentality, he added, was the denial of those natural-rights dogmas whenever they conflicted with the realities of the mechanical standardization of modern industry (17, pp. 327–29).

He believed trade-unionism to be a short-run phenomenon— "on its face, an endeavor of compromise between received notions of what 'naturally' ought to be in matters of industrial business, on the one hand, and what the exigencies of industry demand and what the new animus of the workman will tolerate on the other. . . ." "The latest, maturest contemporary expressions of trade-unionism are, on the whole," he added, "the most extreme, insofar as they are directed against the natural rights of property and pecuniary contract." What is more, "when unionism takes an attitude of overt hostility to the natural-rights institutions of property and free contract, it ceases to be unionism simply and passes over into something else, which may be called socialism for want of a better term" (17, pp. 330–31).

Veblen argued that unions, though they usually play according to the (pecuniary) rules of the game, actually are more than mere self-interest bodies intent on maximizing their economic gains. What they seek, he wrote, is the remaking of the social order along the lines of productive function; in this sense they are really revolutionary institutions. In essence, then, they are the workmen's immediate protective device against the ravages wrought by the machine process on business-minded society. Union aggressiveness reflected the inflexibilities of the natural-rights philosophy and the changes in value schemes made mandatory by technological advance. Unions were, in other words, simply a transitional device stemming from the effect of progress on an outmoded tradition. Ancillary to Veblen's view was the fact of the workers' economic misery, which resulted from economic insufficiency, but he did not originally consider this a prime cause of unionism.

The three theorists to whose writings we now turn were influenced by the Veblen theme. Two of them adduced some empirical evidence to support their theses. Tannenbaum, however, came to somewhat different conclusions. After a consideration of the same factors, he, unlike Veblen, saw trade-unions as the champion of those struggling against the machine in order to preserve old rights.

Carleton Parker: Individual Psychology

Parker's ideas, though preceded chronologically by those of Hoxie, are taken up first, since Hoxie's views strayed further from the Veblenian tradition. Parker's unique approach to trade-

unionism resulted from his interest in the economic consequences of the psychological maladjustment of the individual
worker. His link with the Veblenian system rests on Veblen's observations regarding human instincts rather than on Veblen's
discussions of the conflict between the "pecuniary" and "industrial" value systems. Although Parker's posthumous volume of
essays was dedicated to Veblen by Mrs. Parker, apparently to
acknowledge her husband's deep sense of intellectual obligation, Parker himself noted in one of the essays in this volume
that, in spite of having studied labor relations at four universities
and under Sidney Webb, it was not until he had chanced on two
of Sigmund Freud's books that he discovered a truly scientific
approach to the analysis of labor problems (**10**, p. 27). It is
largely as a consequence of Freud's analysis, and only indirectly
as a result of Veblen's work on unions, that Parker developed
his theory of the psychological causes and purposes of unionism.

Parker added to Veblen's four basic instincts twelve more:
(5) fear and flight, (6) mental activity or thought, (7) housing
or settling, (8) migration and homing, (9) hunting, (10) anger
or pugnacity, (11) revolt at confinement, (12) revulsion, (13)
leadership and mastery, (14) subordination and submission,
(15) display, vanity, and ostentation, and (16) sex (**10**, pp. 141–
54). He considered these "unlearned tendencies to action" (he
disliked the term "instinct") to be most evident in children, at
whose stage of life societal and parental discipline was particularly slack.[2] Working-class youngsters whose parents were too occupied to give them much attention were uninhibited in their
street play and grew without psychic restraint until the time
came for them to go to work. Suddenly freedom was replaced
by the pervasive restraints of factory life.

. . . It seems, however, that the necessary laxness of working home
discipline, the decay among the working population of respect for
conventional rules and law, the favorable opportunities for the chil-

---

[2] Parker believed that people of certain races were less civilized than others,
and cites the case of a Negro child who "was closer to his jungle forebears than
a white child."

dren to quit school, the plasticity of the codes governing street social life, all work in an important manner towards allowing a relatively free and healthy psychic development of the children affected by it [10, p. 47].

This normality was soon perverted by economic necessity as the children had to go to work. Even the terminology of work (i.e., monotonous work, servile work, dirty work, simplified work, etc.) emphasizes this frustration (cf. 10, pp. 48 ff.).

It is no wonder that dissatisfaction and personal frustration developed. This change and the personal maladjustment it brought about were, in Parker's view, the key to the whole labor situation. " 'The real labor problem,' " he noted in a lecture,

". . . is one of individual psychology. What are men when they die as laborers or business men? What kind of grandchildren will follow them? What is their social heredity? What is the psychic balance sheet? It is a relation between a plastic, sensitive, easily degenerated nervous organism called 'man' and an environment. The product is human character. The labor problem is one of character-formation. . . . The importance of the western labor problem is that a *human,* irrational, de-mechanized, dynamite-using labor type rose and functioned . . ." [10, p. 7].

Besides these causes of frustration, however, Parker emphasized the purely economic origins of discontent. Principal among these were miserable working and living conditions. He reasoned that the more wretched one's economic surroundings were, the more strongly inclined one would be to revolt against the prevailing legal and social customs. He concluded from his own observations of western agricultural labor that workers neither respected the law nor felt anything remotely resembling loyalty to the economic order. In one essay he quoted an Industrial Workers of the World leader as saying,

"If you were a bum without a blanket; if you had left your wife and kids when you went west for a job, and had never located them since; if your job had never kept you long enough in a place to qualify you to vote; if you slept in a lousy, sour bunkhouse, and ate food just as rotten as they could give you and get by with it; if deputy sheriffs shot your cooking cans full of holes and spilled your grub on the ground; if your wages were lowered on you when the bosses thought they had you down; if there was one law for Ford, Suhr and Mooney, and another for Harry Thaw; if every person who represented law and order and the nation beat you up, railroaded you to jail, and the good Christian people cheered and told them to go to it, how in hell do you expect a man to be patriotic?" [10, p. 102.]

The economic misery which he saw and so vividly described in several of his essays could largely be alleviated, he wrote, by better organization of the labor market (11). The changes he recommended included positive programs for industrial "decasualization" and the encouragement of certain group relationships that would increase mutual understanding in industry (12). He also suggested that the government and industry should call on university- and hospital-trained psychologists for advice on ways to overcome existing worker hostility. Ultimately, he argued, new standards of social normality would have to be established. There, too, the psychologists would be the obvious leaders.

. . . The problem of industrial labor is one with the problem of the discontented businessman, the indifferent student, the unhappy wife, the immoral minister,—it is one of mal-adjustment between a fixed human nature and a carelessly ordered world. The result is suffering, insanity, racial perversion, and danger. The final cure is gaining acceptance for a new standard normality. The first step towards this is to break down the mores-inhibitions to free experimental thinking [10, p. 59].

Parker was actually more concerned with worker maladjustment and the problems that arose from it than he was with trade-unionism. In one essay he made this point very clear.

As a class, the migratory laborers are nothing more nor less than the finished products of their environment. They should therefore never be studied as isolated revolutionaries, but rather as, on the whole, tragic symptoms of a sick social order. Fortunately the psychologists have made it unnecessary to explain that there is nothing willful or personally reprehensible in the vagrancy of these vagrants. Their histories show that, starting with the long hours and dreary winters of farms they ran away from, through their character-debasing experience with irregular industrial labor, on to the vicious economic life of the winter unemployed, their training predetermined but one outcome. As the Harvard biologist words it, nurture has triumphed over nature, the environment has produced its type [10, pp. 88–89].

During World War I, Parker became convinced that the American labor movement was becoming increasingly more radical.

For those who care to see, there is abundant evidence that the Trade Union movement in the United States has become revolution-ary. . . . [But] no publicist of note has dared to analyze the spread of embarrassing strikes throughout the United States during the past two months, the most critical months of our war activities [10, p. 109].

He felt that the collective agitation was a symptom and that it was mandatory to study the basic social ills if solutions were to be found.

. . . The I.W.W. has importance only as an illustration of a stable American economic process. Its pitiful syndicalism, its street corner opposition to the war, are the inconsequential trimmings. Its strike alone, faithful as it is to the American type, is an illuminating thing. The I.W.W., like the Grangers, the Knights of Labor, the Farmers' Alliance, the Progressive Party, is but a revolt phenomena [sic]. The cure lies in the care taking of its psychic antecedents, and the stability of our Republic depends on the degree of courage and science with which we move to the task [10, p. 124].

The implication in this reasoning is that the psychologist and decent working conditions were the means by which not only industrial disaffection but also the problem of unionism could be solved. Whether this implication was conscious or not, it was there, and it makes Parker a precursor of the personnel-manage-ment movement. Moreover, it is in this framework that his view of unionism, admittedly only a part of his general view of social maladjustment, can be seen to be the first step toward an employer's welfare program that would negate unionism.

Parker's theoretical conclusions differed considerably from Veblen's. Since they were never fully developed, owing to his untimely death, a thorough judgment of them is unwarranted. But their influence was great, and from them as from Veblen's own work stemmed considerable later research. For this reason, if for no other, Parker's contribution is deserving of recognition.

Robert Hoxie: Mass Psychology

Certainly the most influential proponent of the "environmental" or "psychological" approach to the study of trade-unionism was Robert Franklin Hoxie. We have already noted the nature of his academic and intellectual background (see pp. 37–39), but it is pertinent to emphasize again the impressive debt he owed to the work of his close friend and colleague, Thorstein Veblen. He went far beyond Veblen in his analysis of trade-unionism, however, and ultimately disagreed with some of Veblen's fundamental conclusions.

Unlike Veblen, Hoxie had a strong strain of the moral reformer in his make-up and neither could nor would bring himself to accept the inevitable, opaque social conflict which Veblen predicted. He drew on Veblen as a source of ideas, but to these ideas he added his own unarticulated, but nonetheless basic, affinity for something akin to Christian socialism. His desire and unsuccessful attempt to achieve scientific objectivity should also be recognized as a factor in his thinking.

Hoxie, like Veblen, was primarily interested in the interaction between individual temperament (in which heredity and instincts played a major part) and environmental influences. In this sense, he drew most heavily on the parts of the Veblenian analysis least interesting to Parker. Also like Veblen, he originally believed that social development was essentially nonteleological. He went beyond Veblen, however, in arguing that, since workers' organizations avowedly served different purposes and took widely different forms, the forms, aims, and means of posi-tive types of social organization also were unpredictable. He was skeptical, too, of most claims of uniformity in society and social structure and, as we shall shortly note, set up two typologies that he felt took account of the important differences among worker groups.

His interest in instinctive psychology does not appear to have been very keen. He apparently accepted without explicit critical analysis most of Veblen's observations regarding individual mo-tivation and went on directly to classify the individuals who had social roles as unionists. This decision to leap from a con-sideration of the wellsprings of individual motivation to the con-sequences of social decision does not seem to have been, in itself, a denial of Veblen's system. It implies that Hoxie accepted Veb-len's dichotomy in social-value schemes (the "pecuniary" versus the [mechanistic] "industrial" patterns of thinking) and his theory of the destructive effect on workers of the coming of the machine and the machine society to a commerce-minded world.

Hoxie divided unionists into three categories: the leaders, the satisfied rank and file, and the dissatisfied rank and file. He viewed leaders with innate suspicion. He acknowledged that possibly they were disinterested, and that there were significant factors that made them conservative, but nonetheless he dis-trusted their motives and decried the effect of the oligarchy nec-essary for their efficiency and success. Democracy, as he used the term, meant group participation, and there was little of this kind of participation among the majority of unions of the business type.

Rank-and-file members of unions fell into one of two classes, divided according to the keenness of their "supervision" over, or jealousy of, leaders. Those who tolerated powerful leaders who "deliver the goods, in terms of high wages, short hours, and good conditions" were classified as conservatives, or "bread-and-butter" unionists. Those who were "always suspicious and at con-stant war with the [union] officials" were dubbed "radical" unionists. This distinction was not intended to imply that the business-minded bread-and-butter unionists were not at times aggressive. Quite the contrary, when dissatisfied with their leaders they were wont to turn on them "with every conceivable denunciation and rend [them] . . . [and were] likely to run amuck, overbear the authority of the officers, and commit all sorts of acts in violation of constitutional authority" (7, p. 178).

Hoxie observed that the great mass of American workmen were not "conscious revolutionists" or of the "radical" mold. They were, instead, "optimistic opportunists" who "want more here and now . . . [and] are unwilling to leave the path which has been marked out by experience with its slow but sure advance, to plunge into theoretically assumed short cuts charted only by the imagination" (7, p. 159). Personally, Hoxie seems to have had greater sympathy for the radical type and to have entertained hopes that events would lead to popular appreciation of the radical's role. He saw progress being made in the structural organization of unions and commented that the "cooler headed socialists [i.e., radicals] have seen that the American Federation of Labor is normally heading toward [industrial unionism] and that it was their fiery efforts more than anything else that held things back. . . . But the socialists are there in the unions and the sentiment is growing fast even among business unionists" (7, p. 187). Structural organization served as a useful issue with which Hoxie could shift from the discussion of individual unions to union organization in general.

Hoxie proposed a cross-reference system of union types. Although it has become classic, it might be considered as one of his less significant intellectual contributions. He began by disregarding the usual assumption that union types are homogeneous; he looked for differences rather than similarities. These he found by examining the formal structural organization of unions and by assessing the functional purposes they served. His next step was to show the variations in simple union forms. The simplest form was a local or national *craft* union embracing all the workers in a single identifiable occupation. A second basic form was a *crafts* or *trades* union, or federation of unions in different crafts or industries, that generally had three levels: local, state, and national. The third essential type was the *industrial* union, which had jurisdiction over all workers in a single or allied group of industries regardless of their crafts or jobs; this union also had local, state, and national levels. The last basic type was the general *labor* union, which included all workers, regardless of their crafts, jobs, or industrial locations. This type of union is now organized on three regional levels, although in Hoxie's time it was usually limited to local areas (7, pp. 38–41).

Variations of these types could also be identified. There was, for instance, the *compound craft* (or *crafts*) union, an administrative amalgamation of related crafts. The members of these unions did not work in a single industry or for one firm. Hoxie took care to point out the frequent use of this form in lieu of the neater pure craft union. The other variant form was the *quasi-industrial federation,* of which local building-trades councils or the various national departments of the AFL were good examples. Both these variant forms appeared more frequently than did the purer types.

Hoxie considered the foregoing "structural" classification as not particularly useful and preferred one based on "function," by which he apparently meant the philosophic outlook expressed in a tactical program. In this classification, the most frequent type of union was the *business* union, which was "trade-conscious, rather than class-conscious," and which served primarily to raise the real-wage earnings of its membership. Business unionism was generally characterized by strong leaders and the bread-and-butter variety of rank-and-file members. Its policies were usually temperate, pragmatic, and self-interested.

A second functional type of unionism that Hoxie after some hesitation decided to differentiate from business unionism was *friendly* or *uplift* unionism. Like business unionism, it was temperate and generally worked within the framework of the existing economic order. But unlike business unionism, uplift unionism was idealistic, favoring mutual insurance, political action, co-operation, and a high degree of member participation. Hoxie decided to separate these two types of unions after he realized, probably at Commons' urging (7, p. 47), that they were two variant forms of a larger class, termed *bargaining* unionism or *constructive business* unionism.

Hoxie classified a third general group as *revolutionary* unions, which he divided into *socialist* and *quasi-anarchistic* subgroups. Together the two subgroups contained the bulk of the radical unions in the United States. Although both subgroups sought revolution, the former supported social reorganization with an orderly two-pronged (political and economic) program, while the latter repudiated all the orderly processes of government in its quest for free industrial association. Hoxie cited the Western Federation of Miners as typically socialistic and the Industrial Workers of the World (Chicago group) as characteristically quasi-anarchistic, or syndicalistic. He added in a footnote that "syndicalism" was too specialized a term, and that he thought it was easier to discuss in his more comprehensive phrases.

The type of unionism that was unlimitedly selfish and openly antisocial in methods, aims, and purpose he called *predatory* unionism. It took two forms: *hold-up* unionism and *guerilla* unionism. The former, frequently developed in the building trades, was a mixture of businesslike open bargaining and secret bribery and violence. It had a conspiratorial nature, and union leaders in this group often collaborated with employers against business competitors. Guerilla unionism, though similarly antisocial and coercive, might be recognized by its pursuit of immediate ends by secret and violent methods, and by absolutely no association with employers for any reason, good or bad.

Commons appears to have suggested another category to Hoxie. This was *dependent* unionism; it embraced unions that were puppets of employers and unions that could not exist without constant backing from other unions.

It appears that Hoxie, while intellectually intrigued by the dreams of revolutionary unionism, was primarily interested only in the first two functional groups of unions. We have already noted that he acknowledged the possibility that these two groups were related subgroups. He considered that of revolutionary unionism "we shall see more rather than less." He did, however, add the qualification that this judgment rested on continued unregulated immigration.

Hoxie's analysis of factors relating to the adoption by a union of one or another structural and functional form was more successful in its conceptual design than in its analytical realization. He disagreed with Marx's theory that the labor movement was based on control of the means of production, as well as with Commons', that it was based on the control of market distribution. Instead, Hoxie felt that the labor movement results from the interaction of an external (market) stimulus *and* a personal (psychological) stimulus. With a given market situation, the actual form a union takes would depend upon the personal and racial characteristics of the individuals concerned. If their feelings and attitudes were similar, they would join together in united action. Hoxie emphasized this point by noting:

. . . over against environment . . . is another factor, perhaps equally potent and certainly more permanent. . . . It includes temperament and aptitudes, both personal and racial, which show themselves as between different races and individuals in relatively permanent and conflicting feelings, ideals, and attitudes. It is these temperamental differences plus environmental influences that at any moment cause individuals to differ in respect to what is good and bad, right and wrong, just and unjust; which mold and color their social interpretations, and thus, through the primal forces of association, bring about psychological groups with diverse and conflicting viewpoints and programs of action. . . . [The] functional aspect of unionism . . . [is also] explained causally and historically in [these] same terms [7, pp. 66–67].

He attempted to prove his assertion that unions did differ in structure by illustrating the concurrent existence of rival types and by assessing their relative stability. It is interesting to note that he ascribed the failure of the Knights of Labor and similar "utopian" movements to certain economic conditions that were, in his opinion, disappearing. "Unionism today," he added, ". . . seems to show a constant tendency toward higher integration, centralization, autocracy, social idealism, industrialism and political method" (7, p. 99).

The social function to be performed by a union, Hoxie held, was determined by the problems of the specific situation, the attitudes of the people involved, and the economic conditions of the period concerned. This social function in turn became the critical determinant in the formation of a particular union structure. Thus differences in economic environment were the major cause of differences in social functions and therefore of differences in the structure of unions. Hoxie later went on to say that the social function and formal structure of a union could also be influenced by the insights of its leadership and by the effect of *education* (enlightenment) on the membership (7, p. 133).

He felt, for instance, that the AFL owed some of its success to Gompers' leadership. Gompers had wisely determined that the greatest harmony on economic matters could be achieved by integrating the economic problems of each of the international unions. Nonetheless, Hoxie was quick to emphasize the AFL's lack of success in developing real working-class unity or in thwarting progressive management's use of scientific management to stab at the heart of craft unionism. What the AFL obviously needed, in his view, was "practical idealism," which could be used to unite the many working-class factions into one group. In other words, he implied that it would be possible, to say nothing of desirable, to eliminate the functional differences that he had orginally considered basic (7, p. 135).

We have noted Hoxie's expectation that revolutionary unionism would be a continued and growing force on the American scene if unrestricted immigration into the United States continued. It is important to note also something of his belief that reforms, particularly economic ones, could serve to wean would-be revolutionary unionists from their disaffection with the going system.

. . . A large proportion of our organized workers are probably temperamentally conservative and would never become revolutionary unionists no matter what the industrial development. A growing portion of the workers—largely as a result of our recent immigration—are temperamentally radical. In so far as they become unionists at all they are bound to be revolutionaries. Between these extremes are the floaters, the negative mass, perhaps the largest proportion of workers. They will be swayed by their associates and by industrial and political conditions. As skilled workers they are likely to be conservative; as unskilled, revolutionary. In times of prosperity they will become satisfied and temperate; in times of stress, radical. Political disability and casual work, . . . will draw them into the revolutionary camp. Reforms—workmen's compensation, health and safety legislation, old-age pensions—will tend to make them supporters of the existing system . . . [7, pp. 173–74].

Hoxie's various theories of social change were discussed in the last chapter of his posthumous *Trade Unionism in the United States,* a chapter entitled "Social Control." In it he expressed his distaste for the "classical" theory based on the thinking of the English philosophic radicals (7, p. 361). Like Veblen, he dismissed the "universal" character of natural rights described by the seventeenth-century philosophers. The pecuniary society of Hoxie's time, with its individualism and rationality, was no more than a realization of the values of the contemporary businessman. It was an imposition by one class or another of a value system peculiarly adapted to benefit the class that imposed it.

Hoxie criticized the Marxian view as unscientific because of its teleological predictions of future developments and because of its insistence on an unrealistically simple (monistic) explanation of economic development. Furthermore, he had little use for Marx's dependence upon classical economics.

It is his treatment of Veblen's theory of social control that is of greatest interest to us. Attracted at first by its nonteleological form, Hoxie was eventually repelled, as with the Marxian theory, by its dependence upon economics. In writing upon the role played by purely economic developments, he stated:

. . . [The Veblenian theory] places too much stress upon the economic environment as a formative force. Man is the outcome of his total social environment. The individual, according to Veblen, cannot react on this environment; he is not a center of force. But cannot we do something to change this environment by education, shop arrangements, etc.? Again, there are no such rigid economic environments and disciplines. There is much more social interaction than is supposed [7, p. 367].

Thus after dismissing two theories because of their excessively teleological natures, Hoxie also thrust aside the Veblenian core of his own work. He no longer accepted the view attributed to Veblen, of unending, unresolvable social conflict. Hoxie arrived at this point of no return during the time he worked closely with John R. Commons, and there is no doubt that he was impressed with the latter's success in handling industrial problems with sophisticated institutional controls (7, p. 31).

In any case, Hoxie developed a new theory of social control, the "progressive-uplift theory," which admitted the existence of social classes and class conflict, but which held that this was a transitional state due, at present, to "lack of sufficient social interaction, knowledge and understanding." His solution lay in the intervention of "a strong third party—sometimes called 'the people,' sometimes 'the consumers'—unbiased in its viewpoint, standing for social justice, and representing the true social will, a party already capable in ordinary cases of acting as mediator and arbiter between the warring classes." Hoxie concluded that with the growth of the new force and with the extension of self-government in society, "this third party will gradually control the warring classes and ultimately absorb them" (7, pp. 367–68).

Hoxie's formal treatise on the nature of trade-unions came to an unexpected conclusion. From Veblen's theory of brutish social conflict he had reasoned his way to a virtually Christian Socialist declaration of faith. The apparent contradiction evidently bothered him. In any event, he attempted to redraw the Veblen concept of environment so that it would include enough latitude for planned change. John P. Frey quotes a letter from Hoxie, written shortly before Hoxie's death:

I have come to feel very strongly that it is the whole social environment that influences men, and that the most effective influence, after
all, is what we call the educational. Men are no doubt most strongly
influenced by the material forces which touch them, but few men are
capable of interpreting the meaning of these material forces. What we
are in need of more than anything else, if we are to have social progress and social betterment, is interpretation [quoted in 4, p. 892].

It is reasonable to conclude, however, that these final sentiments
were so significantly different from Hoxie's earlier ideas of
Veblen's theory that they bear no resemblance to it.

No discussion of Hoxie's contributions to theory should omit
his detailed work on the conflict between scientific management
and trade-unions. This project, undertaken for the United States
Commission on Industrial Relations, involved an investigation
of the actual operation of several scientific-management schemes
in American industry, as well as an analysis of the nature and
extent of union opposition (6). It was completed with the aid
of two expert assistants, John P. Frey (b. 1871), an official of the
molders' union, and Robert G. Valentine (1872–1916), an industrial counselor active in management circles. The work was
presented as a detailed summary of the conflict between craft
unions and certain scientific-management engineers. It clearly
stated the conviction that if Taylorism destroyed craft unionism
and collective bargaining, they would be replaced by unionism of
another structural form as well as by social control of another
order (6, pp. 130, 131, and 135). This conviction was further
buttressed by the belief that the "dominant" union (of the AFL
type) was therefore fighting for its life in two ways: first, for
what was most essential to its life, the skill of the craftsman;
and second, for the *status quo,* which made the standard rate
(uniformity) possible through collective bargaining (7, pp.
346 ff.). Nowhere in this discussion is there revealed any hope
of a workable resolution of the differences, beyond the pious
hope that education might be a means by which "the content
which he [lost] as a result of increased specialization and the

abandonment of the old apprenticeship system could be restored to the worker's life" (6, p. 136). "Specialize the old line craftsman," Hoxie concluded,

destroy his craft, and however high your ideals and kindly your motives, you are destroying the foundations upon which the dominant type of unionism is reared. Every union leader feels this instinctively; every one who has come into contact with scientific management and who has an understanding of unionism knows that this is what it is doing. Here, I believe, we have the final answer to the question "why organized labor opposes scientific management." Scientific management, properly applied, normally functioning, should it become universal, would spell the doom of effective unionism as it exists today [7, p. 348].

Hoxie's deterministic and intellectually somewhat inflexible study was caustically reviewed in the *American Economic Review* (9) by Charles W. Mixter, of the Yale Sheffield School of Science, who described the work as "a faulty investigation."

It is difficult to assess the weight of Hoxie's influence. Carter Goodrich, a University of Chicago student after Hoxie's time, stressed the importance of the oral tradition that Hoxie inspired (5). Commons lauded Hoxie's investigational techniques, and said less of his conclusions (2, p. 179). We have attempted to demonstrate that Hoxie's classification, so frequently cited as the core of his work, is only a small part of his intellectual contribution. In any event, *Trade Unionism in the United States* has enjoyed continued popularity. This may be partly because it is thought to be in the Veblen mold, although even a casual reading would show this to be false. As long as that misunderstanding continues, however, Hoxie's book will have readers who are not interested in his own ideas.

Frank Tannenbaum: Veblenism Redirected

Tannenbaum's work has spanned several fields. He was born in Austria and came to the United States in 1905. Professionally, he is a member of the Department of History at Columbia

University, where he lectures on Latin America; he has also written on criminology and prison reform. But we are concerned here with his writings on the philosophy of the labor movement—writings which include two books (14 and 15) and several articles. In order to appreciate the significance of his thinking, one must realize that he had considerable firsthand experience as a casual laborer, during which period he was actually sent to jail for a year for vagrancy. Upon his release from prison he took an undergraduate degree at Columbia University, and a doctorate at The Brookings Institution. His long career, with its many facets, has given him unusually rich experience for his analysis of social processes.

At the core of his thinking is his belief that men seek the right to make decisions just as they seek more tangible forms of economic reward (14, pp. 31 ff.). Since society as a whole, although influenced by the machine process, appears to be guided by the notion of contract (cf. 13, p. 11, and 8, p. 170), individuals find that they have had to yield their decision-making right. They have accordingly become increasingly maladjusted. Among workingmen at certain times the institution of unionism has arisen to protect the members' decision-making right, or status, from the progressive technological changes that have threatened to undermine it. Unions, in Tannenbaum's view, are defensive organizations created to preserve something from the past, and they are thus the antithesis of radicalism. They are in the tradition of the guilds, which protected workers from the inroads of commercial competition. Modern unions protect workers not from the market, however, but from a new threat, the dehumanizing effects of the machine process. Thus Tannenbaum radically departs from Veblen's view that the effects of the modern machine process are socially desirable.

Yet Tannenbaum and Veblen agree in the importance attached to the machine process as a dynamic force in present-day life. The machine process reduces those caught up in it to little more than "human bees." Like Veblen, Tannenbaum argued that the machine process and the social wealth it produces are presently controlled by the business community, and that labor has been forced to organize in self-defense. Unions are therefore a result of the employers' ownership of the machine process. Unions exist as the leading means of redress for the industrial worker, and they seek to exercise a type of control similar to that exercised by employers. Unions, in fact, adopt the values of employers, but seek to supplant the employers (here Tannenbaum and Veblen seem to part company). Union efforts to limit the employer's decision-making function strike directly at the heart of the employer's security. Moreover, their success would deprive him of his social status. Inevitably, therefore, a conflict develops between the employer, trying to protect himself, and the union, which exists to serve its membership at the immediate expense of the employer.

Tannenbaum, like Parker, conceived of the individual worker as a wandering, discontented casual—without property, without roots, but not without hope. What he hopes for is a fixed "berth," but even when he gets a comparatively secure job he continues to fear that he might lose it. In fact, so strong is the craving for status that it gives every worker a common feeling. This common feeling, or group loyalty, is sometimes referred to as "class consciousness." To workers it has real meaning and is associated with a set of problems for which remedies exist. But the remedies are possible only at the expense of the employer, who fancies that his status depends upon his power to give and take away jobs capriciously. The opposition of employers to the reforms advocated by workers through their unions can make the workers a power-mad mob, intent upon the destruction of the employers' tangible property. Thus the social consequences of unionism can be revolutionary and just the opposite of what each party, in its rational moments, wants. In this sense, according to Tannenbaum, employer opposition to unionism is ultimately self-defeating for everyone.

Tannenbaum noted that trade-unions, unlike socialism, tend to focus attention on things "in terms of the values, functions and problems with which the worker is always called upon to deal."

Socialism, on the other hand, is concerned *about* rather than *with* these problems. Furthermore, he seems to have believed that the difference between the Socialist program and the one advocated by trade-unions lay in the reformer's revolutionary intentions. What in effect happens, of course, is that the Socialists achieve no results and the "conservative-minded" unions achieve revolutionary results (14, p. 124). This is the consequence of the machine-ridden worker's desire to achieve decision-making status rather than of his class hatred.

Tannenbaum envisioned the unions' ultimate triumph over capitalist opposition. They would take over industry and run it without being hindered by *rentiers* and middlemen. This view of his is guild socialism, which, except for some minor qualifications, reflects the thinking of G. D. H. Cole.[3]

Thirty years after the appearance of *The Labor Movement: Its Conservative Functions and Social Consequences,* Tannenbaum published a second book on the same subject, *A Philosophy of Labor* (15). His position remained essentially unchanged, although he abandoned the conclusion that the labor movement was revolutionary in effect. He substituted instead the view that trade-unions were the great counterrevolutionary agent that would return society from the consequences of "contract" to an emphasis on "status." In one sense this is a play on words, since the net effect in either instance was to be a marked social change. In another sense, however, there is a significant difference; Tannenbaum eliminates his previous obsession with revolution and develops his theory somewhat more consistently. Since his criticism of socialism was its concern for abstract, rather than concrete, programs, his view that trade-unions had counterrevolutionary rather than revolutionary overtones is understandable. Counterrevolution implies a previous condition, which in itself has somewhat more of a precise connotation than does the notion of future revolutionary results. Thus it follows that

---

[3] He objected to Cole's division of the populace into consumers and producers, and argued instead that ultimately all producers were consumers as well. Hence, in lieu of Cole's bicameral legislature, he proposed one house (14, pp. 227 ff.).

Tannenbaum has indeed stood Veblenism on its head: new industrial arts are driving men from dreams of the future to a reliance upon institutions that will fit the individual into a social framework and give him the right to participate in the decision-making process. And revolution, by its aggravation of man's inherent fear of insecurity and his desire for status, causes a renaissance of values once believed to be "outmoded."

References

1. Anderson, Karl L., "The Unity of Veblen's Theoretical System," *Quarterly Journal of Economics,* XLVII (1932–33), 598–626.

2. Commons, John R., *Myself.* New York: The Macmillan Co., 1934.

3. Dorfman, Joseph, *Thorstein Veblen and His America.* New York: Viking Press, Inc., 1934.

4. Frey, John P., "Robert F. Hoxie, Investigator and Interpreter," *Journal of Political Economy,* XXIV (1916), 884–93.

5. Goodrich, Carter, "Hoxie, Robert Franklin," in *Encyclopaedia of the Social Sciences,* VII, 524–25.

6. Hoxie, Robert F., *Scientific Management and Labor.* New York: D. Appleton & Co., 1915.

7. ———, *Trade Unionism in the United States.* New York: D. Appleton & Co., 1917.

8. Maine, Henry, *Ancient Law.* New York: Henry Holt & Co., Inc., 1877.

9. Mixter, Charles W., review of Hoxie, *Scientific Management and Labor,* in *American Economic Review,* VI (1916), 373–77.

10. Parker, Carleton H., *The Casual Laborer and Other Essays.* New York: Harcourt, Brace & Howe, 1920.

11. ———, "Preliminary Report on Tentative Findings and Conclusions in the Investigation of Seasonal, Migratory, and Unskilled Labor in California." Unpublished report to the United States Commission on Industrial Relations. Wisconsin Historical Society Library [1914?].

12. ———, "A Report to the United States Commission on Industrial Relations on a Labor Trouble in Phoenix, Arizona."

Unpublished report to the United States Commission on Industrial Relations. Wisconsin Historical Society Library [n.d.].

13. Pollock, Frederick, and Maitland, Frederic, *The History of English Law before the Time of Edward I.* 2d ed. Cambridge, Eng.: At the University Press, 1923.

14. Tannenbaum, Frank, *The Labor Movement: Its Conservative Functions and Social Consequences.* New York: G. P. Putnam's Sons, 1921.

15. ———, *A Philosophy of Labor.* New York: Alfred A. Knopf, Inc., 1951.

16. Veblen, Thorstein, "The Preconceptions of Economic Science," *Quarterly Journal of Economics,* XIII (January, 1899), 121–50; XIII (July, 1899), 396–426; XIV (February, 1900), 240–69.

17. ———, *The Theory of Business Enterprise.* New York: Charles Scribner's Sons, 1904.

SIX

Unionism As a Welfare Institution

Around the turn of the century certain economists became, for a variety of reasons, dissatisfied with the lack of moral consciousness in the practical application of their discipline (13, pp. 309 ff.). The economist's achievement of scientific disinterestedness, it was felt, was being gained at too high a social cost, and there was concern that the ethical aspects of economic problems were being slighted. In the eighties a similar regard had led to an undirected protest against the tradition of *laissez-faire* political economy. This new concern, however, emerging during the two decades prior to World War I, resulted in an attempt to incorporate certain considerations of welfare into the body of economic literature. These were to provide an operating framework within which economic policy might be formed. Economists in this group, combining the analysis of costs with the judgments of moral right, came to call their study "welfare economics" (12, pp. 38 ff.). They split into two subgroups, one of which eventually leaned so heavily on the accepted geometry of modern economics that in time it tended to de-emphasize the discussion of the meaning of welfare. The other group, influenced by empirically minded social historians like John A. Hobson (1858–1940), went to the opposite extreme and created a mutation of the old economics, something occasionally called "economic institutionalism."

We are concerned here with a type of trained economist who did not abandon formal economic analysis but was nevertheless both interested in and an active advocate of certain policies with specific social goals. These economists went beyond the limits usually set for "disinterested scientists" in their advocacy of social policies that would result in the redistribution of wealth. What separated them from the usual run of reformers was their reliance upon technical economic analysis. Thus they were in the fullest sense economists with a purpose.

The leading examples of this general type obviously include Sidney and Beatrice Webb (1859–1947; 1858–1943) and Arthur C. Pigou (b. 1877), the Cantabrigian don and professor. For geographic reasons, which limit the scope of this study to persons concerned directly with American unionism, consideration of their work is precluded. Nevertheless it is desirable to make explicit the point that the Webbs, in particular, were important influences in the development of thought in America on the subject of unionism. It would be hard to overestimate the impact of the Webbs' *History of Trade Unionism* (18) or *Industrial Democracy* (19) on American writers. However, in the work of George E. Barnett one can find both recognizable evidence of the Webbs' writings and the application of their analysis to the American environment. Like the Webbs, Barnett's study of the economic and administrative problems of unionism incorporated the broad principles of professional economic analysis. And like them he had a positive (although in his case subtle) commitment to the goal of the redistribution of economic shares.

We shall not be able to examine all of Barnett's work. Some of his publications have had to be omitted for the sake of brevity. Among those studies not discussed is his collaboration with David McCabe on *Mediation, Investigation and Arbitration in Industrial Disputes* (9), even though it is an interesting example of his point of view. His influence on his students' dissertations has already been noted.

The Influence of the Economic Science

Barnett's interest in unionism during most of his active life grew out of his search for a more effective way to distribute wealth. In the six years before his death, however, he appears to have lost faith in unionism as a means for achieving his goal and turned his attention to legislative enactment instead. In discussing his work we shall endeavor to emphasize the fact that he was interested in unionism merely as one of the possible means of achieving a prescribed social end, and we shall contrast this view with that of the theorists who regarded unionism as a social movement.

First of the major influences that affected Barnett's attitude toward trade-unions was the original research of Sidney and Beatrice Webb, particularly their *Industrial Democracy* (19). Barnett accepted much of their terminology, and addressed himself seriously to the issue they raised, that is, the economic (efficient) organization of industrial production. Like the Webbs, he considered unions desirable only because of their economic effectiveness, not because of their sociological effect as a movement.

A second major influence shaping Barnett's work was the unfulfilled legacy of the United States Industrial Commission. We shall note later the relationship between the commission and The Johns Hopkins University, and it is well to recall that the commission's interest was in the contemporary operation of unions, rather than in their historical or evolutionary role (see p. 278). This reinforced Barnett's tendency to look at unions as a means of resolving concrete issues rather than as a historical development of prerogatives. This is an important point, since it is one of the reasons for concluding that his inquiry was that of a professional economist (in the formal "alternative ends, limited means" sense). This does not necessarily mean that he approved of all abstract theory or even that he endorsed the application of "theory" to the "real" world. It does mean, however, that he was interested in specific economic questions rather than in those that involved politics.[1] In any case, we wish to emphasize that he was not a social historian and was not intent on making

[1] See Barnett's discussion of J. B. Clark's "The Theory of Collective Bargaining" (11, pp. 45–50).

broad philosophical generalizations about unions. The commission's work did not fully describe contemporary unionism, nor did it deal with the subject quantitatively, nor examine most of unionism's working policies, nor delineate the extent of its formal permeation of the American scene (see pp. 278–79). These were matters that interested Barnett and occupied his attention for a decade and a half after the commission made its lengthy, though incomplete, report.

The third influence that molded his development was his training in, and his belief in, empiricism. David McCabe reports Barnett as affirming that he "had *no ethical* outlook beyond the standards of decency and legality."

Barnett always maintained, to me at least, that his interest in unions was purely "scientific." He prided himself on his objectivity and on his impersonal attitude towards unions and employers. But [he] was a very warm and friendly person and I know he enjoyed having the goodwill and trust of so many union officers and employers. . . . I know he had a very deep interest in the typographical union, even if he would not admit it [16].

This claim implies that Barnett's interest in unionism lay essentially in the statistical aspects of the movement and that, should unions decrease in number, Barnett would immediately wonder whether other institutions were performing the functions once associated with unions. This is what actually happened in 1932, when he can be said to have dismissed the historical importance of the trade-union movement.

Fundamental to Barnett's development, however, was his study of the most efficient operations in contemporary industrial society. The effectiveness of these operations was, for the most part, advanced by the institution of the joint agreement (the end-product of the process of collective bargaining). Therefore, anything that contributed to that end was to him worthy of investigation. Barnett considered the joint agreement as an economic (productive and distributive) phenomenon to be analyzed as a fundamentally administrative operation. His studies were confined to organizational structures and their economic implications; he admitted to no further interest in the subject.

Barnett's examination of administrative methods was based on a survey of the printers' union. In the course of his investigations he examined the growth of collective-bargaining patterns in the printing trades as a whole, including in his study such significant characteristics of the industry as technological innovation, wage-rate structure, and the division of job opportunity.

His early essays on the printers' union, two of which appeared in a volume called *Studies in American Trade Unionism* (15, pp. 13–41 and 155–82), depicted the growth of the organization and the change in its control from the "chapel" to the "local" and then to the "national." He ascribed these shifts in power first to the need for governing the migrations of workmen and later to the appearance of new technological processes requiring the attention of the whole craft, as well as to the increased importance of mutual-insurance schemes. Barnett believed that the growth of the market—partly a consequence of technological change—resulted in parallel organizations of employers, for instance, the United Typothetae of America and the American Newspaper Publishers Association. The employers generally organized their operations most efficiently at the city level, since divisions of interest existed between the master printers, as a group, and the newspaper publishers (15, pp. 155–82). In these essays he also traced the secession of crafts from the original solitary union.

In 1909 Barnett brought out a more comprehensive study of the government of the printers' union, entitled *The Printers: A Study in American Trade Unionism* (8). He incorporated in this book his earlier material, adding considerably to it to illustrate how devices such as the restriction of numbers, the common rule, and techniques of mutual insurance could be applied. In fact, the bulk of his analysis (Part II) is entitled "Mutual Insurance and Trade Regulations." This study, a classic exposition on trade-union government, was the first thorough inquiry into administrative development under union control in a specific industry.

During 1912-13 Barnett published two essays in the *Quarterly Journal of Economics* generalizing his ideas on national patterns of collective bargaining and on the national administration of unions. The first, "National and District Systems of Collective Bargaining in the United States" (6), reviewed a number of causes for the increase in national and local patterns of negotiation. These patterns were largely determined by three factors: the heroic—relating to the personal skill or influence of the negotiators—the economic peculiarities of the trade, and the particular exigencies of the time. It was on the second factor—economic peculiarities of the trade—that Barnett dwelt at considerable length. The topic later served as the basis for his second essay, "The Dominance of the National Union in American Labor Organization" (3).

In the first essay Barnett emphasized the industrial stability possible when wage agreements are national rather than local in scope. He explained this by showing how the forces of economic competition plus the pattern of union demands tended to create a national rather than a local market condition. He noted that, except for the building trades, where the nature of competition was *sui generis,* unions had maximized their advantage when they set up unilateral, systematic sets of working rules applicable to the whole industry. Because there was greater economic stability on the national than on the local level, unions generally sought national bargains. From this he concluded that a tendency existed toward the integration nationally of joint agreements. It followed that employers were forced to form national associations in defense, since the absence of negotiation on any level caused major cost dislocations and, eventually, much industrial disharmony.

Barnett was greatly impressed with the effect of the business cycle on bargaining patterns. At one moment, he noted, an individual employer or group of employers might carry on extended bargaining activities because of the importance of continuing production and because of their desire to minimize industrial warfare. At another moment the same employers, influenced by a shift in the economic outlook, might become intransigent, breaking off all relations with the union.

In the second of his two *Quarterly Journal of Economics* essays, Barnett actually spelled out the implications of this "urge to national bigness." "National" [2] unions could control journeymen and different trades by benefit systems and a more efficient use of financial resources on occasions when small local units would generally fail. The national union, buttressed as it was by a "universal" set of working rules, could meet the individual employer on more advantageous terms. To enhance its power, the "national" had therefore to chip away at the prerogatives of locals, not only at those of small unions that chose to remain unaffiliated, but even at those of unions that "came in." National policies regulating admission requirements, strikes, and working rules therefore became a major part of the union's administration.

At the same time, the national sought to minimize the local's use of its main weapon, political action, particularly on the local level. Barnett pointed out that the nationals generally opposed as a rival seat of power the semipolitical form (the "city federation") which the locals usually adopted. He admitted, however, that in a few infrequent instances the national protected the local's role in the city federation in order to use that power in negotiations with other nationals. Barnett concluded this essay with a discussion of the building trades, whose case was made unique by the absence of national competition.

The generalizations found in these essays were further developed in an unpublished study which he prepared, with considerable staff assistance, for the United States Commission on Industrial Relations (5). The study begins with a review of his reasons for concentrating on the merits of joint agreements. The general conviction seemed to be, he said, "that [they were] the only satisfactory solution of the labor problem . . . ," since "only through such agreements could the standard of living of the workmen be maintained and improved, the workmen protected against arbitrary and unjust treatment, and the industrial peace

[2] The conventional term now is "international."

effectively preserved." Furthermore, these agreements appeared to regulate industry more effectively than did legislation because of the flexibility of the informal governmental machinery. And, finally, ". . . the enormous loss to the country from strikes and lockouts . . . can only be avoided by resort to the joint agreement, as in the absence of such agreement the workers or the employers may at any time which seems favorable resort to force to compel compliance with their conditions."

Barnett pointed out, however, that there were objections to this system: it might lead to restriction of output and thus to higher prices; it might result in closed unions; and it might lead to the imposition of the closed shop. But he concluded that these evils were not as serious nor as certain as some believed them to be.

The Commission is strongly impressed with the desirability of the joint agreement as a means of settling the conditions of employment. It recognizes that joint agreements are occasionally accompanied by unwarranted restriction on production and by monopolistic rule. It appears, however, that the extent of these evils is not large as compared with the entire field of joint agreement. Moreover, it seems clear that the progress of a system of joint agreements is in the direction of eliminating or lessening those evils [5, p. 190].

Thus after "justifying" a system of joint agreements, he went on to define and discuss it.

The term 'joint agreement' is applied to all those arrangements under which the conditions of employment are governed by an agreement made between an employer or an association of employers and a union of which the employees are members. The essential point in this definition is that the conditions of employment are fixed by agreement—that is, they are the result of conference and the interchange of views. Where the employer alone decides upon the conditions and announces them to his workmen, there is no joint agreement even if the workmen as an organized body accept the conditions [5, p. 7].

Here he followed the reasoning and conclusions of his earlier *Quarterly Journal of Economics* articles. In this study, however, he examined in detail the appearance of the early national and district systems of joint agreements and some of the difficulties that were encountered in making and enforcing them. He observed, for example, that it was difficult to select able negotiators. Electing them was generally unsatisfactory; the most efficient way seemed to be to let the union executive select them. He was also severely critical of arbitration, which he believed to be less desirable than genuine negotiation (5, p. 43).

It was in this project that Barnett directed Leo Wolman in measuring for the first time the distribution of union membership. This report, subsequently revised and published in the *Quarterly Journal of Economics* in 1916 (4), included an extensive tabular summary. Ten years earlier Henry W. Farnham had summarized the problems of measurement in an article on *The Quantitative Study of the Labor Movement* (14). Barnett also surveyed the jurisdictional problems of the building industry, which he concluded would ultimately have to be settled by a national body or authority. One of his students, Solomon Blum, who was later a professor at Berkeley, wrote a dissertation under Barnett on this topic (10). The problem of graft, though included in the purview of his discussion, was a topic that, like other negative aspects of joint agreement, he tended to minimize. He found that charges of corruption were leveled at only a relatively small number of unions. Generally they were associated with the practice of authorizing one individual, without adequate supervision, to call strikes or levy boycotts (5, pp. 186 ff.).

Barnett emphasized in his summary the "educative effects of systems of joint agreements upon the individual workman" and their contribution in this way to industrial efficiency.

. . . The making and administration of the agreements have given the individual workers a share in governing the industry in labor matters and this has not only increased his self-respect but it has greatly aided his self-development in two directions. It has given the individual workman an understanding of the nature and wider meaning of organization for production, of the problems confronting his industry and of the limitations under which those who conduct it must move. It has also given the workers a deeper sense of individual responsibility which has in turn led to the exercise of greater self-restraint.

In the joint conferences which characterize these systems of joint agreements the workers' representatives gain a wider knowledge of their industry and its relation to the public wants. In their arguments and discussions with employers they become acquainted with the sources of the materials with which they work and the markets which they supply. . . . They come to realize the various influences which affect their industry, its place in the industrial life of the country and the conditions beyond the control of the employers under which it must be carried on [5, pp. 190–91].

He added that unions were an excellent opportunity for workers to learn to participate in general political life.

A well-developed system of joint agreements is a system of industrial democracy as well. The workers are not only members of a democratic organization of their own for collective action in regard to the terms of employment, but citizens of a dual government for the industry as a whole in labor matters. They elect representatives to a joint legislative body; they participate directly or through their national officers in the selection of members of a joint judiciary which is in many cases also a joint executive with large powers of enforcing its decision. Their action and that of their representatives must be more measured and more considerate of the interest of others than if they are acting for the government of their own organization alone. The workers thus become schooled of necessity in the selection of representatives to whom they trust their interests and in submitting to the laws for the government of the industry which they have helped to make and to the decisions they have bound themselves to accept. The value of this training in representative government and in self-restraint in developing the workers as members of the body politic can hardly be over estimated [5, pp. 193–94].

For several reasons—the advent of World War I, friction among the commissioners, and perhaps their feeling that the work presented nothing startlingly new or practical—this study was never published. The decision is regrettable, since the study is a significant addition to the literature on the subject of joint agreements.

By 1921 Barnett apparently had begun to doubt the social efficacy of the trade-union movement (7). His continued research on the growth of individual unions forced him to conclude that large segments of American industrial society were virtually untouched by the collective agreement. This was so even during World War I, when the ranks of organized labor had swelled from around two-and-a-half million to almost five million.

With the coming of peace the government withdrew completely from all but railroad transportation. Barnett had expected continued union growth and power in this area, but was disappointed to find the outlook so bleak in other areas, particularly during the depression period of 1921. He believed that unions operated best during periods of static prices and, since this period was one of falling prices, he predicted further losses. But the 1921 depression was soon over and prices stabilized, yet unions continued to lose ground. He mentioned the possibility of an open-shop campaign, but did not pursue the subject (7, pp. 50–51).

Despite his discouragement, Barnett continued his research on trade-union policies, and in 1926 published a new book, *Chapters on Machinery and Labor* (2), which was concerned largely with technological advances and adjustments in industry. It was his view that five factors governed the transitional harmony of technological change: (1) the rate at which the innovation was introduced; (2) the mobility within the affected skilled trade; (3) the elasticity of demand for the product; (4) the labor-displacing power of the innovation; and (5) the degree of skill that the new machine required of the operator (2, pp. 117 ff.).

Barnett concluded that American unions had been more successful in maintaining old wage rates than in preventing technological unemployment (2, p. 160). One could not accurately forecast just how a union would deal with the problems posed by the appearance of a new machine, but usually they would attempt to protect their past gains rather than to promote job opportunities. Barnett was greatly interested in the techniques employed. Unions might try to prevent the introduction of a new process; to increase the work opportunity for the older handworkers by cutting the wage rate; to get job-jurisdiction over the new process in order to control the immediate employment dislocations; to cut down entry into the trade; to distribute equitably such little work as remained to the older handworkers; or any combination of these plans (2, pp. 140 ff.). The skilled and senior employees thus generally had an advantage over those less skilled and younger. In brief, unionism tended to favor its "aristocracy." In this way, the unions functioned as conservative institutions that would not, or could not, help to resolve the problem of the economically underprivileged (cf. 2, p. 140).

Six years later, in his presidential address to the American Economic Association, Barnett reverted to the pessimistic outlook he had expressed in 1921. The relative decline in the importance of unions during the twenties was, he argued, in part the result of the relative increase of employment in traditionally unorganized areas such as the mass-production industries. In addition, unions lost membership within the traditionally organized industries because of the introduction of labor-saving and skill-destroying machinery. There was also a marked decrease in the demand for goods produced by unionized skilled craftsmen, and an increase in the demand for products turned out on the assembly line (1).

Barnett went on to conclude that his original faith in unionism had been shaken to its foundations.[3]

. . . American trade unionism is slowly being limited in influence by changes which destroy the basis on which it is erected. It is proba-

[3] The Webbs had come to a similar conclusion. They urged greater state regulation (legal enactment), although they added that collective bargaining should continue in areas where national minima would be ineffective. Cf. 18, pp. 796–806.

ble that changes in the law have adversely affected unionism. Certainly the growth of large corporations has done so. But no one who carefully follows the fortunes of individual unions can doubt that over and above these influences, the relative decline in the power of American trade unionism is due to occupational changes and to technological revolutions.

It would be interesting to speculate on the possibility that American trade unionism as a whole could organize on some other basis than that on which it has organized itself from the beginning of its history. It is possible that something like the Knights of Labor may emerge and dominate American trade-union organization. Many writers have counseled the leaders of the American trade-union movement to abandon their present forms of organization and to move in the direction of industrial trade unionism. There are no indications that anything of this kind will happen in the near future. The changes—occupational and technological—which checked the advance of trade unionism in the last decade appear likely to continue in the same direction. It is hazardous to prophesy, but I see no reason to believe that American trade unionism will so revolutionize itself within a short period of time as to become in the next decade a more potent social influence than it has been in the past decade [1, p. 6].

Barnett then discussed the new role of the trade-union as a result of these changes. He continued by pointing out the existence of a school of thought that

conceives the trade union more as an instrument of social progress, and less as a means of redressing the balance in individual situations. The argument runs somewhat as follows: The labor contract in recent years has become more complex than formerly. It embraces not merely the monetary element ordinarily known as wages but the non-monetary elements of the amount of employment, accidents, occupational disease, etc. It is primarily the business of trade unionism to establish the conditions surrounding these non-monetary elements in the labor contract. When these are standardized for a particular trade, the strictly monetary element of wages will need less effort. Moreover, and this is perhaps the most important part of the argument, these non-monetary elements can ordinarily be brought into standard form only for labor as a whole by legislative action. The role of the trade union should be to experiment with and establish these standard conditions in the non-monetary parts of the labor contract. Compensation for industrial accidents and disease, standardization of the hours of labor, unemployment insurance, old-age pensions established and regulated by the state, constitute the goal towards which the trade union is to be the formative agency.

If the foregoing views are correct, the failure of trade unionism to expand may be partially offset by the adoption by the American states of systems of compulsory social insurance. To be sure, the problem of exploited labor in certain industries seems impossible of solution in the face of the decision of the Supreme Court that minimum wage laws are unconstitutional. But the setting up of systems of social insurance would enormously improve the bargaining power of labor. . . .

The greater part of the large corporations in this country have maintained systems of old-age pensions for their employees; and some of them have attempted to establish systems of unemployment insurance. The need for such provision is clear to their minds. Is it not obvious to both businessmen and workmen that piecemeal attempts to provide for such contingencies as unemployment and old age fail to meet the situation? We are dealing here with a social problem and not a problem of an individual trade or business. The events of the past three years have spoken eloquently in favor of this view. May we not hope that the decade before us will see employers and trade unions jointly urging upon the legislatures of our states the establishment of social insurance systems? [1, pp. 7–8.]

Thus Barnett concluded on a theme that was—for the wrong reasons—vaguely prophetic.

Fundamentally, Barnett's work was that of a competent economist. Its strength lies in its careful presentation and analysis; its weakness lies in its limited scope. Certainly anyone acquainted with the structure and nature of the trade-union movement is well aware of Barnett's contribution, whether his name is explicitly acknowledged or not, for his view was catholic and went beyond wage rates and earnings. His work suffered because he never fully examined his own social philosophy. Limited in this way to the last, he never speculated, except indirectly, on whether the movement whose workings he examined so carefully had a purpose other than maximization of economic ends. Without this speculation his work seems to lack the leavening agent necessary for ready adaptability. These remarks, however, are not intended to minimize his achievement. What he did, he did well, and it is to be regretted that so few men followed his lead. Among those who have, fewer yet have shared his philosophical view.[4] Perhaps, as Dorfman has suggested, Barnett's approach was the product of his youth, and later economists were more ready to discuss at length the standards or goals that they sought to establish. This shift in attitude toward the elaboration of one's social beliefs should not dim Barnett's glory. And his silence about the importance of the redistribution of wealth should not be taken to imply that he was not concerned; his technical contributions as well as his change in attitude belie that conclusion. He was committed to the most economic way to redistribute wealth.

References

1. Barnett, George E., "American Trade Unionism and Social Insurance," *American Economic Review*, XXIII (March, 1933), 1–15.

2. ———, *Chapters on Machinery and Labor*. Cambridge, Mass.: Harvard University Press, 1926.

3. ———, "The Dominance of the National Union in American Labor Organization," *Quarterly Journal of Economics*, XXVII (1913), 455–81.

4. ———, "Growth of Labor Organization in the United States 1897–1914," *Quarterly Journal of Economics*, XXX (1916), 780–95.

5. ———, "Joint Agreements." Unpublished research paper of the United States Commission on Industrial Relations. Wisconsin Historical Society Library, [n.d.].

6. ———, "National and District Systems of Collective Bargaining in the United States," *Quarterly Journal of Economics*, XXVI (1912), 425–43.

[4] A recent exception is Lloyd Ulman (cf. 17, pp. 504–604 and 620–30, especially 601 and 603–4).

7. Barnett, George E., "The Present Position of American Trade Unionism," *American Economic Review,* XII (Supplement) (1922), 44–55.

8. ———, *The Printers: A Study in American Trade Unionism.* "Publications of the American Economic Association," Ser. 3, Vol. X (October, 1909).

9. ———, and McCabe, David A., *Mediation, Investigation and Arbitration in Industrial Disputes.* New York: D. Appleton & Co., 1916.

10. Blum, Solomon, *Jurisdictional Disputes Resulting from Structural Differences in American Trade Unions.* "University of California Publications in Economics," No. 3 (1913).

11. Clark, John B., "The Theory of Collective Bargaining," *Publications of the American Economic Association,* Ser. 3, Vol. X (April, 1909), pp. 24–39; discussion by Barnett and others, pp. 40–58.

12. Clark, John M., "Aims of Economic Life As Seen by Economists," in A. Dudley Ward (ed.), *Goals of Economic Life.* New York: Harper & Bros., 1953.

13. Dorfman, Joseph, *The Economic Mind in American Civilization,* Vol. III, 1865–1918. New York: Viking Press, Inc., 1949.

14. Farnham, Henry W., "The Quantitative Study of the Labor Movement," *Publications of the American Economic Association,* Ser. 3, Vol. VII (February, 1906), pp. 160–76.

15. Hollander, Jacob H., and Barnett, George E. (eds.), *Studies in American Trade Unionism.* New York: Henry Holt & Co., Inc., 1906.

16. McCabe, David A., private communication, November 3, 1952.

17. Ulman, Lloyd, *The Rise of the National Trade Union: The Development and Significance of Its Structure, Governing Institutions, and Economic Policies.* Cambridge, Mass.: Harvard University Press, 1955.

18. Webb, Sidney, and Webb, Beatrice, *History of Trade Unionism.* 1902 ed. London: Longmans, Green & Co., 1902.

19. ———, *Industrial Democracy.* 1920 ed. London: Longmans, Green & Co., 1920.

SEVEN

Unionism As Part of the Democratic Process

We have discussed the trade-union as an economic institution developed along lines characteristic of the traditional, mature English approach to economics represented by Marshall and Pigou. We now take up the ideas of three American economists whose study of trade-unions followed in the broad intellectual tradition of the German historical school, combining economics and jurisprudence. This school was epitomized by Adolph Wagner (1835–1917), proponent of economic reform; Karl Knies (1821–98), cofounder, with Roscher and Hildebrand, of the German historical school and best known for his work on money and credit; Karl Bücher (1847–1930), of the "younger" historical school, whose significant work dealt with the geographic development of European national economics; and Gustav Schmoller (1838–1917), leader of the younger historical school, whose best-known work is in history (43). These men, accustomed to strong central government, viewed economic relationships as the medium from which emerged the jurisprudential product; thus the problems of government and economic distribution were linked inseparably together. It is no accident that this merger of disciplines existed at the core of Marxian thought as well, since Marx was influenced by the same culture and the same *Weltanschauung*.

But simply to point out the base upon which a body of thought rests does not predetermine the nature of its specific conclusions. Originally the Germans, notably Schmoller—and even Marx—had seen the problem as one concerned with the dynamic role of government influenced by or directly influencing economic development. Other Germans, pursuing similar lines of inquiry, had turned their attention to self-governing economic institutions within the political state and had sought to explain the rationale of their existence. In this last group one finds Lujo Brentano (1844–1931), whose earliest study on the history and development of German guilds marks the beginning of a line of research that reached a peak with the appearance of the Webbs' work on trade-unions, and Otto von Gierke (1841–1921), German legal scholar and professor at Breslau, Heidelberg, and Berlin, both of whom did notable research on the English guilds and the *Genossenschaft* theory.[1] This group centered their interest on the dynamic subgroup within general society, a subgroup with some but not all of the characteristics of a political unit. It is in this field of study that we find so much intuitively brilliant as well as scholarly research being done by British writers at the turn of the century. Particularly important in this tradition were Arnold Toynbee (1852–83) with his authoritative essay on the industrial revolution; Frederic Maitland (1850–1906), whose interpretive work on the history of English law surpassed even that of Sir Henry Maine (1822–88); and George Unwin (1870–1925), whose historical study of English industrial organization served as documentary evidence for the theories of the Manchester School.

This was the cultural and intellectual background of a group of American economists whose productive period began in the early eighties, when Henry Carter Adams first became aware of the work being done in the German universities. Later on John R. Commons, influenced by the English scholars men-

---

[1] This theory is well explained in English in F. W. Maitland's introduction to his translation of Otto F. von Gierke's *Political Theories of the Middle Age* (30) and in Sir Ernest Barker's translation of *Natural Law and the Theory of Society* (6).

tioned as well as by the Germans and by Adams, followed the same avenue of research. Adams and Commons fall conceptually somewhere between the English, who tended to regard the state as an evil, and the Germans, who tended to regard it as an end in itself. Both these Americans regarded the German-English juristic explorations as models, and used an adaptation of this approach to explore the American scene, where social and political power rested on a complex network of economic bargaining groups and a constitutional tradition of limited governmental powers. There was in America no simple legal or productive "leviathan."

Their thesis, which we now develop, is that unions are a critical element of the historical democratic process, and that they are essentially social bargaining institutions, aimed at increasing the social status and particularly the economic liberty of working people. In American society, where status depends so clearly upon ownership of property, an improvement in social position is most readily achieved when the basic meaning of property, which historically has always been a fluid term, is expanded to include the right to a job. To this end these theorists have attempted to interpret the labor movement as a historical institution striving to give proprietary significance to job rights; the material benefits coming from the collective-bargaining process were desirable but not inherently necessary by-products.

For present purposes this discussion will be confined to Henry Carter Adams, John R. Commons, and Selig Perlman. Adams not only gave original expression to the job-property concept, but was an obvious link between American theorists and the tradition of the German historical school. John R. Commons made the study of the actual historical documents and records of unions the key to an understanding of union aspirations and the successful public administration of industrial relations, and Selig Perlman formalized the Commons approach into a philosophy or theory. Because Commons and Perlman taught at the University of Wisconsin and for over half a century attracted students interested in their philosophy, the body of their thinking has come to be called, particularly by their critics, "the Wisconsin theory." Their theme, resting upon a base of nineteenth-century historical scholarship but adapted to the specific American environment, has become since 1932 a generally accepted explanation of the American labor movement and at the same time the subject of numerous modifications and criticisms. If nothing else, their work shows the wealth of the German and, above all, of the British research in jurisprudence drawn on by scholars in American universities.

Henry Adams: The Early Vision

Henry Carter Adams may be identified as a link between the American university development of a theory of unionism and the German historical school of economics. He received, in 1878, the first doctorate granted by The Johns Hopkins University, and was strongly influenced in his interest in social reform by the attitude of his family and by his connection with the eminent American economist and academician Francis A. Walker (1840–97).[2] It appears that Adams was in no sense doctrinaire in his opinions, nor was he blinded by his exposure to the prevalent English economics of his time. He set off for Europe with a relatively open mind to learn what he could. Adolph Wagner, professor at Berlin, Adolf Held, professor at Bonn, and Ernst Engel, chief of the Prussian Statistical Bureau, were those with whom he discoursed in 1878–79. Their influence had a pervasive effect on his thinking, but it did not rob him of any of his critical faculties. It did result in the focusing of his interest on the interrelation of economics and jurisprudence and on the usefulness of statistical material. Moreover, his experience abroad confirmed his belief, later paraphrased by him in this way: *"Society* is the organic entity about which all our reasoning should center. Both state action and the industrial activity of individuals are functions of the complete social organism" (5, p. 494).

[2] For further biographical information about Adams see 7; 23, pp. 164–79; and 24.

Adams returned to America in 1879 and for several years taught regularly but on a part-time basis at Johns Hopkins, Cornell, and Michigan. His advanced views ultimately led him into difficulty at Cornell where, in 1887, he was unceremoniously dropped from the faculty. Fortunately a permanent appointment was almost immediately forthcoming at Michigan, where he remained until his death in 1921. There he achieved considerable fame as an economist interested in governmental regulation of railroads. Our prime concern here, however, is with some ideas about unions developed by him and expressed during and shortly after his Cornell period. It is possible to see in them reflections of the German origins of his sociojurisprudential theory of the labor movement.

This is clearly expressed in an early Adams essay that compares the economic methodology of the German historical school with that of the English classicists. He emphasized in this essay the Germans' consideration of the social whole, of which the individual is only a minor part—the antithesis of English thought (see 2, p. 80). Adams argued that "it is impossible for the economist to arrive at just conclusions in economic matters unless he consciously allows his thought to be influenced by a keen appreciation of the science of jurisprudence and also of the juridical structure of the society to which his attention is addressed." That is, the economist must have an awareness of historical sources as well as of the nonindividualistic nature of the ethical values necessary for economic and, thereby, industrial organization. Adams, in some ways favoring the German tradition, felt that social considerations in the form of state control should intervene in certain areas and say to the parties, "regardless of what you may yourselves think you prefer, beyond these defined limits you may not operate." Economic choices should not be left to the free operation of market forces, as the traditional English economists advocated, but should be made subject to some legal regulation.

His contact with the German-inspired economists and legal historians had also made Adams acutely aware of the subtle means by which individual actions could be governed by social practices. Jurisprudence, these Germans taught, reflected group custom as well as natural law, and the weight of old traditions could thus affect conclusively what appeared to be simple as well as completely new relationships. In this way modern law could be seen to be merely the adaptation of old customs to new uses. Since customs are social rather than individual phenomena, the state, acting as the instrument of society, was operating within its normal prerogatives when it intervened in economic matters (cf. 32). Adams' views were buttressed by his reading of the work of Arnold Toynbee (cf. 24, p. 42) and Frederic Maitland.

Adams put forward a second and supplemental theme relating to job rights. He argued that job rights were a normal and "legitimate" historical extension of the juristic principle of property. Obviously, this contention caused him to be regarded not only as one of the bright young men on the scene, but also as something of an *avant-garde* economic radical. That he was one of the five who founded the American Economic Association contributed to the luster (or the glare) of this reputation.

Adams argued that every nation had its own unique historical measure for the degree of state intervention considered desirable (5). In Germany the state's role seemed to be all-pervasive —in England it appeared to be relatively negligible. Adams noted that in America a third, or middle, course seemed to have developed. He therefore sought a formula for the practical intervention of the state in America where the state is "[neither] made out of the chips and blocks left over after framing industrial society, nor, does industrial society serve its full purpose in furnishing a means of existence for the poor unfortunates who are thrust out of the civil or the military service" (5, p. 495). It was not an easily developed formula, for it required an understanding of several somewhat indistinct historical trends.

First, the state should intervene in order to set the minimum level of competition (factory laws). Second, it should regulate the activities of decreasing cost industries (monopolies). Third, the test for further governmental supervision was the administrative effectiveness of the operation, and that, in turn, often depended upon the abilities of public servants. And, finally, labor relations were generally to be exempted from direct governmental action, not because administering them would have presented almost insuperable difficulties, but because the actual American cultural tradition provided a better way. That tradition was "built upon four legal facts: Private property in land, private property in labor, private property in capital, and the right of contract for all alike."

In the area of contemporary industrial relations Adams noted a particular conceptual lag. On the cornerstone of the once novel concept of personal property he felt that there had been erected an insurmountable barrier against further social modification. The labor movement, he pointed out in another lecture, was trying to broaden the original concept so as to give it a more general meaning as well as a less sacrosanct character (4). Where unions had once asked for no more than improvements in wages, hours, and apprenticeship regulations, they now (1886) sought to extend the personal ownership concept to include the right to a job.

. . . What the workmen demand [he said] is such an organization of the industries to which they give their time that certain rights shall be granted to them, even though they are not proprietors, in the ordinary acceptance of that word. . . . Capital can no longer be regarded as bearing purely a private character, and . . . proprietorship in productive agencies can be admitted only on condition of strict responsibility. Such decisions as these may be regarded as prophecies of a new industrial organization [4, p. 8862].

Adams clinched this estimate of the evolution of social values by rhetorically asking whether these union demands did not really follow earlier patterns made by shifts in social and political control.

. . . May not the benefits of proprietorship be diffused, while the nominal or legal residence of property remains where it now is? If men are given tenure of employment, and cannot be discharged except for cause that satisfies a commission of arbitrators, they may be said to be in the enjoyment of an industrial home; if men are promoted from the ranks (that is, according to civil service rules), they may be said to have a vested interest in the industry; if employes are consulted whether hours of work or the numbers employed shall be reduced, they have secured a right to live in hard times from the fund of capital created by them in flush times; and if all these claims—as well as others naturally implied by them—should be so well established that infringement on either side may be taken into the courts, the practical meaning of proprietorship in productive agencies will be radically changed from that which either custom or law now recognizes. It will be virtually a new law of productive property. It will result in the establishment of an Industrial Federation [4, p. 8863].

A further expansion of this view is found in an essay published in 1891. Note the implication that the extension and impersonalization of the market was a prime cause in the reorganization of social relationships and values. Adams presented this as a novel introduction to the Marxian theory of the changing modes of production. He later returned to it and expanded it.

. . . In my opinion, combination among workingmen is a necessary step in the re-crystallization of industrial rights and duties. From the sixteenth century to the beginning of the nineteenth century, the tendency has been towards disintegration in all matters of property and industries. *In early society, when men worked wholly for local markets, when the relation between employer and employé was a personal relation, competition was kept in restraint by custom and by law.* But with the downfall of feudalism, with the discovery of the new world, with the new spirit of personal independence infused into life by the great religious reformation and by the political struggles, all this was changed. Localism gave way to nationality, competition took the place of custom, and wealth came to be used as capital. It was at this point in the development of English society that the era of inventions made its appearance, and the result was what might easily have been expected. The power and the energy previously shown in religious and political controversies now made itself manifest in trade. Great industries sprang into existence, and under the theory of property then prevalent it naturally followed that the new social power generated by the use of machinery fell into the hands of those who were so fortunate as to become proprietors of the mechanism of production [3, pp. 45–46; italics added].

A theory of evolutionary jurisprudence and a theory of "countervailing power" were both explicit in his reasoning.

This is a most important fact if we would understand the industrial armament in which the world stands to-day, for it shows that the concentration of industrial power did not begin with the workmen when they organized themselves into unions, but was an inevitable result of the use of machinery in a society whose legal structure was shaped to meet the conditions of personal competition. It began when employers came to be exclusive proprietors of machinery, of material, and of factory. My point is this. *The birth of a capitalist class, freed from the restraints formerly imposed by custom and law, was the first step in industrial armament, while the organization of labor into unions of trades is to be regarded as a second step, a counter-movement on the part of those whose interests were endangered by the rise of great industries. This is the historical explanation of trades-unions* [3, p. 46; italics added].

One might add parenthetically Adams' further implication that the only government that could work well in industry was self-government. In this way employers and employees would have a continuing institutional arrangement that permitted the continuous interchange of views. The realization of this plan, he concluded,

would require that employers should recognize unions and deal with the men in a body; that they should be willing to submit all matters of internal organization to arbitration; that men already employed in industry should have preference over men outside; and, what is perhaps of most importance, all these should come to the workingmen as their right, and not by the grace of employers. This seems like giving up everything to the workmen, and it would indeed result in a new form of industrial organization in which the wage-earner would receive greater consideration. But it would, I am sure, increase rather than decrease the efficiency of industry and be of mutual advantage to all concerned [3, p. 49].

At the end of 1896 Adams chose for his presidential address to the American Economic Association a summation of his views on methodology, in which he discussed the role of social as contrasted with individual values (1). He reiterated his ideas on state intervention in industrial matters and on the historic development of the aims of the labor movement. Speaking of the concentration of wealth and power brought about by the industrial revolution and the consequent impotency of legal controls that had been developed in an individualistic society, he argued that the challenge to law and order arising from the change in the nature of economic society should not be met either by a resort to seventeenth-century juristic precepts or by an attempt to recreate the balance of wealth and economic responsibility of the earlier age, since both attempts were, as solutions, doomed to failure. He offered instead his solution that the old property concept should be extended to cover workers' jobs. The job right, he assured his professional confreres, was not only a legitimate extension of the Anglo-Saxon code of individual liberties, but was the key to the discovery of industrial peace through industrial liberty. Furthermore, he emphasized that this key was one that had been sought, but not found, by earlier English economists.

The assertion that property is essential to liberty should be the occasion of no apprehension. It is as old as the conception that the essence of liberty consists in a proper correlation of rights and responsibilities. He who reads with a discerning mind those writers who developed the theory of industrial individualism, will perceive that the ability of a careful and energetic man to acquire property, and through property to control the conditions under which he works, was an assumed though frequently an unexpressed premise of all their arguments. The same thought underlies the theories of prosperity incorporated into the writings of professed economists. By reference also to the proposals of industrial reformers which have claimed, or are claiming, the attention of our own time, it will be discovered that they all agree in the assertion that it is impossible for a man to become master of himself without acquiring control over the oppor-

tunities of labor. What else can the doctrine of the English economists respecting the importance of personal savings imply? What
other meaning can be given to the theory of co-operation, the aim of
which is to make all laborers capitalists, if it be not that by becoming
a proprietor one becomes his own master? [1, pp. 27–28.]

In addressing himself to the problem, Adams outlined the way
in which he differed from the classical English position.

. . . Political economy was brought by John Stuart Mill as far as it
was capable of being brought under the eighteenth century conception of property, and the further evolution of industrial theory, as
well as the reconstruction of the legal framework of industrial society,
must begin with the modification of the concept of property, if any
progress is to be made in industrial science or industrial administration [1, p. 32].

Adams concluded his remarks by illustrating the steps by
which industrial government emerged, and by noting in an aside
the opportunity for social service that this evolution offered to
those trained to observe and to understand.

My second thought respecting that which, by courtesy of your
imagination I have termed the workmen's property, is that its clarification will take place through the evolution of collective bargaining
and the formal labor contract. Some steps toward collective bargaining have already been taken. Trades-unions are no longer indiscrimi-
nately condemned; strikes are no longer considered universally il-
legal; the law of conspiracy, also, is coming to be confined within its
legitimate sphere. At the same time it cannot be said that the situation has been heartily accepted by either party to the controversy.
Employers still assert their purpose to bargain with individual employees, and the employees still show a timidity, amounting at times
even to cowardice, in the presence of definitely expressed responsibilities. Both appear to think their liberty to consist in being a law unto
themselves, rather than in the discovery and measurement of their
respective rights in view of the new industrial conditions under which
they are obliged to live. Neither appears to recognize that the sociology of the industrial process has rendered collective bargaining im-
perative, in order that due regard may be paid to the instinct of indi-

vidualism by which both are impelled. The one thing needed is a true analysis of the situation, and a satisfactory exposition of the advantages that would accrue from the labor contract. This service is the high privilege of economy, but it must be an economy that rests on history, that is motivated by a passion for liberty, and that is directed and limited by a knowledge of jurisprudence [1, pp. 32-33].

Needless to say, neither Adams' remarks nor his ideas were eagerly accepted by all of the profession. He was largely ignored, although one outspoken critic, Arthur T. Hadley (1856-1930), did reply to him. Hadley, too, had studied with Adolph Wagner and was at this time president of Yale University and an advocate of extreme economic conservatism. He defined Adams' views of jurisprudence (later they would have been classified as sociological jurisprudence) as erroneous, and pointed out that his conclusions regarding historic changes in economic relation, though possibly correct in direction, were extreme in degree.

It is interesting at this juncture to note the reaction of one of the young economists, John R. Commons, at the time professor of sociology at Syracuse University,[3] who appears to have been seeking a new "theoretical framework." There is a record of what Commons thought of Adams' position in Adams' reply to Hadley.

The impression which is left upon my mind by this discussion, and I need not say how deeply interested I am in it, is that there is some danger connected with using old words for new ideas. Professor Commons remarked to me last evening that it seemed to him unfortunate to employ the word "property" in any but the established and accepted meaning. "For," he remarked, "it tends to introduce confusion into a subject that might be presented more clearly by giving specific illustrations of the new rights which laborers are at liberty to urge on account of new industrial conditions." I appreciate very keenly the pertinency of this criticism, and many of the remarks which have been submitted in the course of the discussion this morning emphasize its pertinence. But before consenting that it is unwise to employ the word property in a new sense, it may be well to inquire

---

[3] Five years earlier Adams had tried to buttress Commons' position at the University of Indiana (cf. letter dated August 28, 1894, in 25, p. 273).

if the confusion of ideas has been occasioned by my use of this word, or does it exist in the situation itself? As it appears to me, one who analyzes the labor situation at the present time, finds himself groping after an idea for which there is not adequate expression. Could it be expressed, however, and become a real thing by being embodied in contracts, it would hold to the laborer the same relation that what we now know as property, holds to the proprietor, his employer. If we look at the matter historically, it is clear that the word property has not always meant the same thing. On the contrary, it suggests to the mind a series of rights that have been acquired from time to time; and if the labor problem is in essence what I hold it to be, the social and industrial changes essential for the working out of that problem will add yet another concept to that series of rights and privileges which the past evolution of the English speaking people has crystallized into the word property. At best, one who discusses this problem is reduced to the alternative of using old words with new meanings, or of coining a new word, which could not be understood until explained. For many reasons, I am constrained to believe that, in the long run, greater advantage will accrue from the employment of the word property with a slightly altered meaning than from the coining of any new expression. It is the common method of historic evolution [1, pp. 45–47].

When Hadley succeeded Adams as president of the American Economic Association and gave the next presidential address, "The Relation between Economics and Politics" (28), he made a point of touching on Adams' speech. Hadley insisted that economists were not trained to explain historical evolution but, on the contrary, should be academically prepared to enunciate the eternal verities of economic theory. Commons' reaction to Adams' ideas during this period may have been somewhat ambiguous, but Commons' opinion of Hadley's criticism was as clear as it was outspoken. Commons replied to this speech by saying, "The function of the political economist is to show that the standpoint of a class is the best standpoint; and he does this even when he claims to speak from the standpoint of society as a whole; for, then, he is arguing in favor of the class which benefits by leaving private property as it is. Economists have not lost influence as a whole—only those who stand for a class which has passed the day of its political power" (**19**, p. 112). This position reflects neither Adams' nor Commons' later views. Quite naturally, Hadley rejected Commons' view, and contented himself with remarking that "economic theory is as true and as important as geometrical theory."

Adams wrote several books that stand as academic landmarks. None dealt with the "labor problem"; his writing in that area was limited to essays, which are not a popular form. For this reason alone, his contribution to trade-union theory appears to have gone largely unrecognized. Indeed, only his contemporaries or those who had read his work in other connections knew of these essays at all. Although Adams played a minor role in the labor discussions of the American Economic Association after 1900, when professional interest in that field expanded, his work provoked a good deal of discussion, and as a well-informed fore-runner of modern trade-union theorists he was unsurpassed.

John Commons: Theorist As Policy Maker

Commons, with the details of whose life we are already familiar (see pp. 31–36), deviated from the line of economic orthodoxy early in his career, when he published his *The Distribution of Wealth* (**11**). Despite adverse reviews in most professional journals, Commons persevered stubbornly in his independent think-ing and continued to formulate novel juxtapositions (cf. **23**, pp. 284–85). In time his ideas went through several phases, obviously shaped by his reading and by a variety of personal professional experiences. The record he left as a pioneer on the frontiers of public administration is actually the basis for his considerable reputation. But we are presently concerned with the evolution of his ideas regarding the social role of labor unions, and will there-fore spend little time on his administrative career. Suffice it to say that his knowledge of trade-unionism greatly enhanced his activities as a public administrator.

Toward the end of his long career, Commons combined his

labor interests, the lessons in practical administration learned
from his own numerous public activities, and some ideas gained
from reading philosophy, into a formal recapitulation of economic doctrine. The complex amalgam which resulted makes
the task of assessing his labor contribution somewhat difficult,
particularly since his ideas merged with those of his student,
Selig Perlman, and are not always distinguishable.

One would be hard put to it to demonstrate that Commons'
thinking changed its course as a direct result of Adams' AEA
presidential address alone, since Commons had read, or was
then in the process of reading, not only Schmoller and Bücher
but also several English writers whose original inspiration came
from the German historical school. Joseph Schumpeter cites Commons' *Documentary History of American Industrial Society* (22)
as illustrative of the influence of this school in America (44). In
any event, it is apparent that the pioneer works of Sir Henry
Maine and Frederic Maitland in the fertile area of legal history,
as well as those of George Unwin and William Ashley on the
development of economic institutions in England, had a marked
effect upon Commons.[4] He quoted their ideas in a long series of
articles written at Syracuse during the period in which his views
were changing. These articles are particularly useful to us because they hint at his growing reliance upon historical records as
a source of social generalizations.

I have designated these papers [he concluded] "A Sociological
View of Sovereignty." It remains to justify this title and further to
distinguish the sociological from other views. These are, as already
stated, the philosophical, the legal, the political. Philosophical views
turn upon the ideal, or ultimate purpose, of the state, as the expression of universal reason or of the development of human character.
They tend to personify the state, and to abstract the idea from the
actual historical institution. The sociological view is concerned not so
much with the ultimate purpose as with the detailed processes of the

---

[4] The citations in his subsequent work bear evidence of the extent and nature
of his readings (cf. 12 and 20). His complete bibliographic history can be found
in his *Economics of Collective Action* (12).

state's evolution. It is an inductive, comparative study of historical societies with reference to the part played by sovereignty, and its aim is to discover the actual laws governing the emergence of the state. The legal view is the view of the lawyer and the judge whose problem is a practical one. He must decide between two claimants for control in a definite matter of life, property, or other privilege. For this reason the legal view is entirely separated from the scientific purpose of sociology, and, if projected by the legal mind into social theories, it tends to abstract the state from the remainder of society and to set it overhead as something external and mechanical. Political science, which has borrowed its concepts from jurisprudence and has been prosecuted by lawyers, falls also into this fault [20, VI, 86–87].

Like Adams, Commons immediately began to discuss the property concept that was basic to the understanding of value.

. . . Private property is but another name for that coercive relation existing between human beings through which the proprietor commands the services of others. This also is sovereignty, and in its mediaeval law "the one word *dominion* has to cover both proprietary rights and many kinds of political power; it stands for ownership, lordship, sovereignty, suzerainty." [The quotation is from Maitland, 29, p. 344.] Up to this point, therefore, in European history the state had not yet clearly emerged. Private property is strictly competitive, a necessity of the struggle for life, and has no ethical implication. Neither is it subject to the will of any person outside the proprietor himself. When, therefore, order and right are injected into property, we may say the state has appeared. Sovereignty and private property, then, constitute the two branches of this all-pervasive social relation, coercion, or *dominion* [20, VI, 87–88].

Commons, using *histoire raisonnée,* felt constrained, however, to establish a causal relationship between the property concept and formal social organization.

But private property, contrary to the legal view, is not the creature of the state, nor is it subject to the state. It is pristine and anterior. It springs from the very nature of man. The state is rather the creature and offspring of private property. It arises quite late in the history of property, with the rise of reflective thinking and the capacity for rational coöperation. The legal view, seeing only the unity and immense power of the modern state, has reversed both the historical and the psychological order. The state is not sovereign, except to the extent that it has actually become so, *i.e.,* except as it has actually extracted coercion from private property, and has, at the same time, acquired for itself the organization for expressing and enforcing its will. The state expresses the coöperative or mutual-veto will of that part of society which is politically organized for this purpose. Private property expresses the individual will of the several private owners, or of the private chief, whether patriarch, pope, suzerain, boss, or industrial monopolist, who is at the head of the particular institution. The sociological view, being strictly inductive, does not impart to the theory of the state that which is potential and ideal, but only that which is actual and historical. At the same time, by recognizing the state as a process and not an entity, it allows for its further growth and extension, and even its ultimate absorption of all private property. Only in the latter event could it be rightly said that the state is absolute and ultimate, as maintained by the legal view [20, VI, 88].

It is worth repeating that Commons' subsequent experiences with the U.S. Industrial Commission and the National Civic Federation turned him from a consideration of abstractions and conjecture (*histoire raisonnée*) to concrete social groups and alignments. Commons was something of a reformer but, like H. C. Adams, he had relatively few illusions about the inherent power of the state when it confronted dynamic semiprivate institutions. In fact, he shared Unwin's view that the government, whenever it intervened, tended to bungle the job.[5] But he set himself the task of devising workable methods for progressive governmental supervision of technical industrial problems, and eventually achieved considerable fame. The Wisconsin Industrial Commission Act of 1911, in particular, serves as a memorial to him and to his knowledge of industrial relations.

We find that the development of Commons' interest in the field of trade-unionism went through four major phases. His early

---

[5] Unwin emphasized the dynamic qualities of the self-defined economic units in post-Elizabethan England. Ashley, by way of contrast, stressed the role played by the political government.

interest in Christian socialism as represented by Richard T. Ely has already been indicated. This was the first of his developmental phases and appears to have lasted until the mid-nineties (see 9 and 10). It was succeeded by a second, somewhat confused period, which is most aptly characterized by his extended comments on Arthur T. Hadley's presidential address to the American Economic Association.

As economists I believe we would stand on safer ground if, when our conclusions lead us to champion the cause of a class, or of a group of classes, or to expose another class, we should come squarely out and admit that it is so; not because the class interest is foremost in our minds, but because the class is the temporary means of bringing about the permanent welfare of all. . . . We should never be blindly bigoted nor partisan nor committed irrevocably to a class position, with its bad as well as its good. We should be broadminded like Adam Smith. But we should admit that we differ among ourselves, and that our fundamental differences coincide in general with class antagonism in society. We are a part of the social situation. History alone will decide between us. Our present vision is limited. For this reason we ought to acknowledge that no one man is great enough and good enough to stand solely and at all times in practical politics for the nation as a whole, but that all men in a free republic are also moved by the same spirit of patriotism. We ought to acknowledge that the nation as a whole is represented by the accredited representatives of all classes; that no man can honestly represent a class in which he does not believe. It is out of the combined result of public-spirited men contending for their own convictions and authorized to speak for others whose convictions are the same, and who are capable of making concessions in the true interest of all, that all of society is truly represented. Not the individual economist, but the *associated economists,* represent the permanent interests of the nation as a whole [15, pp. 69–70].

Years later, in 1934, Commons expressed an implied criticism of the type of thinking he had done during this second phase of his development. He mentioned that Thorstein Veblen's knowledge of economic institutions had been confined to the case material presented to the U.S. Industrial Commission (1898–1901), thus "his [Veblen's] notion of intangible property ended in the Marxian extortion and exploitation" (14, p. 4). But it is useful to remember that Commons' own sources were the same as Veblen's. That this was true is evident in an essay presented to the American Sociological Society at the end of 1906, in which Commons dealt with industrial psychology and incentive schemes.

. . . The psychology of the workman is analyzed and experimented upon as accurately as the chemistry of the different kinds of coal. A time-keeping department is created for this purpose, with experts, card records and a testing laboratory, and a new engineering profession springs up with industrial psychology as its underlying science. Wonderful and interesting are these advances in harnessing the forces of human nature to the production of wealth. The pioneers in this field, calling themselves "production engineers," may well be compared with the great inventors of the turbine and the dynamo in what they are doing to reduce cost and multiply efficiency.

But in doing so they are doing exactly the thing that forces labor to become *class*-conscious. While a man retains individuality, he is more or less proof against class feeling. He is *self*-conscious. His individuality protects him somewhat against the substitution of some one else to do his job. But when his individuality is scientifically measured off in aliquot parts and each part is threatened with substitution by identical parts of other men, then his sense of superiority is gone. He and his fellow-workmen compete with each other, not as whole men, but as units of output. The less-gifted man becomes a menace to the more gifted as much as the one to the other. Both are then ripe to recognize their solidarity, and to agree not to compete. And this is the essential thing in class conflict [15, pp. 74–75].

Later on Commons also stressed that his experience in drafting bills for legislative consideration, and his concomitant study of court decisions, collective bargaining, and arbitration cases, had contributed to the development of a completely different theory of economic activity. This we term the third or "Wisconsin theory" phase, and he moved into it at the University of Wisconsin during the decade prior to World War I.

It is significant that Commons took pains to point out, in the first essays connected with the project on the documentary history of industrial society, the extent of his rejection of industrial class consciousness as a motivating force in American history. He found in American historical records clear proof that unionism had preceded industrialization and technical changes in the modes of production. Commons did not argue that unionism preceded industrialism, but that unionism, as a phenomenon, was not dependent upon the prior existence of industrialism. He acknowledged that in many instances unions developed after industrialism had occurred (cf. 16, especially pp. 683–84).

Whatever may have been its origin in other countries, the labor movement in America did not spring from factory conditions. It arose as a protest against the merchant-capitalist system. The factories were as yet confined to one branch of cotton textiles, employing mainly women and children. These did not take part in the organized movement. The effort, indeed, of the New England Association of Farmers, Mechanics and Working Men to secure the coöperation of the factory operatives was distinctly a failure. But the merchant-capitalist system, with its extension of the markets through improved transportation, with its enlargement of credits through the banking system, with its option of purchase over wide areas of competing producers, had begun to reduce both the journeyman and the master-mechanic to a common level of dependency. With the rapid growth of cities and the appearance of the speculative capitalist-builder the same sweat-shop methods invaded the building trades. "We would not be too severe on our employers," said the building mechanics of Boston in 1834, "they are the slaves to the capitalists as we are to them" [22, V, 23–24].

Commons added that the social dividing line in America was always between the "producer" and the nonproducer, the poor and the rich, and only ultimately (and then not always) between the worker and the owner. Moreover, when Commons traced social alignments he was led to conclusions that were strangely reminiscent of those of Maitland, and at the same time anticipated those of Roscoe Pound.

From the accepted standpoint of their time, [the workers' "equal citizenship"] demands were not inspired by a just regard for equality, but by "agrarian" thirst for other people's property. Their stand-point was the naïve theory, even yet animating our jurisprudence, that thinks only in terms of property, and conceives of labor and wages only as one kind of property to be treated like other kinds. It is because our modern view has shifted unconsciously from the stand-point of property to the standpoint of man that we fail to see either the consistency of those who opposed the demands of 1829 or our inconsistency in asserting the equal treatment of capital and labor. In this we have accepted the working men's point of view as it was in 1829, unwitting that in so far we give precedence, not equality, to labor over capital.

This was done, not by virtue of partisanship for labor, but because experience of the new political and economic conditions had gone far enough to show that oppression of the working man brought down the social fabric with him. Compulsory militia service had become a source of dissipation; absconding contractors and imprisonment for debt had demoralized the laborer, and discouraged his efforts toward honest industry; an ignorant electorate was a political menace. Thus a nation whose industrial progress was bringing forth a class of wage-earners endowed with suffrage could well afford to give to labor priority over capital before the law [22, V, 29–30].

Commons went on to test certain of the class-conscious (Marx-ian) theories prevalent at the time. His research in the history of conspiracy among shoemakers, besides confirming the existence of a pre-industrialization labor movement, demonstrated that one of the prime purposes of unionism was protection against the competition of cheaper labor. In other words, the job rights of certain individual workmen rather than the interests of a sup-posed general economic class were to be protected. In pursuing this topic further, he discovered that the organized journeymen often realized that it was not their masters who caused their misery, but rather the oppressive forces of economic competition. Lower prices for the consumer brought lower wages and more misery for the workingmen.

The menace of competition may conveniently be described as in-ternal and external. The former arises within the area of the existing market, the latter proceeds from cheap producers abroad. With the ever-widening area of political control these external menaces become internal, and it is this moving frontier that determines the scope and character of protective organization and protective legislation.

Throughout the course of industrial evolution the part played by the merchant stands out as the determining factor. The key to the situation is at all times the price-bargain. It is the merchant who controls both capital and labor. If the merchant has a market, he can secure capital. Even the modern "manufacturer" is first of all the merchant. The "conflict of capital and labor" is a conflict of market and labor, of merchant and wage-earner, of prices and wages. With the extension of the market the merchant-function is the first to separate, unless prevented by guild or other regulations, and with each further extension the separation is greater. Just as the first "masters' society" of 1789 was really a retail merchants' association, so the modern "manufacturers' association" is a price-regarding association. Capital follows the merchant, and the manufacturers' protective organization is an organization to protect prices. When the extension of the market provokes the conflict of prices and wages, the wage-earners resort to independent protective policies. Then the manufacturer turns, for the time, from the market and faces the workman . . . [15, pp. 261–62].

Ultimately the conflict is one between the consumers' interest and that of the producer:

. . . Wherever the consumer as such is in control, he favors the marginal producer, for through him he wields the club that threatens the other producers. Consequently, the producers resort either to private organizations equipped with coercive weapons to suppress their menacing competitor, or else they seek to persuade or compel the government to suppress him. In this way the contest of classes or interests enters the field of politics, and the laws of the land, and even the very framework of government, are the outcome of a struggle both to extend markets and to ward off their menace [15, p. 262].

Labor spared itself no efforts in attempting to limit the effects of competition. It embraced the tariff principle to keep out cheap foreign goods (the external menace). And it agitated for the right to form its own private organizations to suppress the physical influx as well as the economic effects of cheaper labor in the home market (the internal menace). When it could not effectively suppress cheap labor through private collective action, it mustered its political resources to secure legislation curbing the employment of children and women—to say nothing of prison labor. Labor, like the employer, also sought to cultivate the consumer and affixed, in lieu of "Made in USA" trade-marks, the union label. In these efforts what labor sought was relief from the effects of competition—the competition of cheap ware and, above all, the competition of cheaper labor.

Thus it was that Commons came to formulate a completely non-Marxian explanation of the rise of unionism. His emphasis on the changed nature of physical distribution was in direct contrast to the classical Socialist belief that it was the industrial revolution and the changes in machine ownership that mattered. For the concept of class Commons substituted the lesser but more historically demonstrable unit, the self-interested or job-possessing faction. And for class hatred he substituted the fear of the external menace (goods) and the fear of the internal menace (cheap labor). Unionism was, in his view, simply an interest group that was striving to protect and better working conditions for its membership. The workingman's emphasis on holding his job or on wage concessions rather than on class solidarity merely demonstrated his adaptation of the vested-right concept which the German social theorists had first "isolated" and which Adams, in particular, had identified with American unionism.

But Commons was also concerned with the idealistic side of unionism. Having eliminated the concept of altruistic class loyalty, he felt obliged to formulate a reasonable and demonstrable substitute, which he insisted upon calling "idealism," although it would have been easier to comprehend if he had termed it "working philosophy." In his essay, "An Idealistic Interpretation of History" (15, pp. 25–50), he suggested that idealism could be discovered on two levels: the higher or transcendental, and the lower or pragmatic. The final paragraphs show Commons' reasoning and his profound respect for the complexities of the motives that lead to "steps in the right direction."

I have attempted to sketch the origin and evolution of the two species of idealism that struggled for existence in this epoch of American history. This biology of ideas exhibits both adaptation to, and rejection of, the contemporaneous economic development. The transcendentalism of New England, with its humanized God and its deified man, was rather a protest against, than a product of, the new economic conditions. As the years advanced and industrial anarchy deepened, the protest turned to reconstruction. But the tools and materials for the new structure were not politics and legislation, but an idealized, transcendental workingman. Transcendentalism resurrected man, but not the real man. It remained for the latter, the man in the struggle, to find his own way out. By failure and success, by defeat, by victory often fruitless, he felt along the line of obstacles for the point of least resistance. But he, too, needed a philosophy. Not one that would idealize him, but one that would help him win a victory. Shorter hours of labor, freedom to escape from economic oppression, —these were the needs that he felt. His inalienable "natural right" to life, liberty, land and the products of his own labor,—this was his philosophy. Politics and legislation were his instruments.

It is easy to show that "natural rights" are a myth, but they are a fact of history. It was the workingmen's doctrine of natural rights that enabled the squatter to find an idealistic justification for seizing land and holding it in defiance of law. "Natural right," here as always, was the effective assailant of legal right. Had it not been for this theoretic setting, our land legislation might have been piecemeal and opportunist like the English—merely a temporizing concession to the squatters on account of the difficulty of subduing them by armed force. Such an opportunist view, without the justification of natural rights, could not have aroused enthusiasm nor created a popular party. The Republican party was not an anti-slavery party. It was a homestead party. On this point its position was identical with that of the workingmen. Just because slavery could not live on onehundred-and-sixty-acre farms did the Republican party come into conflict with slavery [15, pp. 49–50].

It is worth adding that the rightness or wrongness of the pragmatic idealism did not stem from its being inherently good or bad for workingmen. Quite the contrary, its moral value was judged along traditional lines that emphasized liberty and self-realization. But the superiority of the pragmatic idealism was the combination of its moral rectitude and its actual social success. Commons was a pragmatist of sorts.

It is erroneous to conclude that Commons derided abstract idealism. What he was wont to stress, however, was the pragmatic or lower level which, in spite of its crude trappings, had yielded beneficial results. From the vantage point of historical reflection, Commons was relatively curious about how the right things got done, although he did not emphasize the socially significant role of heroic pioneers. He thought that social development resulted as often from the demands of untutored, parochial-minded workmen as it did from the more articulate demands of upper-class reformers, whose position and sense of personal mission made them considerably less anonymous. Although this conclusion is more closely related to an analysis of social administration than to a theory of union development, nevertheless the impact of its consequences on a theory of unionism should not be overlooked. Commons was always working on a "practical idealism" that would link the future with the present, and altruism with self-interest. Later his student Selig Perlman was to term this practical yet idealistic *élan* "organic unionism," but at the time Commons worked out his theory its full implications were not elaborated.

Commons' obscure literary style and his lack of method as a historian detracted from his written work. However, in his introduction to the *History of Labour in the United States* he presented the characteristic intuitive generalizations which typify the best of his third or "Wisconsin" phase.

Labour movements in America have arisen from peculiar American conditions, and it is by understanding these conditions that we shall be able to distinguish the movements and methods of organisation from those of other countries. Out of these conditions have sprung certain philosophies, or certain modifications of imported philosophies, and it is the union of these conditions and philosophies that explains the movements. . . . The labour history of the country is here treated as a part of its industrial and political history. It is the story of how, in the course of three centuries, the wage-earner, as a distinct class, had been gradually, even violently, separating himself from the farmer, the merchant, and the employer, and coming to feel that his standing and progress in society depend directly on wages and not directly on prices, rents, profits, or interest.

The condition which seems to distinguish most clearly the history of labour in America from its history in other countries is the wide expanse of free land. As long as the poor and industrious can escape from the conditions which render them subject to other classes, so long do they refrain from that aggression on the property rights or political power of others, which is the symptom of a "labour movement" [21, I, 3-4].

Commons went on to discuss the origin and role of government.

Even more fundamental than free land is that political institution which alone could make land a political issue. At least two or three generations before labour in other countries, whether peasant or wage-earner, had won the first great point of vantage for which it fought, labour in America had received with scarcely a struggle the boon of universal manhood suffrage. . . . When, therefore, in the 'thirties, the first glimmerings of his condition as an unprivileged class awakened him from sleep, the "working man" entered promptly into that political struggle, which has ever been his hope and his undoing. The tragedy, the credulity, the fiasco, the lessons learned, forgotten, learned again, the defection of leaders, the desperate reaction to violence or anarchism, the disintegration of unions—these are the moving picture of eight decades of that universal suffrage, for which the labourer would give his life, but by which he has often followed a mirage. The repeating cycle of politics and trade unionism, political struggle and economic struggle, political organisation and economic organisation, marks out the course of this history of labour.

The vast area of the United States, coupled with free trade within that area and a spreading network of transportation, has developed an unparalleled extension of the competitive area of markets, and thereby has strikingly distinguished American movements from those of other countries. It is almost as though the countries of Europe, from Ireland to Turkey, from Norway to Italy, had been joined in a single empire like China, but, unlike China, had passed through a century of industrial revolution. . . . It is the historical extension of markets over this broad expanse, from colonial times to the present, that has changed the character of competition, intensified its pressure, separated manufactures from agriculture, introduced the middleman, produced new alignments of social classes, and obliterated the futile lines that distinguish the jurisdiction of States . . . [21, I, 5–6].

Other factors molding the American labor movement besides the "wide expanse of free land" were the easy attainment of popular self-government, a geographically large free-trade economy which gradually became economically integrated, the diffusion of political powers among the many levels and the three branches of government, and the "influx of immigrants" of diverse "races, nationalities and languages [not to mention freed Negro slaves] thrown together into a single competitive area." As he wrote,

. . . The problem of assimilation and Americanisation is thrust directly upon labour as a class, for immigrants and races come first as wage-earners, and it is only by the assimilating power of labour organisations that they can be brought together in a movement that depends for success on their willingness to stop competition and espouse co-operation. Property values, business profits, and professional incomes are elevated by the very competition of immigrants which depresses the wage-earning classes, and, while the beneficiaries may look with complacency on the incoming multitudes, the labourers themselves are reduced either to the invidious necessity of resisting their coming, or to the patriotic burden of assimilating them after they come. . . . It is in meeting this problem of races and immigration that American labour movements have displayed their most violent exclusiveness and their most humane fraternity. At the one extreme are the exclusion of the Chinese by law and the exclusion of immigrants by the "closed shop," at the other is the affiliation in the same union of whites and blacks [21, I, 9–10].

It was this *History* that capped Commons' reputation as a labor historian, not so much because of the infinite detail (for which his associates were actually responsible), but because it showed the breadth of his social interest.

Commons' ideas on the social control of labor relations

stemmed from his National Civic Federation experiences, were further excited by his reading of Hector Denis' *Histoire des systèmes économiques et socialistes* in 1907, and blossomed with his creation and shaping of the Wisconsin Industrial Commission. Despite the personal frustration and bitterness of his painful experience with the U.S. Commission on Industrial Relations in 1914–15, which we will discuss elsewhere and which was only a temporary discouragement, Commons retained his earlier conviction that the foundations of "constitutional" government in industry could be consciously laid. Walsh and his other critics did not think that Commons' recommendations would lead to industrial stability, but he persevered with his private administrative analysis. He did not proceed blindly—quite the contrary, the wealth of his pre–World War I personal experience in Wisconsin gave him real confidence. Thus it was that he entered the fourth phase of his intellectual development, the one characterized by him as emphasizing "industrial goodwill."

The administration of the labor force, he argued, was usually conceived in two shortsighted ways (13). One considered labor as a commodity and conceived of wages as a consequence of the interaction of supply and demand. The other considered labor as an adjunct of a machine whose output determined labor's value. For these two views Commons had little respect.

. . . The commodity theory is the merchant's theory of buying and selling. The machinery theory is the engineer's theory of economy and output. Man is, after all, the most marvelous and productive force of all the forces of nature. He is a mechanism of unknown possibilities. Treated as a commodity, he is finished and ready for sale. Treated as a machine, he is an operating organism to be economized [13, p. 14].

To supplement these two incomplete views, Commons suggested a theory of social wholeness or integration which he called "mutual concession." In his own words,

Scientific management, since it begins and ends with individuals separated from their fellows, has the defects of autocracy. It means government by experts. An expert comes into the factory and makes a study of the operations of the selected individual. That individual and his fellow-workers are much concerned about his time studies, his stop-watch, his cold calculations, which decide for them the amount of work that shall be portioned out for the task. But they cannot be consulted. They are objects to be investigated, not investigators.

But goodwill is reciprocity. It is not government at all, but mutual concession. It yields as much to the prejudices and passions, to the conservatism and even suspicions of patrons as it does to scientific knowledge of what is good for them. Goodwill is not necessarily a virtuous will, or a loving will, it is a beneficial reciprocity of wills, and whether there is really a benefit or really a reciprocity, is a matter of opinion and mutual good feeling as much as a matter of science.

Goodwill is productive, not in the sense that it is the scientific economizing of the individual's capacities, but because it enlists his whole soul and all his energies in the thing he is doing. It is that unknown factor pervading the business as a whole, which cannot be broken up and measured off in motions and parts of motions, for it is not science but personality. It is the unity of a living being which dies when dissected. And it is not even the personality of a single individual, it is that still more evasive personality to which the responsive French give the name, *l'esprit de corps,* the spirit of brotherhood, the solidarity of free personalities.

It is this corporate character of goodwill that makes its value uncertain and problematical. A corporation is said to have no soul. But goodwill is its soul. A corporation owns its goodwill, and the value of goodwill is reflected in its stocks and bonds. It is the soul of a going concern, the value of the unity and collective personality that binds together all its parts in a living organism [13, pp. 19–20].

Commons thus had moved from an examination of concrete historical institutions to an attempted formulation of the spirit of industrial progress. Later he wrote somewhat wistfully that the employers who knew his theories and work had learned that the "best way to beat the unions was 'to beat them to it.'" This development was something he had not expected, but, if it had any effect at all on his thinking, it merely induced a philosophical or reflective attitude (18, p. 189).

In summary, Commons moved from the particular to the general, and in three major books (**17**, **14**, and **12**) spelled out his ideas of the meaning of group control and group action in modern industrial society. He argued that bargaining between collective socioeconomic groups tended to supersede individual political expression as the sovereign power in a democratic state. An exception to this was governmental determination of the rights of bargaining groups. He felt that disinterested experts could and should seek to mediate between competing groups. Through their technical ability, he believed experts capable of bringing reason and order to the borders of social hegemonies (**12**, pp. 266–84). Commons' explanation of this process, which was a unique analysis as well as an interpretive history, is not easy reading. The points he made have since been summarized by W. C. Mitchell and others (**31**, pp. 313–41; **33**). Our conclusion is merely that his interest in labor and trade-unionism was superseded by an older interest, dating from the time of his *Distribution of Wealth,* in creating a more perfectly descriptive economic theory.

Commons' contribution to trade-union theory went far beyond Adams'. His interpretation of the effect of the extension of the market on the position of social alignments puts him in company with the leading critics of Karl Marx. The insights in his exposition of the two types of idealism, although not fully developed by him, constitute major additions to social thinking and to historical research. But these points pale by comparison with Commons' contributions as patron of a school of public administration. It is from this phase of his career, as we have noted, that his reputation derives. The Wisconsin Industrial Commission, the Wisconsin Unemployment Compensation Act, and the development of principles for evaluating public-utility investments stand out as his memorials as much as, if not more than, his work in trade-union theory. It is possible that it was because of this administrative phase of his energetic interests that it was not he, but Selig Perlman who went on to synthesize what Commons had done and to add additional insights and research. The work of these two men, teacher and pupil, represents the full evolution of the "Wisconsin theory." Perlman, coming to Madison near the beginning of Commons' third phase, served his apprenticeship at an exciting time, and eventually succeeded "the master" as the working head of a research group studying the social history of labor movements.

Selig Perlman: Social History and Theory

Selig Perlman was born in tsarist Russia in 1888. He began his education in a *Realgymnasium* and spent a year in Italian universities prior to coming to the United States. In Europe Perlman was a member of the Jewish Bund, a revisionist Marxian trade-union organization, and as such was a follower of Marx. He emigrated to America in 1908, and in 1909 was sent on to the university in Madison by William English Walling, who was at the time active in the Socialist movement and in Marxian groups.

Madison in 1909 was enjoying its golden age, with both the university and the state government achieving importance as intellectual and experimental centers. The happy combination of a progressive legislature and a socially oriented university had resulted in "McCarthy's Bill Factory" at the state capitol, which provided both positive enactments and excellent job opportunities for ambitious and diligent students. Furthermore, the university was at the zenith of its fame, including on its faculty such men as Frederick Jackson Turner and E. A. Ross. It was an exciting place and an invigorating period, with plenty to do and an atmosphere favorable to original intellectual endeavors.

Although Perlman wrote an unusually erudite baccalaureate thesis (34) for Commons, on the emergence of "realistic" (pragmatic) socialism in Milwaukee from 1893 to 1910, it is apparent that Turner, who offered him an assistantship, was the first to be impressed by him. But when Commons intervened and suggested that Perlman work on the labor-history project then in progress, Perlman came to join Commons' staff. Because Perlman was conversant with the tortuous evolution of Socialist thought and could read German, a language in which many contemporary American union journals and documents appeared, he was assigned to the section dealing with the rise of the "foreign" labor movement in the eighties. It was as the result of his search through these union materials that he evolved a theory of the origins and nature of the redefined type of unionism that developed in that period as the AFL.

Perlman had from the first been impressed with Commons' historical findings on the shoemakers. A theory that combined concrete historical data with an extension of the market theory supplanted his original Marxian orientation. This shift in point of view resulted in his desire to systemize Commons' technique and specific findings. To do this, Perlman was forced to make somewhat broader generalizations than had Commons. He took from his teacher the conclusion that the traditional American labor organization had emphasized the ultimate reliance of the individual upon a form of self-employment, a political bias toward small-scale enterprise, and a transcending faith in easy-money solutions to business-cycle problems. In the American scene of that time, Perlman found that these traditional ideas were the nucleus of the philosophy of the Knights of Labor.

Yet his own European background and some of the material he found in his investigations led Perlman to make a startlingly new evaluation of the Socialist movement in America. He noted in particular the emergence in the eighties of a new kind of labor leader—one who came from the ranks of the Socialists but had abandoned his class consciousness and faith in general social reform in favor of a trade consciousness and a belief in the efficacy of immediate, albeit limited and parochial, gains. These former Socialists, unhampered by the anticapitalist feelings of the traditional American reformer and shorn of the faith of the orthodox Marxian or Lassallean determinist, were compelled subsequently to fight a two-front campaign against the Knights and the Socialists. Their victory marked the emergence of the modern labor movement. These ideas, as expressed in a few paragraphs in Perlman's section of the *History of Labour in the United States,* marked not only his significant contribution to the study, but also the major advance that the *History* as a whole made over Commons' earlier work in the *Documentary History*. In Perlman's view, modern unionism emerged from a reoriented Socialist philosophy and a recast Knights of Labor method.

. . . The half wage-conscious and half middle-class philosophy of the trade unionism of the sixties was entirely absent from the new trade union movement which started towards the end of the seventies. Yet that philosophy was preserved simon-pure in the Order of the Knights of Labor, which can be looked upon as the direct heir and successor to the unionism of Sylvis, Trevellick, and Cameron. The aspiring mechanic of the trade unions of the sixties had transmitted his faith in voluntary co-operation, social reforms, and politics to the humbler and machine-menaced member of the Knights of Labor. But the new trade unionism got, in place of the lost philosophy, the wage-consciousness of Marx and the International, purged of its socialist ingredients.

Socialism had also undergone an evolution. Starting out with the trade union philosophy of the International of 1864, it successfully endured a brief but painful period of attempted inoculation with the "isms" of native American reformers of the intellectual class, only to be overcome later by the "politics-first" philosophy of Lassallean-ism. Out of the strife and turmoil of factional struggle, the small group of Americanized Internationalists in the East withdrew to build up a potent trade union movement upon the basis of a wage-conscious but non-socialistic philosophy. . . .

As to methods. The trade unions of the sixties had made their appeal exclusively to the skilled man, and they succeeded in time of prosperity. Their disintegration during the years of depression in the seventies reduced the skilled man to practically the same position as that of the unskilled, so that henceforth the appeal to organise was extended to him also. Although the wage-conscious and semi-social-istic appeal of the International Labor Union to the unskilled ended in failure, the Knights of Labor succeeded in accomplishing in the eighties what McDonnell and Sorge had failed to do in the seventies. But the new trade unions, like those of the sixties, restricted their appeal to the skilled mechanics. The experience of the seventies taught them to eschew politics, but in the Knights of Labor every political movement started by workmen or farmers was sure to find a warm response [21, II, 353–54].

This new kind of union philosophy, which accepted the wage system, had little or no prejudice against large and integrated economic organization, and appealed to the self-help impulse among skilled and semiskilled laborers. In his part of the *History,* Perlman took pains to emphasize that the end product of the new philosophy was an era of joint agreements, or "constitutionalism in the relations between labor and capitalism." More than this, it was an admission that labor and capital had an approximately equal degree of bargaining power because the jobber was eliminated and the relationship between the capitalist (now a manufacturer) and the laborers was direct. Perlman went on immediately to qualify his statement and to point out that the jobber was not always eliminated by a reorganization of production methods. In some instances jobbers were eliminated by a change in patterns of ownership-control—that is, if a trust emerged, replacing jobbers as well as individual manufacturers. Then there would be no equality of bargaining power; quite the contrary, trusts resulted in unipartite control by the employer of all the labor force.

Perlman noted that another source of opposition to those who sought joint agreements was the prerogative-minded employer, of whose philosophy the open shop was an ideal expression. Despite this opposition, Perlman added, the joint agreement had become "one of the most generally accepted principles in the American labour movement . . . professed by the 'pure and simple' trade unionists and by the great majority of their socialist opponents. Those who reject it are a very small minority composed principally of the sympathizers with the Industrial Workers of the World" (21, II, 527).

Perlman took pains to explain why the focusing of attention on joint agreements tended to reduce political action to a secondary role. At the same time he emphasized that American unionism was aware of the necessity of keeping the public attitude favorable; the power of public opinion was seen even in private labor contracts. "Wish as it might," Perlman wrote, "the Federation could no longer [after 1904] remain a purely economic organisation. It was obliged to seek influence in elections" (21, II, 531). Yet this was a secondary activity and little real attention was paid, except by the Socialists, to labor legislation as a "cornerstone" of the unions' program. What they sought from the government was not general protective legislation but freedom of economic action vis-à-vis the employers and, particularly, the courts.

Perlman concluded that the AFL still paid, either by choice or by force, too much attention to political and legal action. As a consequence, too little effort was made to organize the unskilled workers. And the unskilled, forced because of this to look to a radical or "one big union" movement, put pressure on the semiskilled and their organizations. The semiskilled, convinced of the usefulness of the joint agreement but still somewhat less than completely convinced of the desirability of all aspects of the wage system, therefore turned to industrial unionism (to preclude the development of a competitive menace in the persons of the unskilled) and to limited political action. These two groups were getting far less attention from the AFL leadership than they deserved and needed. As a result, Perlman saw them forming a bloc against the "upper stratum" of skilled workers. The skilled were not responsive to the others' needs because of the nature of their own jurisdictional problems and the effect of these on the degree of concerted action possible among the various skilled crafts, particularly in the building trades. Perlman ended his essay by saying that until the skilled crafts could set up an organization that did more than provide for the absorption of the weaker by the stronger, the hiatus between the unskilled, the semiskilled, and the skilled workers would constitute the major problem for the AFL.

Perlman used his section of the *History of Labour in the United States* as his doctoral dissertation, and received his degree in 1915. After World War I he was hired to rewrite Richard T. Ely's 1905 revision of *The Labor Movement in America.* Perlman's revision did not follow Ely's Christian Socialist viewpoint and, quite naturally, something of a chill in their personal relations ensued. The disputed manuscript was published in 1922 as *A History of Trade Unionism in the United States* (35), and included, in addition to a condensation of the two-volume *History of Labour,* some lengthy theoretical "inferences" of Perlman's own, which in the main he had based on Commons' essays in the *Documentary History.*

Perlman proceeded to point up the "extension of the market" theme, with its attendant theses of the "competitive menace" and the divorce and ultimate stabilization of the price and wage bargains. Then he noted that the unions were alternately dependent upon long-range and short-run altruistic programs and self-help programs, which Commons described in his essay on "An Idealistic Interpretation of History," and how this fluctuation was associated with the vagaries of the business cycle. Finally, he turned to some of his own theories about the American labor movement. He addressed himself particularly to the reasons for the absence of a real labor party and the economic conservatism of most trade-unionists in America. These last topics concerned him even after the appearance of this volume, and in 1928 he published a new book, *A Theory of the Labor Movement* (39), which dealt with these two questions. This presented both the "Wisconsin school" approach to unions and the author's criticisms of the Marxian Socialist theory of labor-union action. In these criticisms he made an obvious attempt to do for the Wisconsin theory what Marx's historical sociology had done for the Marxian approach.

Perlman's historical orientation is to a great degree assumed in *A Theory of the Labor Movement.*[6] Nevertheless, he emphasized

---

[6] A criticism of this point can be found in Gulick and Bers, "Insight and Illusion in Perlman's Theory of the Labor Movement" (27). For a defense of the Perlman thesis see Ellenbogan, "The Development of Labor Movement Theory" (26).

the importance of concrete historical knowledge, and made it clear that he did not consider labor, as he put it, "an abstract mass in the grip of an abstract force." Quite the contrary, he considered it an observable unit with a group personality, a group history, and, in some instances, a group objective. In order to show the development of this group Gestalt, he compared the labor movements of the United States, Britain, Germany, and Russia, and in each instance tried to analyze the causes of their similarities and differences. He examined in each country the diffusion of economic wealth and power, the role of ideological reform movements, and the amount of experience in trade-union self-government. This examination led him to the conclusion that, other things being equal, the greater the diffusion of wealth, the imaginative resilience of private entrepreneurs, and the amount of experience in self-government, the less influential the idealism of the intellectual reformers and the more stable the labor movement. From this starting point Perlman proceeds, as a social historian, to develop his theory. It is worth repeating that this three-pronged hypothesis is methodological—his theory, insofar as it conforms to the English-American model of trade-unions, tends to be based predominantly in the third area on concrete records left in constitutions, convention proceedings, and, above all, in the working rules of trade-unions.

It was Perlman's evaluation of working rules which led him to conclude that the overwhelming majority of unions able to survive the vicissitudes of the business cycle and the hostility of the employer and the public centered virtually all their attention on issues directly concerned with job problems. Earlier, Commons had referred to this phenomenon as "wage consciousness" and had mentioned that it involved an acceptance of the wage or "capitalist" system. But Perlman went further and argued that, in its fullest sense, the concept embraced a modified, yet complete, property concept. "In the evolution of the psychology of the American wage earner," he wrote,

the fruition of this "job and wage conscious" unionism and its eventual mastery of the whole field . . . meant a final and complete rupture with the old "producing classes" point of view, which saw the road to economic democracy in a restoration to the individual, or to intimately associated groups of individuals, of access to economic opportunity in land, marketing, and credit; this opportunity once restored, competition alone would suffice to preserve it all around. . . . In contrast, the ideology of the American Federation of Labor was both an urban and a wage earner's ideology. It was based on a consciousness of limited job opportunities,—a situation which required that the individual, both in his own interest and in that of a group to which he immediately belonged, should not be permitted to occupy any job opportunity except on the condition of observing the "common rule" laid down by his union. The safest way to assure this group control over opportunity, though also a way so ideal that only a union as favored as the printers' . . . was able to actualize it entirely,—was for the union, without displacing the employer as the owner of his business and risk taker, to become the virtual owner and administrator of the jobs. Where such an outright "ownership" of the jobs was impossible, the union would seek, by collective bargaining with the employers, to establish "rights" in the jobs, both for the individual and for the whole group, by incorporating, in the trade agreement, regulations applying to overtime, to the "equal turn," to priority and seniority in employment, to apprenticeship, to the introduction and utilization of machinery, and so forth. Thus the industrial democracy envisaged by this unionism descended from Marxism was not a democracy of individualistic producers exchanging products under free competition, with the monopolist banished, but a highly integrated democracy of unionized workers and of associated employer-managers, jointly conducting an industrial government with "laws" mandatory upon the individual [39, pp. 198–99].

Having thus established the proprietary attitude of unionism toward job rights, he analyzed at length why in the United States the AFL, with its refusal to espouse revolutionary goals or even a political labor party, represented a significant adaptation of the essential ideas of unionism to the particular American national environment.

. . . The unionism of the American Federation of Labor "fitted," first, because it recognized the virtually inalterable conservatism of the American community as regards private property and private initiative in economic life. It, too, accordingly arrayed itself on the same side, demanding only that the employers should concede the union's right to control the jobs through "recognition" embodied in the trade agreement; and in this attitude it remained unperturbed in the face of all the charges by socialist intellectuals of treason to labor or even of corruption.

This unionism "fitted," secondly, because it grasped the definite limitations of the political instrument under the American Constitution and under American conditions of political life. . . . It went into politics primarily to gain freedom from adverse interference by judicial authority in its economic struggles;—it did not wish to repeat former experiences when trade unions standing sponsor for a labor party found themselves dragged down to the ground by internecine political strife. The American Federation of Labor made itself felt politically by exercising pressure on the old parties; but it kept politics at arm's length from its own cherished trade union organization. . . .

Thirdly, the unionism of the Federation was a fit unionism to survive because it was under no delusion as to the true psychology of the workingman in general and of the American workingman in particular. It knew that producers' co-operation was a beautiful but a really harmful dream, since it only caused labor to fritter away its spiritual and material resources by shouldering itself with an impossible task of winning in the unequal competition between the capitalist-managed business undertakings, which marched like an army, and co-operatively managed ones, which were governed more by debating clubs.

This unionism was also without illusions with regard to the actual extent of labor solidarity. It knew that where wage earners were held together by the feeling that their jobs came out of a common job reservoir, as did those in the same or in closely related crafts, their fighting solidarity left nothing to be desired; provided that their unity was safe-guarded by vigilantly uprooting "dual" unions as so many noxious weeds and by enforcing a military discipline against "outlaw" actions within the union itself. The leaders of this unionism also knew, however, that they had to go slow in pressing on to greater solidarity. Where conditions made co-operation between different craft groups urgent, it was best obtained through free co-operation in "departments" of unions in the same industry,—each union reserving the right to decide for itself in every situation whether to co-operate or not [39, pp. 201–3].

But he took care to point out that this adaptation had led to organizational complacency and even to senility. In the past certain intellectuals, willing to forgo their dogmatism, had shaped a new movement from the upheaval of the seventies, and Perlman now wondered whether there might not have to be a similar group to shape a new movement for the future.

. . . Every union leader admits that the organization of labor must be expanded into the basic industries—steel, automobiles, farm machinery, electrical supplies, etc. But at the first encounter with the difficulties of the task,—difficulties which are admittedly enormous, made up as they are of the employers' active opposition and of the inertia on the workers' part begotten by the Coolidge prosperity and by "welfare capitalism,"—or in many cases even before such an actual encounter, union officers and organizers lose their heart for the task, and rarely proceed beyond expressions of good intentions. . . . [They] settle down to a smug survey of well oiled machinery of their little organizations, which suggests at least a suspicion that these leaders might not entirely welcome too many new members, whose alignment in the politics of the union would at best be uncertain.

. . . [The] American labor movement had acquired in the seventies, with Gompers and Strasser, the philosophy of stable trade unionism, so indispensable to its later growth, because a group of "left wingers" of that day, taught in the school of American experience, exchanged their class-consciousness for a job consciousness, and, later, in the eighties, made job conscious unionism prevail throughout the whole labor movement over the theretofore impregnable philosophy of "anti-monopoly." Might it not, therefore, be that the movement in our own day, no longer facing the problem of its own stability, which is already assured, but that of expansion across the double barrier of "open shop" and "welfare capitalism," will eventually recover the indispensable "will to action" by drawing upon a modern "left wing" group, which, like its predecessor of half a century earlier, will have discovered a true path for labor's advancement in the same experimental school of American industry and society? [39, pp. 232–33.]

So much for the shaping of the group personality of the union! But Perlman felt it necessary not only to analyze the group, but also to ask why individuals adhered to the group. Again he refers to the methodology involved in the search.

A theory of the labor movement should include a theory of the psychology of the laboring man. The writings of socialists, syndicalists, anarchists, communists, and "welfare" capitalists abound in embroideries on the theme of "what labor wants" or "what labor aspires to." But the safest method is to go to the organizations of labor's own making, shaped and managed by leaders arisen from labor's own ranks, and to attempt to discover "what's really on labor's mind" by using as material the "working rules," customs, and practices of these organizations.[7] A study of such "rules" and customs, the products of long drawn out, evolutionary developments, will aid in distinguishing fundamental from accidental purposes [39, p. 237].

Here Perlman turned to Werner Sombart's analysis for an answer. Sombart had pointed out the differences in the general motivations of medieval and modern population groups, and Perlman found these same distinctions in contemporary society.

In an economic community, there is a separation between those who prefer a secure, though modest, return,—that is to say, a mere livelihood,—and those who play for big stakes and are willing to assume risk in proportion. The first compose the great bulk of manual workers of every description, including mechanics, laborers, farmers, small manufacturers, and shopkeepers (since petty trade, as Sombart correctly points out, is also a manual occupation); while the latter are, of course, the entrepreneurs and the big business men. The limited or unlimited purpose is, in either case, the product of a simple survey of accessible economic opportunity and of a psychic self-appraisal. The manual worker is convinced by experience that he is living in a world of limited opportunity. He sees, to be sure, how

[7] "Unorganized workers, where they are subject to less than an iron discipline, are found to observe practices and usages identical in their purposes with the usages of organized labor. However, it goes without saying that the practices of unorganized labor are of too elusive a nature and are frequently also too unformed to serve as anything better than corroborative facts here and there" [footnote in 39, p. 237].

others, for instance business men, are finding the same world a storehouse of apparently unlimited opportunity. Yet he decisively discounts that, so far as he is himself concerned. The business man, on the contrary, is an eternal optimist. To him the world is brimful of opportunities that are only waiting to be made his own [39, pp. 238–39].

But why was the wage worker so fearful?

The scarcity consciousness of the manualist is a product of two main causes, one lying in himself and the other outside. The typical manualist is aware of his lack of native capacity for availing himself of economic opportunities as they lie amidst the complex and ever shifting situations of modern business. He knows himself neither for a born taker of risks nor for the possessor of a sufficiently agile mind ever to feel at home in the midst of the uncertain game of competitive business [39, p. 239].

Perlman believed that the scarcity consciousness characteristic of manual workers found logical expression in the working rules which he had earlier argued were the clearest evidence of the spirit of unionism. In his view this body of rules served in an almost paradoxical fashion. The unionism from which the rules sprang and which they guided was simultaneously individualistic and collectivistic: it served to protect and broaden opportunity for the individual, yet it also restricted that individual's private interests. From this seeming paradox the altruistic side even of "business unionism" could be seen to emerge.

. . . In truth, unionism, even "business unionism," shows idealism both in aim and in method; only it does so in the thoroughly unsophisticated way of "Tom, Dick, and Harry idealism." All unions sooner or later stress "shop rights," which, to the workingman at the bench, are identical with "liberty" itself,—since, thanks to them, he has no need to kowtow to foreman or boss, as the price of holding his job. And, after all, is not this sort of liberty the only sort which reaches the workman directly and with certainty [8] and that can

---

[8] "Frequently workingmen are willing to resign themselves to 'boss control' in their union for the sake of this liberty in the shop. In other words, they are willing to sacrifice their 'political' liberty in the union so long as they may have 'economic' liberty on the job" [footnote in 39, p. 275].

never get lost *en route,* like the "broader" liberty promised by socialism? For, in practice, that other liberty may never succeed in straining through the many layers of the socialistic hierarchy down to the mere private in industry. Secondly, a union which expects its members to sacrifice for the group on a scale almost commensurate with the sacrifices which patriotism evokes, cannot be without its own respectable ideology. Frequently, therefore, the "materialism" of unionism proves only the one-sidedness of the view of the particular observer [39, pp. 274–75].

The analogy of patriotism and unionism was a useful one. It provided an insight as to the practical limits of union solidarity, and at the same time made it possible to guess at revisions which might in time occur. "Many are the influences affecting union job control," Perlman concluded,

the legal status of unionism, the policies of the government, a favorable public opinion, and others. Thus every union soon discovers that the integrity of its "job-territory," like the integrity of the geographic territory of a nation, is inextricably dependent on numerous wide relationships. . . . We know from history that the most craft-conscious bodies that ever existed, the mediaeval gilds, left nothing to be desired so far as solidaristic action against the common overlords was concerned. There is, however, a practical limitation upon labor's solidarity, and this limitation is a very vital one, namely that, in a labor movement which has already gone beyond the emotional stage and acquired a definite rationale of its own, an appeal for common class action, be it through a sympathetic strike or through joint political action, will only be likely to evoke the response which is desired if the objective of the proposed common undertaking be kept so close to the core substance of union aspiration that Tom, Dick, and Harry could not fail to identify it as such [39, pp. 276–77].

And like nations in periods of stress, unions in depressed industries can often be depended upon to take extraordinarily selfless and farsighted measures.

Just as we find job conscious unionism far from devoid of idealism of a kind, so its ultimate industrial vision need not at all be limited to the job itself. In truth, such a unionism might easily acquire a lively interest in problems of management without previously undergoing mutation. It is not at all unnatural that a unionism which is intent upon job opportunities should join with management in a joint campaign to reduce the cost of operation and raise efficiency—all for the "conservation" of the current job opportunities. However, to grant so much is far from making the claim that labor might be brought to embrace "efficiency" as its primary concern instead of merely pursuing it secondarily to the primary interest in jobs. Thus it grows out of the preceding that whether one is trying to "improve" labor's "ideology," to broaden its solidarity, or to awaken its interest in "efficiency," one will indeed do well, in order to avoid wasted efforts, to steer close to the fundamental scarcity consciousness of the manual worker, which rules unionism today as it ruled the gilds of the past [39, pp. 277–78].

Throughout Perlman's work there is a running criticism of "intellectuals," who were, he felt, constantly tempted to lead or try to lead workingmen away from their "lower" idealism to one more transcendental and abstract (see 45). These "higher idealists" he classified as ethics-oriented, efficiency-minded, or socially deterministic.

Every one of these three types of "intellectuals" projects from his own abstract conception of "labor as a mass in the grip of a force" a mental picture of the workingman as an individual. Consequently, every one of these pictures differs widely from the real person whom employers and union leaders know. The Marxian pictures the workingman as a class-conscious proletarian who, at the dawn of a real revolutionary opportunity such as a world war or a similar upheaval, will unhesitatingly scorn all the gains in his material conditions and in his individual status which as a trade unionist he has already conquered from the employers, and will buoyantly face an uncertain future—all for the sake of the dictatorship of his class.

Unlike the Marxian, who makes a virtue of thinking in terms of the "mass," the "ethical" intellectual places the highest value upon the liberated human personality and consequently is obliged to keep the individual in the center of his vision. Yet he too falls short of a true vision, since he arrives at his individual workingman by separating him out as a molecule from the abstract labor "mass." By this process, curiously enough, the individual workingman emerges bearing a very striking spiritual resemblance to his maker, the "ethical" intellectual. To the latter, industrial freedom means the complete disappearance of all authority from above, and an opportunity for everyone to participate in the total creative planning of industry. So his "workingman," too, feels that he is still being denied his rightful chance for development of personality, if he has merely been given the opportunity, under the protection of his union, to enjoy an inalienable right to his job.

Lastly, the individual workingman of the "efficiency" intellectual, as we shall come to see, is a creature who has forever given up any claim to a vested right in any particular job, or, in common with the others in his group, to any particular "job-territory"; but is, on the contrary, totally indifferent as to who gets the job or jobs, so long as the employer observes the union standards of wages and hours. This "workingman" has presumably arrived at such a thorough oblivion of self and of his nearest group in the vital matter of securing his opportunity, because he has realized that, with such an arrangement, the employer would be free to select the fittest worker for the job and that hence the way would be opened to the highest "efficiency." Truly, the "workingman" of the "efficiency" intellectual should have no trouble in getting admitted to the Fabian Society or even perhaps into a somewhat reconstituted Taylor Society of America [39, pp. 283–85].

Perlman's continual reiteration of these points undoubtedly reflected some personal estimate of his own earlier ideological affiliation. But he often repeated that "intellectuals" performed vitally necessary and useful functions for the labor movement and that his criticism of their historic role was confined simply to their continual desire to shape the goals toward which the movement was ostensibly moving. His criticism appears to have been intended as a boost for working rules or job-conscious unionism rather than as a damnation of the intellectuals' transcendentalism.

A Theory of the Labor Movement is in some ways handicapped in its presentation. It is not written as a "scientific" paper, and thus embodies some verbal imprecisions stemming from cultural usage (see 27). Moreover, it contains many quotable expressions which, although useful in crystallizing ideas, tend to obscure the wealth of historical qualification. And without any doubt, Perlman, writing in the mid-twenties, took little account of the social movements of an aroused middle class, and consequently gave virtually no hint of the effects on labor of totalitarianism—Nazism, fascism, or ultranationalism. Despite these drawbacks, his book now appears to be basic, and is the point of departure of some subsequent work as well as the subject of considerable criticism.

In 1934 Perlman expanded his theory to include developments in Fascist Italy and Nazi Germany (37). The xenophobia found in both societies stemmed from the same scarcity consciousness that was present in the medieval guilds and modern unions. In Italy and Germany there had been a precapitalist atavism, which attempted to restore control to the "native" groups who had held it prior to the rise of nineteenth-century economic liberalism.

. . . Capitalism broke down both attitudes of the guild system. It broke down the solidarity within the group. It liberated the individual heretofore lockstepped with his group, and gave him a chance to become a businessman, a speculator, or a developer of new businesses and a seeker for new opportunities. It also broke down the distinction between the legitimate and the illegitimate competitors. In other words, anyone that could come in was considered a legitimate competitor, and the inside groups were abolished, or relatively so. . . . [Nevertheless,] the older attitudes persisted and they persisted in the lower strata of the population.

They persisted in Europe, for instance, among the handworker class, the handcrafts men, the peasant, the small merchants, the shopkeepers, and the white collar people after a while. . . . The long chain of developments which we need not, of course enter into, in Germany have brought about revival to power of the spokesmen of these forgotten classes, the peasants, the handcraftsmen, the lower middle classes in general, the white collar classes and the university students who are the sons of the petty bourgeoisie.

These forgotten classes, having come to power, reflect through their activity or through their behavior this ancient mentality of dividing people into insiders and outsiders, of looking upon opportunity as being strictly confined and strictly limited and the natural monopoly of a legitimate group—the outsider need not apply [37, p. 12].

It should not be inferred, of course, that Perlman thought that collective control was generally used only for atavistic purposes. Quite the contrary; it was most frequently used to secure improved status for all sorts of inferior groups—organized labor being the example par excellence. In an article appearing in 1936 he generalized his conclusions about the goals of the collective-bargaining process in democratic industrial society, and noted that they were progressive in character and were associated with giving labor more than increased benefits in the shop alone. Rather, collective bargaining was used to secure equal rights—rights commensurate with the employers' older, more accepted, property rights.

Collective bargaining is not just a means of raising wages and improving conditions of employment. Nor is it merely democratic government in industry. It is above all a technique whereby an inferior social class or group carries on a never slackening pressure for a bigger share in the social sovereignty as well as for more welfare, security, and liberty for its individual members. As such it is not confined to a single arena, the industrial one, where employers and labor unions meet directly, but manifests itself equally in politics, legislation, court litigation, government administration, religion, education, and propaganda. Nor is collective bargaining only a phenomenon of modern society. On the contrary, its clearest and most comprehensive manifestation was shown by the urban communities in the Middle Ages—the boroughs and the guilds in the struggle against feudal lords.

Collective bargaining as a technique of the rise of a new class is quite different from the class struggle of the Marxians. It is nominalist instead of realist. It is pragmatic and concrete instead of idealist and abstract. It is much less concerned with algebraic formulae summing up basic economic trends than with problems of building discipline in organization and of training leadership. It derives its emotional impetus not from the desire to displace or "abolish" the "old ruling class," but from the wish to bring one's own class abreast of the superior class; to gain equal rights as a class and equal consideration for the members of that class with the members of that other class; to acquire an exclusive jurisdiction in that sphere where the most immediate interests, both material and spiritual, are determined, and a shared jurisdiction with the older class or classes in all the other spheres [38, p. 154].

After speculating on the implications of his historical comparison, Perlman turned his attention to the various attitudes taken by public authorities toward rising groups, and listed them in sequence as (1) suppression, (2) grudging toleration, (3) benevolent toleration, (4) promotion, and possibly (5) absorption. The purpose of his discussion was to raise not only the obvious caveats about the fifth stage, which involved the nationalization of unions, but to point out the dangers inherent in governmental promotion of unionism. For, as he wrote, "it is a rare governmental promoter of collective bargaining who will resist the temptation to try to impose his own views of what is rational and good for the labor movement. Genuine reform," he concluded, "even in the labor movement, can come only from within."

The final two volumes (making a total of four) of the original Commons and Associates *History of Labour in the United States* appeared in 1935. The fourth volume (42), covering the history of organized unions from 1896 to 1932, was written by Perlman in collaboration with Philip Taft, one of his students. In this volume Perlman by and large continued his earlier emphasis on job control as the key to an understanding of union ideology and structural organization. His critical attitude toward the intellectuals' attempts to influence the development of the American union movement did not diminish, but he added that with increased governmental intervention in economic matters, "the use of the intellectual as [an] expert is bound to increase."

It is probably fair to say that he saw the problems of leadership and union structure as the big issues in the American movement. He mentioned that "the chief strategic blunder [in the period 1896–1932] was made in the steel industry," and that the existence of graft within particular unions would have been prevented or minimized by wiser top leadership, even though, he noted, the AFL's formal disciplinary powers over its constituent unions were virtually nil. The manuscript of this last volume was completed before the secession movement that resulted in the formation of the Congress of Industrial Organizations, however, and Perlman appeared to credit the same leadership with more flexibility and perception than was warranted.

During the forties Perlman wrote relatively little. A series of lectures given to an Officers' Institute of the International Ladies' Garment Workers' Union appeared in printed form (36), as did two articles in a book edited by T. C. T. McCormick (41). He also prepared a classification of unions in the post–World War II period (40).

We have indicated in our discussion something of the intellectual heritage on which Perlman drew. Using historical generalizations about past periods, he developed a theory of why men join unions and, incidentally, of the historical role of collective bargaining. He used Commons' concepts of the market and of the other general cultural forces that shaped institutional development. His conclusion that the job is the focal point of union activity showed his debt to Adams. In his methodology, too, Perlman revealed the influence of the work of these predecessors.

Commons had been essentially interested in problems of social administration. His students did not confine their efforts to the field of labor unionism, and the generalizations he reached were applied by them to many problems quite far afield from labor administration. Perlman, by way of contrast, stayed close to the topic of unionism, and his students also tended to remain specialized.

We have stressed the origins of this sociohistorical theory of unionism and noted that its development in the American environment gave it a national flavor uniquely its own. The three scholars whose work has been discussed took for granted the fact of cultural heterogeneity, and thus, unlike the Marxians, explained the rise and operation of trade-unions not as the result of the phenomenon of industrialization alone, but as the consequence of the action of historical and economic forces peculiar to this country. Even Perlman, who went beyond the formulation of the American "problem," took great pains to emphasize the many forms which political traditions and capitalism take in different societies. Each has a unique effect on the development of its native labor movement.

These writers argued that, in the Anglo-American tradition, the most basic social concept involved the institution of private property. Thus, they concluded, unionism used the property concept, but stretched it to include the right to a job of the employed workman. From this conclusion it followed that unions were essentially conservative in nature, although their desire to reshape old concepts to cover new needs was not, of course, always viewed with equanimity by those who lost thereby.

To Malthus' and Hobson's tradition of pessimistic economics, Perlman added his own theory that workingmen were affected by their consciousness of the scarcity of opportunity. To this combination he then added Commons' argument regarding the idealistic, yet pragmatic, philosophy of working rules as the latter affected the job and social controls external to it. Thus he and Commons evolved between them a "theory" or "philosophy" of organic labor, and used the historical record to illustrate what they meant. But a "philosophy" of organic labor itself is merely the reflection of a social movement that follows from the motivation.

This leads us to the conclusion that the Adams-Commons-Perlman theory is an analysis of American unionism as a social movement. It views organized labor not as a simple means to moral, political, or economic reform, nor as a direct psychological protest against the dehumanizing consequences of the industrial or machine society. Though it is partly a means to these ends as well as a protest, it is most of all something of an end in itself.

Unionism is a national historic force combining many features and capable of creating its own traditions. The history of unionism, with its jurisprudential implications, becomes a guiding force for later generations.

References

1. Adams, Henry C., "Economics and Jurisprudence," *Economic Studies,* II (1897), 7–35; "Answer to Discussion," 45–46. (Reprinted in 24, pp. 135–75.)

2. ———, "Economics and Jurisprudence," pp. 80–91 in R. T. Ely (comp.), *Science Economics Discussion.* New York: The Science Publishing Co., 1886.

3. ———, "An Interpretation of the Social Movements of Our Time," *International Journal of Ethics,* II (1891–92), 32–50.

4. ———, "Labor Problem," *Scientific American,* XXII (Supplement) (1886), 8861–63.

5. ———, "Relation of the State to Industrial Action," *Publications of the American Economic Association,* Ser. 1, Vol. I (1886–87), pp. 465–549. (Reprinted in 24, pp. 57–133.)

6. Barker, Ernest, "Introduction" in Otto F. von Gierke, *Natural Law and the Theory of Society, 1500–1800,* trans. Barker. Cambridge, Eng.: At the University Press, 1934.

7. Bigelow, S. Lawrence; Sharfman, I. Leo; and Wenley, R. M., "Henry Carter Adams," *Journal of Political Economy,* XXX (1922), 201–11.

8. Brentano, Lujo, *On the History and Development of Gilds and the Origin of Trade-Unions.* London: Trübner & Co., 1870.

9. Commons, John R., *The Christian Minister and Sociology.* "Christian Social Union Publications," No. 4. Baltimore: Guggenheimer, Weil & Co., 1892.

10. ———, "The Church and the Problem of Poverty in the Cities," *Charities Review,* II (1892–93), 347–56.

11. ———, *The Distribution of Wealth.* New York: The Macmillan Co., 1893.

12. ———, *The Economics of Collective Action.* New York: The Macmillan Co., 1951.

13. Commons, John R., *Industrial Goodwill*. New York: McGraw-Hill Book Co., Inc., 1919.

14. ———, *Institutional Economics; Its Place in Political Economy*. New York: The Macmillan Co., 1934.

15. ———, *Labor and Administration*. New York: The Macmillan Co., 1913.

16. ———, "Labor Movement," in *Encyclopaedia of the Social Sciences*, VIII, 682–96.

17. ———, *The Legal Foundations of Capitalism*. New York: The Macmillan Co., 1924.

18. ———, *Myself*. New York: The Macmillan Co., 1934.

19. ———, reply to Hadley, *Economic Studies*, IV (Supplement) (1899), 108–13.

20. ———, "A Sociological View of Sovereignty," *American Journal of Sociology*, V (1899–1900), 1–15, 155–71, 347–66, 544–52, 683–95, 814–25; VI (1900–1901), 67–89.

21. ———, and Associates, *History of Labour in the United States*. 2 vols. New York: The Macmillan Co., 1918.

22. ———, and Others, *Documentary History of American Industrial Society*. 10 vols. Cleveland: The Arthur H. Clark Co., 1910–11.

23. Dorfman, Joseph, *The Economic Mind in American Civilization*, Vol. III, 1865–1918. New York: Viking Press, Inc., 1949.

24. ———, "Henry Carter Adams: The Harmonizer of Liberty and Reform," pp. 3–55 in Dorfman (ed.), *Relation of the State to Industrial Action and Economics and Jurisprudence*. New York: Columbia University Press, 1954.

25. ——— (ed.), "The Seligman Correspondence," *Political Science Quarterly*, LVI (1941), 107–24, 270–86, 392–419, 573–99.

26. Ellenbogan, Jack, "The Development of Labor Movement Theory." Unpublished Ph.D. dissertation, University of Wisconsin, 1954.

27. Gulick, Charles A., and Bers, Melvin K., "Insight and Illusion in Perlman's Theory of the Labor Movement," *Industrial and Labor Relations Review*, VI (1953), 510–31.

28. Hadley, Arthur T., "The Relation between Economics and Politics," *Economic Studies*, IV (1899), 7–28.

29. Maitland, Frederic W., *Domesday Book and Beyond*. Cambridge, Eng.: At the University Press, 1897.

30. ———, "Introduction" in Otto F. von Gierke, *Political Theories of the Middle Age,* trans. Maitland. Cambridge, Eng.: At the University Press, 1900.

31. Mitchell, Wesley C., *The Backward Art of Spending Money*. Reprint. New York: Augustus M. Kelley, 1950.

32. Nettleship, R. L. (ed.), *The Works of Thomas Hill Green,* Vol. II, *Lectures on the Principle of Obligation*. New York: Longmans, Green & Co., 1889–90.

33. Parsons, Kenneth C., "John R. Commons' Point of View," *Journal of Land and Public Utility Economics,* XVIII (1942), 245–66.

34. Perlman, Selig, "History of Socialism in Milwaukee (1893–1910)." Unpublished MS, 1910. Private copy.

35. ———, *A History of Trade Unionism in the United States*. New ed. New York: Augustus M. Kelley, 1950.

36. ———, *Labor in the New Deal Decade*. New York: International Ladies' Garment Workers' Union, 1945.

37. ———, "Present Day Economic Trends and Their Effect on Jewish Life in America," *Proceedings of the National Conference of Jewish Social Service, May 26–30, 1934,* pp. 11–15.

38. ———, "The Principle of Collective Bargaining," *Annals of the American Academy of Political and Social Science,* CLXXXIV (1936), 154–60.

39. ———, *A Theory of the Labor Movement*. New York: The Macmillan Co., 1928.

40. ———, "A Theory of the Labor Movement." Privately processed essay, 1949.

41. ———, and Knowles, William H., "American Unionism in the Postwar Period," Chap. 2, pp. 33–48, in T. C. T. McCormick (ed.), *Problems of the Postwar World*. New York: McGraw-Hill Book Co., Inc., 1945.

42. ———, and Taft, Philip, *History of Labor in the United States,* Vol. IV, *Labor Movements, 1896–1932*. New York: The Macmillan Co., 1935.

43. Schmoller, Gustav, *Grundriss der allgemeinen Volkswirtschaftlehre*. Leipzig: Duncker & Humblot, 1900–1904.

44. Schumpeter, Joseph, *Economic Doctrine and Method,* trans. R. Aris. New York: Oxford University Press, 1954.

45. Sturmthal, Adolf, "Comments on Selig Perlman's *A Theory of the Labor Movement,*" *Industrial and Labor Relations Review,* IV (1951), 483–96.

EIGHT

Assaying the Five Theories

We have implied in our earlier discussion that unionism is a multifaceted institution in which each observer will perceive unique characteristics. We have suggested that the literature from its inception until the New Deal can be clustered in five groups and we have examined the theories underlying each of these groups. In organizing our material in this manner we have given this study its framework.

Each group of theories concentrates upon a single facet of unionism and deals with questions intended to illuminate that facet. Thus the observer will tend to be attracted to that theory which best explains the particular aspect of the institution in which he is most interested.

But what shapes his original interest? What makes him more sympathetic to the discussion of one aspect of unionism than to another? The answers to these queries generally are to be found in an examination of his background. What are the prevalent social, ideological, and economic patterns found in the society about him? Has he been trained in a specific academic discipline? Has his thinking been influenced by the creed of any social movement? No less significant will be his personal willingness to challenge the explanations that have been given to him and thence to reason inductively or deductively to his own conclusions.

Each of us will accept in each theory only as much as we are prepared to consider relevant in the questions that the respective theory asks. And the questions posited by that theory are directly related to the theory's basic assumptions or postulates regarding social structure. We can, therefore, with some confidence stress the relativism of the theories, emphasize that from each theory comes its own set of insights, and consider each theory as but an elaboration of one set of premises as they affect a particular question.

We are concerned now with questioning the relevancy for current use of each of the five groups of theories. We seek to provide an over-all view of the five theory groups, and to explain why certain of the theories appear to have lost, at least for the present, their usefulness. In brief, we are concerned with assessing the value of the early literature and suggesting why some writings now seem less significant.

Our discussion will consist of five divisions; the first is a recapitulation of the five groups of interpretations, which we will regard rather as five distinct theories: the moral-conditioning theory, the social-revolutionary theory, the psychological-environment theory, the economic-welfare theory, and the social-institution theory. The second division is a brief comparison of their salient features. The third is a short examination of one major implication of the methodology involved in this study. The fourth part provides a synoptic digression on the meaning of the New Deal to unions as it might be seen from the vantage point of a proponent of each theory; and the fifth and last part presents what seems to us to be the most useful combination of theories for understanding unionism.

Synthesizing the Theories

THE MORAL-CONDITIONING THEORY

This is an ethical, not a historical, theory of unionism. It assumes that unions can be organized by right-thinking individuals who, by using persuasion, will inspire individual workers to improve their ethical behavior. These leaders do not have to be themselves workers, but can be and often are self-appointed social reformers from all kinds of backgrounds, particularly the pulpit or the professorial chair. They consider that the value of unions lies in their ethical consequences, which can be judged at the social and the individual level.

At the social level, unions are considered essentially educational institutions which teach habits of propriety, self-restraint, and decent self-expression. Through unions, workers are enabled to rise to the point where they can be permitted to have the controlling voice in industrial decisions. Ultimately, the factory will enjoy the benefits of full representative government (producers' co-operation) in every aspect of its activity. Quite naturally, day-to-day union policies are to be determined in the light of their educational implications.

The individual will be attracted to unionism because it is a schooling institution designed to help him to help himself to realize his maximum personal potential in the factory, just as the church and the public school are there to perform similar functions in his religious and political activities.

The Social-Revolutionary Theory

This theory, in its many forms, is based on what is believed to be a dispassionate, scientific understanding of the historical process. Technological advances in production techniques have caused changes in the relationships between the bourgeois, property-holding classes and the working, propertyless classes. Inevitably and increasingly, the *bourgeoisie* has exploited the workers. One way in which the workers frequently, if not always, retaliate is by forming unions. Thus the immediate cause of unionism is class conflict; the immediate cause of class conflict is bourgeois exploitation of the working class; and the immediate cause of this exploitation is technological changes in production techniques. It then follows that unions are caused originally by technological advance.

What specific unions do at any one time in any particular situation depends upon the union leader's appreciation of the historical process. Unions acting in ways that further the revolutionary ends of the working class are considered to be acting wisely.

Unions that accede to the demands of their bourgeois employers or that temporize their revolutionary purpose in favor of shortsighted pecuniary and nonpecuniary concessions are thought to be useless and undeserving of their historical sanction. Ultimately, only the Socialist theorist who comprehends the full historical consequences of any given act can be trusted to judge between the good and the bad. And it is unanimously agreed that any union leader who tries to make peace with the bourgeois employer is a faker and a traitor.

According to this philosophy, unionism is a device useful in the workers' class war against the *bourgeoisie*. But when a Socialist society is achieved, unionism will have to develop a new purpose, since its old one will have been completely fulfilled. Unions in the Socialist state would continue to organize the workers, but to increase productive efficiency rather than to promote class warfare.

Why would a worker join a union? Because in a capitalist society it gives him, as a member of the working class, protection from bourgeois exploitation, and because it offers him a chance to play a progressive role in the historical process. Every informed and loyal worker understands that the historical process is the law of destiny. Through his union, the worker can help to shape the future. What about the worker who refuses to help the revolutionary cause? He is either uninformed or selfish —in both instances he has to be salvaged by a program of vigorous reorientation.

Two things stand out in this revolutionary theory: its teleological nature and its dependence upon a "proper" understanding of the historical process. The former stimulates moral certainty and confidence in the future. The latter creates dissension in the ranks, since any human action or program of intended actions, regardless of the ostensible motives involved, encourages speculations about the "real" consequences. As a result, the revolutionary theory has had numerous advocates, each of whom has tended to give his own interpretation of the historical meaning of any action.

The Psychological-Environment Theory

This theory grew out of the psychologist's interest in human behavior as affected by physical and cultural stimuli. By and large, it is conceded that some human responses are instinctive or unlearned, while others are conditioned by ethnic or cultural traditions. Only in the sense that the psychologist, with his emphasis on science, admits the importance of historical experience on cultural developments might this theory be considered historical.

Adherents to the psychological theory view unionism as a movement controlled by the interaction of three factors: (1) the cultural lag associated with technological change, (2) the effects of economic insecurity on the attitude of workers, and (3) the manifestations of certain basic human instincts, which vary according to the ethnic or cultural group to which the worker or group of workers belongs.

At any given time union policies are decided by the members' understanding of the evil confronting them. Whether their reaction is a moderate one (leading to negotiation) or a violent one (leading to revolution) depends upon the three factors mentioned above. Individuals who believe that workers form unions for psychological reasons imply that an employer, aided by a skilled and experienced psychologist, can within certain broad limits control the nature of worker response (union policies). Whether or not unionism will continue indefinitely into the future depends upon the nature of the interaction of the three factors, with the possibility that experienced psychologists can affect the course of events. Veblen evidently believed that they could not, and predicted that industrial disorder could not be prevented. His conviction of the inevitability of unending blind conflict was not shared by others who agreed with his general point of view.

This theory suggests that the worker is attracted to unionism because of certain drives about and within him. It also implies that an employer, by using a conditioning program or by a successful educational policy, can influence the individual worker so that he becomes antiunion rather than pro-union. It is not difficult to see why a form of this theory has often been adopted by personnel administrators attempting to break a union.

THE ECONOMIC-WELFARE THEORY

There are those who believe that general dissatisfaction causes workingmen to band together and to develop institutional controls that will guarantee greater job security, higher wages, and improved working conditions. Of the various methods used by workers to achieve these ends, collective bargaining has in recent history produced the quickest and the best results. Hence the union, the most efficient administrative unit for carrying on collective bargaining, becomes the most important unit in the labor movement. This is primarily an economic theory, for it is based on the idea that unions are the least costly way to achieve certain objectives, but the theory has its historical implications in its reliance on historical records to demonstrate why collective bargaining has been more successful than mutual insurance or legal enactment in improving the worker's lot.

According to this theory, union policies are determined by a rational ordering of the goals chosen by the union, combined with a rational estimate of the efficiency of various alternative solutions. Since the decisions that must be made often involve highly technical considerations, it follows that unions should rely upon trained experts. This implies that a sympathetic trained expert can provide a considerable part of the day-to-day union leadership.

Whether or not collective bargaining will remain the means of negotiation most favored by the labor movement is uncertain, and it is probable that if some other means becomes more economical, the usefulness of the trade-union as the prime working-class unit might become less than that of a political labor party.

Many persons who maintain this point of view feel that legal enactment will prove superior to collective bargaining as a means of handling such economic problems as unemployment, industrial accidents, and superannuation. They criticize the unwillingness of the labor movement to abandon its historical commitment to unionism, as an irrational dedication to an ineffective institution. Implicit in this criticism, of course, is the belief that unions are not social ends in themselves, but merely administrative devices.

THE SOCIAL-INSTITUTION THEORY

In this approach to unionism, unions are considered to have an importance in the western European democratic social structure quite apart from their ability to raise wages and improve working conditions. Unionism is the technique through which social inferiors band together to secure social and industrial rights. Once having secured these rights, workers use unions to protect themselves from the effects of rigorous market competition, which through history has been intensified by the growth of markets (bringing once separate communities into direct economic competition) and changes in production techniques (resulting in competition among the workers in any one area). Thus unionism has been both an offensive and a defensive institution, but invariably it has intended to promote the social interests of its membership. This approach to unionism developed from a study of historical records showing how specific workingmen sought to protect their jobs. These records were found in court trials for conspiracy and in the development of job customs or working rules in particular trades or industries.

The primary intent of union policies, according to this theory, is to protect job opportunities for the group of workmen concerned. As a rule, the older a union gets, the more it tends to draw on its own historical experience. In other words, it tends to rely upon the "common will," as interpreted by union leaders. Consequently, unions are reluctant to follow the advice, however well-intentioned, of outside well-wishers and experts. Unions generally attempt hegemony over a limited job territory only, having discovered by experience what limits are most effective. In Anglo-American countries, unions pursue policies intended to give to job possession the type of property rights already guaranteed to real estate and chattel ownership. In this sense, when workers bargain collectively they are acting in the tradition of the barons at Runnymede and the Protestant reformers of the sixteenth and seventeenth centuries.

Social-institutionalists assume the existence of social pluralism. The union exercises hegemony over job rights, just as the state does over civil rights and the churches do over religious rights. Unions, according to this theory, are therefore an inherent and essential part of modern representative democracy. Their primary justification rests on the social role they play in giving order and stability to an important phase of community life and to a lesser, although still important, extent on the economic role they play in maximizing workers' gains.

Comparing the Theories

These five groups can be compared and contrasted. Doing so points out the ways in which different writers treated the same or similar aspects of trade-unionism. It also serves to emphasize that for the most part the writers within each of these theory groups were concerned with distinctly different matters. Some emphasized normative standards which they felt unions should adopt; others merely tried to explain what unions did. This variation of emphasis makes a systematic comparison somewhat difficult, yet it also serves to underline the value of understanding the intellectual media in which the theories grew.

Two contemporary writers (1, 3) have suggested a useful set of four questions, discussed in the following sections, that bring out the principal comparisons.

1. *What were the original causes of unions?* Technological change and the upsetting of values and relationships cause unions to develop as agencies for *revolutionary* change or as agencies formed by workingmen who feel a *psychological* need to band together. Growth of the market, bringing the intensification of competition and the need for stabilizing controls, was the main

cause of the development of unions in a representative democracy, according to the *social-institution* theory. A rational comparison of the net-cost advantages of unionism, group self-insurance, and political action in augmenting labor's share of the national income largely explained the rise of unionism, according to the *economic-welfare* theory. Spiritual poverty caused by economic misery led to the *moral-welfare* approach to unionism and the stress it put on the moral aspect of unionism.

Thus three factors emerge as causes: technological change, market competition, and the desire to improve the workingman's lot. Elements of each factor are probably present in each theory, but so great are the variations of emphasis that they serve to differentiate the theories from one another.

2. *What considerations should control policies?* For those who regard unions as *moral-conditioning* institutions, the significant factors in the union's determination of policy are the ethical consequences. Those who regard unions as *revolutionary* believe that union policies should be largely determined by the anticapitalistic results to be obtained. If unions are considered to be *economic-welfare* institutions, a rational analysis of the economic costs and the benefits gained by union action will be taken as the explanation of most tactical decisions of the labor movement, although it will be understood that miscalculations are possible. When unions are considered primarily as *social institutions,* the common will (embodied in written and oral union traditions and expressing the group's desire for social recognition and power) is thought to be the main determinant of union policy. The theory that regards unions as products of *psychological environment* holds that there are three factors—cultural lag, economic insecurity, and human instincts—determining union policies; it implies that something can be done to control the collective response to the three stimuli.

Of great importance in the history of unionism is also the influence of men outside the union movement. The *moral-conditioning,* the *revolutionary,* the *psychological-environment,* and the *economic-welfare* theories all agree that "outsiders" (non-workers) should help to steer the labor movement. Only those who believe that unions are *social institutions* attempt to explain why there is an inherent distrust in union circles of the outsider or expert, even though the expert is sympathetic and produces results. The explanation they offer is that no one outside the unions can generally interpret the common will in a fashion satisfactory to the regular membership.

3. *What will be the future of unionism?* When unions are considered as products of the environment, there may be no future for unionism if employers use skilled and experienced laboratory psychologists to solve the problems of the workingmen. Should the employers not use these experts—or, according to Veblen, should the experts fail—unions would continue as protest institutions. The *economic welfarists* also indicate that the future of unionism is uncertain, and that straight participation in politics may be the best course for workers to take. The *social-institutionalists,* on the other hand, stress that there are areas of democratic community activity, such as religion and industrial production, which are not suited to the usual forms of political control. Thus in a democratic society enlightened private-interest groups, of which unions are one, will have a continuing function to perform. Both the *moral conditioners* and the *revolutionaries* predict that unions will play ever greater roles in industry in the future. In the end, they say, workers will run the factories and make all industrial decisions.

4. *Why does unionism appeal to the worker?* According to those who believe that unions are *social institutions,* unionism appeals to the typical worker because he feels insecure and unable to hold his own in his daily struggle for economic security. This "scarcity consciousness of the manualist," to use Selig Perlman's phrase, explains why most workers will exchange some of their personal freedom for the "community protection" of the union. The *social revolutionaries* and *psychological environmentalists* believe that workers join unions because of rebellion against exploitation and poor living conditions. A realization that he can strengthen his moral position or maximize his eco-

nomic position explains, according to the *moral conditioners* and the *economic welfarists,* why the worker joins a union.

In each instance the explanations are not mutually exclusive, and this question (almost ignored except by Hoxie, Tannenbaum, and Perlman), points up least satisfactorily the significant differences between the theories.

A General Theory?

We have found that the literature can best be understood by employing a fivefold theoretical classification. Thus there are five theories—each with its own set of postulates and its own range of interpretations. Each theory raises its own set of questions, and develops an appropriate set of answers. Yet the questions and the answers are meaningful only to those who appreciate the relevant postulates. For this reason, the postulates are of critical importance. They serve to focus attention on one or another facet of unionism. And they serve to classify different writers.

Within each theory there tend to be differing interpretations. But the variation between these interpretations is of an altogether different order from the wide differences between the theories. In the former case there is agreement on the postulates; in the latter there is not. With such an agreement, it is possible for different writers to come to some sort of integrated understanding. They are communicating in the same language, asking much the same questions, considering similar answers. Ely's and Ryan's works are compatible; as are those of Adams, Commons, and Perlman. Even the various "scientific Socialist" writers (the Marxians) understood one another's arguments, although full agreement on details was not forthcoming. Veblen, Hoxie, Parker, and Tannenbaum all had a common bond. Such differences as existed merely reflected individual estimates or values imputed to one or another of the general factors considered.

But where there are separate sets of postulates, the task of integrating the five theories becomes nearly if not completely impossible. The sole common denominator for all five was that each discussed unions. And there the common features end. Some discussed unions as they have been; others discussed unions as they should be. Some discussed unions within the context of a capitalistic society essentially private in character. Others considered unions under social arrangements of quite another character.

Therefore in approaching the literature one cannot lay too great a stress on the differences in postulates. They create the theories, they separate them, they give to each its particular tone. For that reason it is useful to summarize them as they apply to each theory.

1. The *moral-conditioning theory* subsumes the desirability of producers' co-operation and thereby the ownership and control by workingmen of the factories in which they are employed. Unions, therefore, are devices to prepare the workingmen in a given factory for the responsibility of owner-managership.

2. The *social-revolutionary theory* purports to be scientifically teleological. As such, it postulates economic determinism and the ultimate abolition of all forms of private ownership of the means of production. Unions, consequently, serve to marshal the working class for the day when the nonproductive *bourgeoisie* will be overthrown. Then production decisions will be made by disinterested experts. And then the workers in a given factory will work for the good of society as a whole—not merely for themselves or their exploiters.

3. The *psychological-environment theory* stems from an estimate of the causes of maladjustment of workers within a socially disoriented world. Great emphasis is put on the unhappiness of the individual. Hence unions and union policies reflect socially the individual workman's felicific calculus of misery, degradation, despair, and unhappiness. It further implies that under some conditions controls can be developed. Improve the adjustment of individuals, it seems to say, and the picture will change.

4. The *economic-welfare theory* is based on the critical as-

sumptions that labor wants only to improve its material lot (maximizing its returns), and will do so rationally by employing the least-cost means. Thus unionism can be *the* economic way to achieve a given end; it can also be otherwise. Unionism is used when it is economically efficient; other more desirable means will be used when they prove more economic than unionism. In any event, there is nothing deterministic about social organization—workers may or may not be inherently maladjusted. What can be believed, however, is that workers will strive to get as great a net material return as possible.

5. The *social-institution theory* posits both the existence and ethical desirability of groups within society generally and among workers specifically. It further hypothesizes that workers are concomitantly members of many groups, and that in most organized social activities the individual achieves self-expression, material security (that is, the right to property), and moral realization only by joining with others. Democratic government or control is achieved through the interaction of responsible groups or factions, to which the individual belongs by free choice or because of some psychological or economic necessity. Thus democracy in industry, as in all other sectors of society, can be attained only through collective bargaining of some sort. Unions are the collective-bargaining instrument in industry. From all of this it follows that unionism is not a transitional instrument to a new and better world, but a part of the new and better world. Unionism and industrial democracy are indistinguishably interrelated.

From this comparison it is apparent that irreconcilable differences between the postulates exist. This is particularly so when each set of postulates is pursued to the extreme. And because every theory must rest firmly on postulates, it becomes evident that one cannot construct a general theory that will include all the conflicting theories discussed in this book. Thus there are five theories, not one grand one. But this is no cause for despair. Each theory provides insights of a kind, and as such can lead to the understanding of different aspects of the subject. And the empirical work done in the name of any one theory often contains information that will be useful to scholars or others concentrating upon another theory.

In sum, theorizing about unions and the labor movement is like theorizing about all other living institutions. The truth is larger than the mind; the mind can only benefit by making use of the results of varied approaches to the truth. This is the justification for any study of the history of ideas; it is also the reason for this comparative study of the theories of unionism.

The Great Depression and Thereafter

A convenient point at which to terminate any discussion of the early trade-union theory is the Great Depression, when for the first time the whole structure of American industrial society became a matter for serious governmental reconsideration. By 1933 economic activity had fallen to the point where virtually all sectors of the American community were willing to reassess the theory and the practice of the previously predominant "old order." That old order had not been sympathetic to the rise of trade-unionism, and had emphasized individual rather than collective bargaining. If it had at times produced high wages and rising standards of living, these had been the products of basic, impersonal economic forces and of employers' unilateral decisions—although, to be sure, the specter of unionism and the need to meet economic competition frequently prompted the employers' moves.

The Great Depression marked the end of one era in the government of American industrial society. It was a time when it was universally admitted that individual bargaining was insufficient—when a national illusion that the ruggedly individualistic worker could cope with the vicissitudes of the business cycle and the vagaries of employer attitudes was shattered. Yet if an old belief had been destroyed, just what would replace it was not necessarily immediately apparent. In historical perspective the New Deal was a melting pot of ideas, speculations, and theories—a mélange of influences striving to reshape the American mold. And the five theories of unionism, too, were put into the melting pot.

For the sake of intellectual curiosity it is interesting to review some of the New Deal programs as they were proposed, in order to associate them with each of our five theories. At the same time it is also of interest to indicate where the "end product," the post–Great Depression American trade-union movement, deviated from the lines suggested by the theories. In other words, where do the theories fit into later developments? In this fashion it is possible to estimate roughly some aspects of the current relevance of the theories.

1. *The moral-conditioning theory.* In its purest form this theory found its earliest expression in the National Industrial Recovery Program. Section 7a of that Act, later spelled out as the Wagner Act, sought to establish through enlightened governmental leadership, more than through a program of punitive measures, the copartnership in production of management and labor. Labor, in this case, was encouraged to seek self-expression through union organization. That the NRA—a halfway house on the way to factory and industry councils—failed, first functionally and then legally, is beside the point; what is significant is the emergence of an action plan based on the type of thinking urged initially by educators and reformers of the stamp of Ely and Monsignor Ryan.

The other elements of the New Deal program intended to help those who cannot help themselves—child labor laws, minimum wage–maximum straight-time hourly pay laws, aid to impoverished students and youths, and particularly the assertion of federal responsibility for the old, the very young, the ill, and the indigent—also may have borne the stamp of the type of thinking propounded in this theory. The spirit of charity, once effectively the symbol of the humane rich, was written into law and acquired a professional priesthood of civil servants.

Yet if the New Deal contained these program elements, it is even more apparent that much of what this theory had to offer was rejected. Producers' co-operation, the key to this theory, was virtually forgotten. The wage system was not abandoned; in fact, it emerged from the Great Depression as dominant as it had been in the twenties. Even "labor banks," perhaps the closest most American unions got to achieving one form of managerial status, disappeared. And where unions continued to handle large sums of investment funds, greater reliance was put on the usual market channels. By the fifties, the avowedly pro-capitalist firm of Merrill Lynch, Pierce, Fenner & Beane enjoyed a staff (advisory) relationship with many onetime socialistic unions.

The general view of unionism as a ladder to higher educational achievement and greater moral protection also seems to have waned. The change may be due to a diminished need, as a result of expanded public educational opportunity, and to the effects of increased social mobility. The latter has also led to less self-conscious *noblesse oblige,* a change that may be more apparent than real, but which nonetheless results in fewer self-designated "friends of the workingman."

Most of all, there is little mutualism seen in industrial relations today, unless it is the pseudo-mutualism which every seller must perforce find in any buyer. What prevails instead is a market or business bargaining relationship, more geared to positive "deals" than to normative standards. Labor now considers itself as good as management; and fewer managements act as though they honestly believed themselves the protectors of their employees.

In sum, the major failing of the moral-conditioning theory was simply that it did not foresee the actual course of development of American unionism. On the industrial scene its major themes, that is, producers' co-operation, leadership from the "upper classes," and full social co-operation between economically competitive groups, did not materialize. The type of reform which did occur, and which was advocated by Ely and Monsignor Ryan, was not of the union movement. The role of unions was incidental and subordinate. The Ely-Ryan approach was not validated by the postdepression union movement, if it was validated at all.

2. *The social-revolutionary theory.* If one can abstract from the dogmatism of the Socialists and Communists, one can see many aspects of their earlier thinking written into the law and the customs of the land. [1] What they had preached had been the leveling of economic benefits, the taking away of their economic advantages from the aristocrats of management and labor, the brotherhood of the industrial and agricultural worker, and the nationalization of enterprise in order to prevent cyclical unemployment and victimization of the worker. Moreover, they had sought to make the government the critical instrument in the social process, and to awaken worker interest in governmental programs of significance to him.

At first glance, the record does indicate developments along these lines. For a time there were active political coalitions between farmer and union groups, which had action programs supported alike by rural "individualists" and the urban quasi-proletariat. Nor should one minimize the leadership exerted by unions, and particularly by the CIO leaders, in state and national politics. Especially in New York, Michigan, and California, labor played a dominant, if brief, role.

More specifically within the trade-union field, stimulation and even protection was given by the government, through the National Labor Relations Board, to the new industrial type of union comprised of those unskilled and semiskilled industrial workers who theretofore had been unable to secure recognition for themselves. By "running interference" for these industrial unions, the government indirectly aided the CIO revolt against the *status-quo,* jurisdiction-minded AFL leadership. Within ten years several of the large industrial unions, notably those of the steel, auto, and rubber workers, had become pacesetters in

---

[1] The dogma tripped them; it became for some more important than the goal of heightened living standards and levels of social opportunity. For they condoned not only cunning, but also outright deception and avoidable violence. No wonder that as time progressed the ranks of the Marxists became bitterly divided between social-democratic moderates and dogmatic "actionists."

American industry. The development of government owner-ship reflected yet another aspect of the revolutionary theory. The large western dam projects, the Reconstruction Finance Corporation, the Tennessee Valley Authority, and the Com-modity Credit Corporation are but a few of the more obvious examples of what the 1912 right-wing Socialists, at least, had longed to see. And even if one will grant that most of the changes were not the result of direct Socialist activity (the Socialists had never claimed that history needed them to ac-complish its inevitable purpose), it may still seem clear that the social-revolutionary theory foretold much about future devel-opments.

But this is not the case. The truth is that economic class lines are not rigid in America. Economic misery has not increased. And Marxism depended upon the rapid development of class consciousness among the proletariat as the cornerstone of its theorizing. Insofar as this did not occur, socialism failed to provide the answer.

Even public ownership—the simplest and most direct step to-ward the "new society"—proved to be no panacea. All the in-dustrial-relations problems known to private industry remained evident in the governmentally owned sector. Moreover, the right to strike, guaranteed to private industry's employees, is virtually denied to public employees. Unions are today no closer to engaging in direct political action—that is, becoming part of one party's political machine—than they were in 1912.[2]

From evidence of this type one may safely conclude that the social-revolutionary theory did not dominate. Assessed histori-cally, it even played a minor role.

3. *The psychological-environment theory.* Several develop-ments during the two decades since the depression can be listed

[2] It is important to note that Gompers' "political voluntarism" did not pre-clude engaging in politics. Unions have always taken an active role in political fights, particularly on the local (municipal) level. But they have never concluded a blanket alliance with a national party machine; endorsement of leading candidates and some limited financial aid has been the extent of their political action.

as active validations of this theory. During the depression the prevailing misery caused by unemployment led to a popular realignment of social values. One important change was the new faith in collective bargaining as the means to prevent individual and group distress. The exposures publicized by the La Follette committee hearings on employer infringements of worker civil rights did much to awaken the public conscience and to reorient opinion regarding unionism.

The reaction of employers, too, is of importance. Although in the twenties many employers believed that worker morale depended upon high wages and pleasant physical working conditions, the new thinking emphasized "humanism" in industrial relations. It is not for bread, or even butter, that men work; rather do they want to be treated as significant personalities. In short, one version of the new gospel preached the necessity for worker expression, even through unions. Let the worker have a voice, let him ask his own questions, voice his own demands, and this act of self-expression alone, regardless of what he is given, will do much to make him happier. And a happy workman can, with proper managerial supervision, become a more productive worker.

Thus "human relations in industry," an awkward title for much that comprises humanistic industrial psychology, became a source for a certain type of union recognition. Some of those who studied the effect of factory environment on worker attitudes noted that high wages, pleasant physical working conditions, and short hours were insufficient without an instrument for "upward communication." Something else was needed, and unionism was suggested. But the suggestion carried implicitly, if not explicitly, the message that the union could be manipulated. "Management gets the kind of unionism it deserves," was the articulated slogan. What was meant but often left unsaid was that a smart employer could outmaneuver any union.

A survey of the record since 1932 leads to the conclusion that this theory has much to commend it as an explanation of developments. It does not require ingenious reinterpretation to see positive evidence of its influence. Where previously it had been argued that unionism was the reaction to economic misery, it is now said, as we have already noted, that it is the controlled humanistic element in environment, as expressed in contrived attitudes, that gives employers "the kind of union they deserve." Thus, with modifications, the old theory seems to stand.

Notwithstanding the "validity" associated with this theory, it really explains only how to control worker response, not the social purpose to be served by unionism. "Treat a man right, and he won't hate you," is the message. But if this indicates indirectly, for the employer's purposes, why a man joins a union, it does not tell what that man's own reasons are for joining or not joining. Quite the contrary, it merely implies that under certain conditions, an employer utilizing certain techniques can "wheedle" cost-reducing, tension-eliminating co-operation. In its application, therefore, this is an "employers' theory." It explains possible, but not sufficient, conditions for unionism.

The disciplines of psychology and sociology are doing much to fill the gaps in our knowledge of the limits of effective "use" of unions by employers. As yet, however, research is principally on the narrative or observational plane, although some experiments, such as Elton Mayo's historic Hawthorne study, have yielded theoretical conclusions about motivation. It is to be hoped that in time additional findings will fill more gaps, so that this theory can become fully operational. Nevertheless, the psychological-environment theory, because of its assumptions, will most probably always be management-oriented—that is, a means to serve employers' ends. As such it does not have a broad enough application to cover most of the aspects of the kind of unionism that has developed during the last twenty-five years. It may explain why employers think that they should "tolerate" unions; it does not explain much more.

4. *The economic-welfare theory.* The many ways used to achieve economic benefits for workers during the liberal-reform period of the thirties is the significant point in assessing the effect of this theory. Where the method of legal enactment was

believed to produce better results than the method of collective bargaining, the former was used. Witness, for instance, the complex of social-security laws and benefits, the use of national minimum-wage legislation for workers too weak to organize unions, and the use of federal and state authorities to obtain union recognition and prevent victimization of individual workers.

On the other hand, where collective bargaining purportedly worked best—where it was the more economic method—it was embraced and endorsed, even to the point of making strong unions actively oppose some of the efforts of the public authorities intent upon helping those workers unable to help themselves.

A spectacular instance of the shift from one method to another was the AFL endorsement of minimum-wage legislation in 1937. Previously the AFL had opposed minimum-wage fixing because it feared governmental intervention, but in 1937 the leaders of the AFL, having become all too aware of the threat of factory migration to low-wage areas in the South, reversed themselves and sought to have the government do for their members what they themselves had been unable to do. Granted that this was being done in the name of underpaid southerners, nonetheless Messrs. Green and Woll knew how desirable for their own ends the natural consequence would be.

During World War II, when governmental policy made money-wage increases unlawful, unions sought fringe benefits to get "more and more and even more" for their members. And when after World War II taxation on personal money income remained high, the use of fringe benefits was expanded in order to maximize the net take-home earnings of labor.

While it had become apparent that the method of legal enactment was preferred for most social-security benefits, it was no less obvious that labor pressure on Congress alone could not effectively expand the federal program. Thus unions used collective-bargaining pressure upon large employers, and won concessions resulting in supplements to the regular social-security benefits, knowing full well that the employer would then have particularly strong economic incentives to join forces with unions in pressing for increased coverage through the national system. This technique was tried first for pensions and later for supplemental unemployment insurance. In both instances, as in all the cases previously mentioned, the goal was an increased share of the national product for organized workers; the selection of the appropriate means had become essentially a problem in the economics of alternatives.

We have repeatedly noted Barnett's postulate that unionism was generally believed by workers to be the most economic means of increasing their share of the national dividend, and that as long as this conviction prevailed, unionism had a future. The old organizing cry of "Join the CIO [in order to] win a 10-cent hourly increase" is essentially a confirmation of this view. The opinions of Dunlop (2, pp. iii–v) and Ulman (4, pp. 594–604, esp. 601 and 603–4) that unions serve primarily to achieve material goals in an economic fashion are further elaborations of the theory developed by Barnett. The very fact that their research has appeared, written as it was long after Barnett had sung the swan song of unionism, is at the same time indicative of the reasserted vigor of "his" theory and an indication that his 1931 assessment was untimely and wrong.

Although there is much in the economic-welfare theory to commend it as the explanation of the post–1932 trade-union movement, it does lack at least one important element. Just as Barnett failed utterly to see the noneconomic driving force in unionism at its most critical hour, so this theory today still overemphasizes the calculating aspect of the trade-union movement. American workers have frequently not acted as this theory predicted that they would. They have not been as calculating or as "rational" as they should have been if they were trying to maximize their net advantage. Instead they have often chosen to fight lost battles and sacrificed more where by abandoning their union they could have sacrificed less and achieved the same result. This point is discussed further in the following section.

5. *The social-institution theory.* The industrial-relations field was staked out in the United States in the thirties and forties not by government civil-servant "surveyors" alone, but also by self-interested "communities" or pressure groups. If the Wagner Act gave the "workers' communities" the license of freedom and recognition of "full" citizenship, the "gift" was viewed by the government only as desirable, not as essential to American social order. Thus unions could not rely on the government; although they could use the government, they had to rely on themselves. In this sense the postdepression decades, a period when organized groups "found themselves," saw one group in particular exert pressure upon society, or upon the general community which makes up political subdivisions such as the state and the nation. It saw the rapid rise of unions and union pressure. But all of this did not develop in an orderly fashion. One union community was opposed by another; all union communities, by blocks of business and professional interests. Consequently a retrospective view yields a picture of factional dissension and continual bickering—control by pressure rather than by logic.

The fact (not the theory) of social justice seems to be to give to the lion the lion's share. But some erstwhile lions, such as the old AFL unions, were forced to learn that to hold their own they had to develop strength in more parts than the larynx. The social-institutional theorists can point to the flux of group organizations during the postdepression decades, to the claims voiced by each regarding its right to hegemony (in other words, the property concept), and to the patchwork of jurisdictional divisions which resulted, as examples of their correct understanding of the American social process. The result was not simply increased economic benefits; it was the assertion of the property rights of first-class citizenship by several groups. And even when these assertions brought the small community into conflict with the state, the method of resolution was one of trial by combat—and the state, as represented by the NLRB, often came out second best. Within the "house of labor" the new industrial groups forced the "old guard" first to reform itself, and then to give to what had been considered rival and dual unions the stamp of legitimacy.

Increased emphasis on grievance procedure as well as on union security clauses is another example of the application in positive practice of this theory, which stresses the property rights of citizenship. The workers' ownership of job opportunities and the union's right to recognition and continued existence were the goals; the only appropriate means inevitably was, in the last analysis, the procedure of collective bargaining—either over the bargaining table or by group pressure put on the three governmental branches. Great significance was attached to the means, since it was believed that without the existence of a means of group expression, no economic gains, regardless of their size, were secure. Thus this theory emphasized that economic benefits alone were less important than the job right, viewed in all of its complexity—apprenticeship rules, seniority rules, stint rules, and so on.

The record of willingness of union membership to strike and thereby forgo economic benefits for the cause of union security is additional telling evidence of the insight which this theory yields. The number of examples of member dedication to the cause of the union is certainly high enough to corroborate the point. In fact, the New Deal and Fair Deal decades serve as excellent examples of unionism as a way of life for social or bargaining inferiors.

Yet even when unions turned over to the civil government the responsibility for the administration of any program, they frequently lacked confidence in the fairness or understanding of civil government; there was a belief that the handling of the area was directly affected by the strength of the union, standing as watchdog. Thus what the social-institutionalists point to in the two decades after 1929–32 are not the pure gains economically "won" by unions, but the increased scope of collective bargaining, the moves toward representative democracy in industry, and above all, the establishment of the right to the job as defined and guaranteed by the group as an integral part of the constitutional rights to life, liberty, and property.

With all of this, the social-institution theory seems unable to explain some of the things to which the economic-welfare theory gives insight. The rush to unionism since 1932 can be only partly explained by a devotion to industrial democracy per se. It must also be admitted that union ranks swelled because unionism proved during the period to be the most efficient instrument for securing higher wages and better working conditions. Our conclusion is simply that this theory may explain much of the hard core of unionism, but it does not entirely explain the great waves of union growth after 1933. For example, it does provide an understanding of the jurisdiction issue, in that it explains why unions have pressed claims long after the cause seemed hopelessly lost. It even explains why some unions will not negotiate such claims. But it does not by itself provide an explanation of membership lethargy, antiunion political activity by union members, and the like. These, too, are part of modern unionism and need explanation. For the "complete" explanation, one cannot turn to any single theory.

Toward a Reasonable Eclecticism

In any work dealing with the history of ideas, it is incumbent upon the author to make every effort to deal as objectively as possible with the thoughts and sentiments found in the data he examines. It is also desirable for him at some point to make clear his own views, even if he feels confident that he has made an objective analysis. In this postscript we outline very briefly our position. We do so with no apologies—it is included merely to make the picture complete.

As already noted, for most purposes we find the economic-welfare and the social-institution theories most valuable in giving insight into American unionism. Thus we acknowledge an intellectual dualism which, for reasons indicated earlier in this chapter, should not and possibly cannot be harmonized into a unified theory. Nevertheless it may be possible to explain our position by referring to the same ambivalence in complexity and multiplicity of goals in the American cultural environment.

The American heritage emphasizes social opportunity and material advancement. There are two goals: one of social self-realization or recognition, and one of ease in getting additional goods and services. These goals are not uniformly complementary or uniformly interchangeable. Which goal one seeks is determined by considerations of the time and by the impact of contemporary events. So it is with American workers and unions—they want the social prestige of job ownership and the social security it affords; they also want to get material things as effortlessly as possible.

Job security via job ownership is obviously important, but under some conditions workers seem to become hypnotized by the belief that job security can be achieved more effectively through legal enactment and the resultant due process. But in a contracting market workers are perforce brought to realize the full meaning of unionism to job ownership. After impressive instances of victimization, they are extremely conscious of the necessity for unions to stand as guarantors of the job right. Seniority, seen in this light, has the overtones of a political right, and remains the heart of unionism today.

Under other conditions the ease of getting and holding increased real wages tends to minimize the general need for job security. Here it is not relative poverty alone that seems to make workers willing to agitate for more material things. Often a belief exists that there is little chance of prolonged unemployment as a result of a demand for more—a belief that one can get another job quickly. In this event, union-guaranteed job security may be forgotten, and the union may be simply the best (least-cost) mechanism to get material results. An example of this is the case of some tugboat pilots who, knowing the value of their irreplaceable skill, use their union boldly and simply as the most effective instrument to "hold up" metropolitan communities such as New York City, rather than as an essential to industrial democracy. When instances of victimization are rare, when the job market is full of opportunity, when workers feel their mutual interest is easily evident to all, then the commitment of workers to unionism and collective bargaining may be limited to unionism's getting them what they want more economically than some other means. At such times the economic-welfare theory seems to us to be the best explanation of union behavior.

But this discussion is not to say that one's choice of theories can be made by a simple determination of the state of the business cycle or the prevalence of fairness in industrial discipline. For some workers there is never sufficient job security—to them the need for union controls over the job is omnipresent. These men, to our mind, represent the inevitable adherents of the social-institution theory. To them the *right* to the job—jurisdiction, if you will—is always the critical question. And only unionism can provide a satisfactory answer. They are over the years the backbone of the trade-union movement.

Yet the bulk of union membership probably does not at present share this concern. After fifteen years of unrivaled prosperity, many of the rank and file may have forgotten the historical mission of elevating workers to the rights of full industrial citizenship. Instead they are concerned with material plenty in the here and now. This has been an increasingly evident phenomenon since 1946; and, as we have already indicated, is best explained to us by the economic-welfare theory. By implication, the economic-welfare theory also explains why it is difficult for American labor to stay organized, since the goal of achieving material wealth may appear at times to be attainable most easily by agreeing to well-paying yellow-dog contracts. Hence this theory can and does indicate why unions fail during periods of prosperity as well as during depressions.

Whether an American union in a particular situation and at a given time reflects the economic-welfare or the social-institution theory depends upon what its policy makers seek. But a knowledge of these theories of unionism can provide an appreciation of some of the implications of the choice.

We find two of the five theories most useful today. Yet we do not wish to imply that any of the others will never have more than curiosity value. Were the American cultural environment to change, it seems obvious that our preferences might have to be modified. If American social life were more frequently and more strongly motivated by Christian ethics, for example, the moral-conditioning theory might have appeal. Similarly, if the Great Depression had led to greater economic stratification and thence to revolution, a variant of the revolutionary theory might have seemed particularly meaningful. Or if we thought that the "invisible hand" was really under the control of a human engineer (or a Madison Avenue advertising shark), our ideas would be considerably different, and would make the psychological-environment theory more useful. But because we do not hold any of these three sets of postulates to be currently relevant, the theories which they support do not appeal to us.

Yet if a theocratic national dedication such as Moral Rearmament were to occur, brought about by some natural, scientific, or military catastrophe, the usefulness of the moral-conditioning theory could increase. Similarly, if owing to an economic or military defeat a "proletarian" movement should develop in the United States, then the value of the social-revolutionary theory might also grow. Needless to say, such changes do not presently appear likely.

References

1. Dunlop, John T., "The Development of Labor Organization: A Theoretical Framework," Chap. 7, pp. 163–93, in Richard A. Lester and Joseph Shister, *Insights into Labor Issues*. New York: The Macmillan Co., 1948.

2. ———, *Wage Determination under Trade Unions*. New ed. New York: Augustus M. Kelley, 1950.

3. Taft, Philip, "Theories of the Labor Movement," Chap. 1, pp. 1–38, in *Interpreting the Labor Movement,* "Industrial Relations Research Association Publications," No. 9, 1952.

4. Ulman, Lloyd, *The Rise of the National Trade Union: The Development and Significance of Its Structure, Governing Institutions, and Economic Policies.* Cambridge, Mass.: Harvard University Press, 1955.

Four Congressional
Investigations

This Appendix supplements the discussion of the five theories. It is intended to illustrate four things: (1) the refinement of basic concepts that was necessary before the theories could be developed; (2) the stages of maturation of several of the theories discussed earlier in this volume; (3) the expression of the views of several labor leaders on the labor movement; and (4) the pattern of acceptance and rejection of the various theories by public investigators.

The Appendix is concerned with four sets of Congressionally authorized public hearings and the records of testimony and research monographs associated with them. To give perspective to these materials, it should be recalled that the integration of the American economy and the industrialization of the Northeast were greatly accelerated during the Civil War period and the decades immediately following it. Since then America has been at times concerned with such social problems as professional hoboes, large numbers of unemployed industrial workers, and demands for the social and economic relief of urban citizens. Previously these had either been unknown or been known to such a small degree that for all practical purposes they could generally be ignored. The ills of industrial society, however, manifested themselves in ways which prevented their being overlooked. Starting in the late seventies, Congress was repeatedly reminded that the working and living conditions of vast segments of the urban population were less than satisfactory, and that remedies were needed if the endemic unrest, bred by dissatisfaction, were not to flare into more serious revolt.

Congress responded by considering the nature of the evils alleged to exist and then by debating possible remedies. Students of trade-union theory would probably not give this normal Congressional procedure a second thought were it not that the investigators unearthed much valuable material. By reviewing the material preserved in these investigations, one can see how certain theories of trade-unionism matured, and how these came to have relatively wider acceptance as substantiating evidence was amassed.

Congressional studies were equally useful in refining the concepts basic to the study of trade-union theory. For instance, the problems of the industrial worker were initially confused with those of the chronic poor, and the separation of these two groups was essential if any understanding of their problems was to be gained. Also, the distinction between unionism as an institution and unionism as a movement had to be made clear if unionism were not to be continually confused with other, more general notions of social reorganization, such as easy-money schemes, programs for female suffrage, and various types of electoral and ballot reform.

Together with a clearer understanding of the meaning and place of unionism came the need to consider greater and greater masses of evidence. The problems of industrial relations appeared to multiply at something like a geometric rate, and it became increasingly difficult for the members of Congress to assimilate all the data. Thus the techniques of investigation changed, and greater reliance came to be placed upon men who were university-trained as specialists on labor problems.

Yet as Congress took up these investigations, the labor movement itself was growing and becoming more institutionalized. Its attitude toward the various branches of the government changed, and it is interesting to observe the effects of these changes. In some instances labor became bitter, and in others, somewhat disillusioned. Witnesses who had seemed like suppliants in 1879 had in 1914 been succeeded by others who were acting like established middle-class petitioners. Indeed, in a few instances, witnesses were even behaving like self-appointed judges.

The four we shall consider were not the only investigations of labor matters during the period. However, those selected convey well the various points suggested earlier. They illustrate how the theories and the elements within them were evaluated over a period of time. And perhaps most interesting of all, they contain some of the clearest expressions of the philosophies of various figures active in the union movement.

The Hewitt Hearings, 1878–79

Pressure upon Congress in 1878 to do something to mitigate the effects of the long depression that had started in October, 1873, resulted in the naming by the House of a seven-man Select Committee to inquire into both the causes of the depression and its effect upon labor (8, VII, 4754). This committee was directed to devise and propose measures for the relief of labor. Abram Hewitt (Dem., N.Y.), a manufacturer, was named as chairman.

Under his firm leadership, the committee heard numerous witnesses, many with bizarre notions both as to the nature of the problem and its cure. A transcript of the sessions was prepared and most of it published (34). It is the discussion available in this first document that is of particular significance to us, rather than the final, formal report, which was tendered after prosperity had returned.

Few witnesses separated the specific misfortunes of working people from the more general monetary problems. Carroll Wright, for instance, recommended greater efficiency in government, and thus lower tax needs, as a direct aid to the unemployed (34, p. 295). Professor William Graham Sumner (1840–1910) of Yale, an advocate of free trade and *laissez faire,* minimized reports of general economic misery, and endorsed the income tax as a means of obviating the few problems that he felt existed (34, pp. 181–208). Many witnesses argued for "soft" money; others demanded deflation. Some suggested programs of public works, though many, like Wright, held that the solution to labor problems was outside the scope of governmental activity.

George E. McNeill, a former deputy-commissioner of the Massachusetts Bureau of Statistics of Labor and at the time president of the International Labor Union, which had between seven and eight thousand members, made one of the clearest of the statements heard by the committee when he asked for the establishment of a federal bureau of labor statistics, "since many things that appear impracticable may appear practicable when there are statistics available." Unlike most of the witnesses he did not seek to discuss every economic problem imaginable. Instead, he sought a hearing for the problems peculiar to labor, as distinct from an investigation of the problems of taxation.

Adolph Strasser, president of the cigar makers' union, was even more specific than McNeill. He reported that he could speak only for his own industry, which he said was economically depressed because of the competition of coolie and tenement-house labor (34, pp. 99 ff.). He did not propose unionism as an institutional cure, but merely observed that unions were useful in gathering statistical knowledge.

Some witnesses did speak of unionism and the methods used by certain unionists, but few expressed much confidence in workers' organizations. One employer noted that unions were good as far as they went, but that the Constitution and statutory law stood between them and successful action (34, pp. 110 ff.). Andrew P. van Tuyl, an employer, held that only the government could provide the solution, and voiced distrust of the ambitions of union leaders. Chairman Hewitt personally favored unionism because he felt that it provided employees with a bargaining voice and was therefore a help to their economic prosperity. He favored arbitration and conciliation—given stable representation for the worker (34, pp. 386 ff.)—and saw the need for and incidence of strikes reduced by collective bargaining (34, p. 482).

Hewitt, it should be added, was less than sanguine about the

efficacy of positive governmental programs, and his evident belief that unequal economic distribution could not be changed,
added to the fact that he had a considerable private fortune,
made him appear unsympathetic to some witnesses. A careful
reading of the testimony, however, reveals that he was fundamentally committed to realistic self-help and did not feel the
callous indifference usually ascribed to the rich. Although Hewitt
himself frequently spoke of the evils of something called "monopoly," one cannot escape the impression that he strongly criticized
anyone else's lapse into such imprecise generalities.

The depression "ended" in the spring of 1879, and by the time
the Select Committee was ready to make its report, business activity was once more on the upswing. Hewitt was not re-elected
to Congress in 1880 and the newly named committee failed to
publish the testimony it heard. Instead, it prepared a majority
report calling for the abrogation of an immigration-treaty agreement with the Chinese government (19) that the House did not
approve (24, pp. 131, 217, 814, 931–32). Thus the Hewitt investigation achieved no more than an early airing of some views
that were to mature during subsequent years. To us as students
of social history the Hewitt investigation is a convenient reference point. There was no real theory of unionism advanced before it, but there were refinements of the concepts necessary to
a consideration of the theories of unionism. The problems of the
industrial unemployed, as a group, were differentiated by some
of the more discriminating witnesses from the problems of the
poor as a whole and the problems of the general economy. The
need for reliable statistical information about labor was reaffirmed,
and it was made abundantly clear that the lack of factual knowledge handicapped everyone—legislator, worker, and employer.
In this way these hearings give a picture of the environment
from which theories of trade-unionism sprang.

The Blair Hearings, 1883–86

Whereas the Hewitt hearings were concerned with the causes
of and the problems arising from the long depression of the

seventies, the Blair hearings examined the chaotic industrial situation in a state of "normal health."

American social organization changed markedly in the eighties. Business prosperity returned and brought with it drives to organize unions. Rapid growth of the Knights of Labor as well as of the independent "craft" or trade-unions was accompanied by much industrial unrest that Congress viewed with some alarm.

The Knights of Labor was first organized in 1869 as a secret organization, but it abandoned secrecy in 1878. Between 1881 and 1882 the Knights doubled its membership, growing from approximately nineteen thousand to approximately forty-three thousand. Many craft unions were founded in the fifties and sixties, but their growth was arrested by the long depression. Afterward they resumed their expansion. In 1881 several of them organized the Federation of Organized Trades and Labor Unions of the United States and Canada (from which the American Federation of Labor later grew) to lobby for legislation on the national level.

On August 7, 1882, Senator Henry W. Blair (1834–1920, Rep., N.H.), chairman of the Committee on Education and Labor, proposed that his committee sit during the Congressional vacation and hear witnesses discuss the relations between capital and labor, the state of wages and hours, the conditions of the laboring classes in the United States as compared with those abroad, the causes of strikes, and the agencies behind the strikes. In addition, the committee was to recommend ways and means to promote industrial harmony (8, XIII, 6996). These hearings extended over the next year and a half, and the committee, generally under the chairmanship of Senator Blair, traveled extensively. It brought forth no recommendations, however, and the records it left are of use only to those willing to read through more than four thousand printed pages of diverse views.

By and large, all segments of organized labor, including representatives from Socialist organizations, the Knights of Labor, and several key trade-unions, responded to invitations to testify. They voiced repeated demands for an organization to gather federal labor statistics, for controls on the immigration of low-cost labor (one witness from New England called the French Canadians "the Chinese of the Eastern States" [4, I, 66]), for the incorporation of trade-unions, for the establishment and enforcement of the eight-hour day, for control of child labor, for enactment of an employers' liability law to cover industrial accidents, and for relief from such evils as company stores, blacklisting, and the prosecution of workmen's organizations as conspiracies.

In general, the committee listened attentively and, in the light of later hearings, tolerantly. The power and influence of the federal government was not particularly evident in the eighties, and the elected representatives of the states did not take offense when their witnesses spoke sharply. Committee members themselves frequently expressed the sentiment that unions were necessary protective organizations against the pecuniary power of the capitalists. The committee members understood the effects of wage changes and of competition, and they were on the whole receptive to suggestions of what constituted a fair wage. They were interested in discussing the radical and conservative tendencies in the labor movement and did not hesitate to frame one witness' answer in the form of a question to another witness. For instance, Charles Lenz, a German *émigré* Socialist and newspaper editor, stressed the radical trend in the American labor movement caused by the intransigence of the American employer (4, I, 237 ff.). Samuel Gompers, another witness, replied, "As to the views Mr. Lenz holds, I think very little heed ought to be paid to them, for the reason that the views he now expresses are not the views he expressed a year or two ago, and what he expressed a year ago he expressed views contrary to and acted in conflict with a few months ago, and he turned another somersault here. I would rather answer an independent question. . . ." (4, I, 375.)

Of the more than 250 witnesses, only a few discussed at length the role and theory of trade-unions, and most of those who did confined their remarks to the problems of their own

organizations. Naturally the views held by the Knights of Labor and the various independent "craft" unions (many of which
had taken part in the ill-timed Pittsburgh convention of the
Federation of Organized Trades and Labor Unions) were
predominant, but even so, a few Socialist opinions, as well as the
views of the (Socialist) Central Labor Union of New York
City did get thorough representation.

Early in February, 1883, Robert D. Layton, Grand Secretary
of the Knights, appeared as the first witness. Layton conceded
that his organization was really controlled by the telegraphers,
miners, and printers (4, I, 4), but he sought in his testimony to
make it clear that rational knowledge and self-restraint were at
the heart of the policies advocated by the Knights (4, I, 16 ff.).
He felt that as long as the wage system continued, the reason
for workingmen's unions was to prevent oppression, the precise
degree of which could be known only if employers' books were
open to public investigation. It was his opinion that producers'
co-operatives would ultimately replace privately owned institutions, and that education, in which he professed the most
profound faith, would succeed in overcoming all economic problems. Like the other Knights of Labor representatives, Layton
felt that education meant knowledge of facts, and thus he advocated as an immediate necessity a federal statistical agency. When
facts were available, the issues in industrial relations could be
weighed publicly through arbitration, and ninety-nine cases out
of one hundred would thus be solved.

Layton defined arbitration as follows:

. . . a certain number of employés should meet an equal number of
employers; they to select an umpire, whose decisions should be final.
Then let the men make their demands, and let the employers produce their books, and if it appears that they cannot afford to comply
with the men's demands, that decision will be made, and must be
final. But we hold that we cannot have arbitration on any fair basis
without having organization combined with it, as we must have
some delegated body authorized to accept or refuse any offer that is
made . . . [4, I, 23].

Layton was a peculiar mixture of naïve reformer and so-phisticated observer. Although professing to be an idealist, he had no illusions regarding the motivations of individuals.

Q. [by the Chairman]: Which do you believe is the happier man, the employé or the master—which gets the most out of this life?

A. [by Layton]: I cannot give any positive information on that point, but I can state my belief. If I were to judge by the actions of these men, I would consider that the man that had the most money was the happier, from the way they grab at it and the sordid means they use to get it [4, I, 28].

Another Knights of Labor witness was Frank K. Foster, a Massachusetts printer and like Layton a member of the Interna-tional Typographical Union. Foster thought that legislative ac-tion was necessary to overcome the evils of black-listing and other, similar union-destroying tactics (4, I, 79). He also asked to have the child-labor problem dealt with by legal enactment, when that was possible (4, I, 91). Like Layton, Foster put great faith in arbitration, in which public sympathy and co-operation could be used effectively (4, I, 87, 91). He felt that economic competition and the unwillingness of employers to make con-cessions caused most strikes, and urged the necessity for factual investigation. He considered statistical knowledge to be an all-important factor in the development of harmonious industrial relations, and expressed himself as believing that a bureau of labor and statistics would be at that time the greatest benefit that could be conferred on labor (4, I, 87). Foster also spoke of the desirability of legal incorporation for unions—a step which he believed would preclude the further possibility of their prosecu-tion as conspiracies.

The most outspoken Knights of Labor witness, one whose views were admittedly somewhat in advance of those of the organization (4, I, 222), was John S. McClelland, a telegrapher from Hoboken, New Jersey, and secretary of the Executive Board of the Knights. McClelland, examined in August, 1883, was put through a vigorous questioning by Senator Aldrich (Rep., R.I.) (4, I, 221).

McClelland argued that the profits accruing from the introduction of labor-saving machinery should be divided between the inventor and the man operating the machine, and should not add to the profit of the capitalist, who "under the present system of government or of political economy . . . gets everything" (4, I, 138 ff.).

He advocated that workingmen rely on the power afforded them by a fully informed public as well as on the strength of their own organizational unity (4, I, 201 ff.). His most outspoken comments were against a political and social system that gave "capital the power it has" and against "the uses made of it" (4, I, 217–18).

The committee also heard extensive evidence given by two other workingmen's organizations, the Federation of Organized Trades and Labor Unions, of which Samuel Gompers was the guiding spirit, and the socialistic Central Labor Union of New York City. The Federation had its 1883 congress in New York City in August, and Gompers, with the co-operation of Senator Blair, managed to get each of the delegates an opportunity to testify (15, I, 234–35, 237).

Gompers' colleagues represented the "conservative core" of the labor movement, and what is impressive is their hard-headed insistence upon confining their views to specific grievances and particular cures. Several had at one time or another traveled the Socialist road, yet in spite of several digressions into philosophical reveries and occasional lapses into the idiom of class consciousness, virtually every one of them, at the time of the hearings, insistently proclaimed his interest in results rather than in "mere theory."

William McClelland, a delegate from the Amalgamated Society of Engineers, advised the committee to refrain from passing additional labor legislation, beyond the limitation of the use of child labor and the encouragement of school attendance.

As for legislation, I think a good plan might be to leave us alone. By that I don't mean that things are to be left as they are. I do not mean that my idea is that a committee of this kind should return from whence they came and do nothing more. . . . I mean to leave us *free*. Sweep from the statute books all the laws having a tendency to discriminate in favor of one class or another; . . . simply leave us to take care of ourselves, without any special legislation . . . [4, I, 680].

Peter J. McGuire, general secretary of the carpenters' union and later secretary of the American Federation of Labor, was another who testified at length. He advocated the immediate establishment of a federal statistical bureau, arguing that neither the Hewitt nor the Blair hearings were sufficiently systematic— that a regular bureau was needed. He likened a bureau of labor statistics to a weather bureau, the one to warn of economic storms as the other did of storms at sea (4, I, 327–28). He also supported the enactment of an eight-hour day, the prohibition of the importation of contract labor, and the right of incorporation for trade-unions (4, I, 340 ff.). McGuire expressed confidence that there would be fewer strikes if employers would recognize unions and treat workmen as equal human beings. "Flirting" with socialism virtually all his life (3), he reverted to his earlier political convictions when he said:

. . . A strike . . . is a revolt against the class rule of the capitalists, and such revolts, although sometimes organized, are oftener unorganized; for, in proportion as labor becomes organized, just in that proportion are strikes less indulged in by the workers. . . .
Hence, to diminish the number of strikes, all that is necessary is to promote and encourage labor organizations, and protect them and their property by legalizing their existence the same as in England and France [4, I, 321–22].

W. H. Foster, a Cincinnati compositor, member of the typographical union and general secretary of the Federation, was another who spoke out for the eight-hour day and the right of incorporation from trade-unions. In his opinion, legal recognition of trade-unions by the state would force employers to bargain collectively (4, I, 404). He also promoted legislation to make employers liable for industrial accidents, "as many employers are negligent about having proper guards to machinery and such things as that" (4, I, 406). Foster assured the committee that fair treatment of labor would retard the growth and spread of Socialist or Communist ideas (4, I, 412).

One of the most impressive witnesses was Adolph Strasser, acting president and secretary of the cigar makers' union as well as editor of its journal. Strasser, who was also a witness before the Hewitt committee, came with a prepared statement covering the history of his own organization and of American labor organizations in general, a review of the economic conditions of his industry since 1864, and a summary of the organization of cigar makers in Europe.

He noted that there were four stages of union development in America, each ending with a general depression: (1) the Jacksonian stage, ending with the panic of 1837; (2) the period of agitation for the ten-hour day and producers' co-operativism, ending with the panic of 1857; (3) the advance of free labor and the agitation for the eight-hour day coincident with the Civil War and the development of the National Labor Union, ending with the economic collapse of 1873; and (4) the contemporary era, which he prophesied would end between 1885 and 1887. Panics, Strasser testified, could be mitigated, though not altogether avoided, if patterns of consumption were improved and stabilized. He added that panics would never result in more than a temporary setback of the union movement (4, I, 457–60). He felt that unions did not have visionary or idealistic reform programs; they concentrated instead on the precise issues affecting a particular trade.

. . . I look first to the trade I represent; I look first to cigars, to the interests of men who employ me to represent their interests. . . . We have no ultimate ends. We are going on from day to day. We are fighting only for immediate objects—objects that can be realized in a few years. . . . We want to dress better and to live better, and become better off and better citizens generally. . . . We are all practical men [4, I, 460].

Strasser informed the committee that his theory of unionism was based on the actual experience of British and American worker organizations, and that, while he realized that every course of action had some theoretical roots, he wished to emphasize that he was particularly interested only in practical results. He made four specific demands: (1) the right of incorporation for trade-unions to protect their funds and to help in getting employer recognition, (2) the enforcement of the eight-hour day legislation and its extension to the manufacture of all products protected by patent laws, (3) the establishment of a federal bureau of labor statistics, and (4) an amendment to the excise revenue act that would prevent the production of cigars in prisons and penitentiaries (4, I, 461–63).

Strasser expressed some concern about the expansion of federal powers, but he did not explain his fear of the growth of "a national police and the breaking down of our republican form of government" (here he was quoting Abram Hewitt, whose phrase this was). He concluded his testimony by strongly assuring the questioners that there was no growth of "socialistic feeling" or of similar "vague theories" among the members of the cigar makers' union. "The members . . . are simply practical men, going for practical objects that can be accomplished in a few years; they are no 'trimmers'" (4, I, 465–66).

Samuel Gompers had emphasized this antisocialism a few days earlier when he reported that, although where were some sincere Socialists in the trade-unions, they subordinated their personal convictions to the general good of the whole movement. He granted that there were others who tried to conquer the unions in order to propagate their socialism, but he felt that their efforts were resisted by the trade-unionists who, like himself, accepted the continued existence of the wage system (4, I, 366, 374–75).

Gompers told of the inadequacy of arbitration as an instrument, since no arbitrator could prevent an employer from cutting wages when the latter was confronted by competitive pressure. Strikes were, he added, too frequently criticized; they had their good points as well as their weak ones, and often they were the only effective action available. Gompers was vitally concerned with the tendency of industrial relationships to become impersonal and with the growing habit of regarding "labor" as a commodity or even as a social abstraction. He thus considered unionism's major task to be one of bargaining for status and thereby obtaining the respect of the employer. Unions, he told the committee, adopted benefit features to hold the membership in times of economic adversity, when employers tended to take advantage of individual workmen. He held that unions went beyond the immediate questions of wages and hours, however, and gave workmen the sense of security that comes from belonging to a community that will help them in times of personal distress, although their most important function was their protection of the workers' rights to their jobs (4, I, 371, 375 ff.).

Like the others, Gompers supported the right of incorporation for trade-unions. This view, which he was later to reverse, was based on his examination of relevant English, French, and Swiss laws, certified copies of which he gave to the committee (4, I, 378 ff.).

As a result of his contact with the committee, Gompers became an enthusiastic supporter of Senators Blair and George (1826–97, Dem., Tenn.), both of whom were, as Gompers put it, "converted to the cause of labor and strongly impressed with the necessity for the thorough organization of the working people into trade unions." Senator Blair actually called on Gompers' considerable oratorical abilities in his 1884 campaign, when Blair's re-election was being opposed by two of the major New England railroads (15, II, 81–82).

The Central Labor Union of New York City was another body whose views were systematically presented, although its request for the right to subpoena and examine witnesses had to be denied (4, I, 502–3). The union's official spokesman, Louis F. Post, declared that in spite of the great increase in national wealth, labor's share had diminished. The major beneficiary of this wealth had been the land-holding class, which did not deserve to benefit. At this point the committee directed the witness' attention to more specific matters, and pointed out that there were real limits to the committee's powers. Post then presented several specific proposals, including, besides those advocated by the Federation spokesmen, public ownership of the telegraph and telephone system. He also recommended nationalization of the railways, reorganization of the currency system so that only the government would issue credit, and a modified Henry George proposal for collection of the economic rent from land (4, I, 783–806, 821–35).

The most interesting testimony from the Central Labor Union was that given by Edward King, a typesetter and later an active leader in Bishop Potter's Church Association for the Advancement of the Interest of Labor. It was King's optimistic belief that labor organizations would move from "a selfish or narrow view of the interest of a particular trade" to a broader and more social one. This change, which would result in greater attention to political action, was inevitable. ". . . My observation," he said,

teaches me that on the failure of every great effort by what are called economic means there is a falling back upon the idea that the thing cannot be done in that way; that there is no relief for the working-men except by political action [4, I, 559].

However, King had prefaced this observation with an unusually candid statement that the "conservative bodies of workingmen . . . have heretofore found that their only peace was to keep all political issues, and every issue but their distinctive trade issue, out of their deliberations" (4, I, 559). Later he explained this contradiction by saying that, although it was generally recognized that one should not mix politics with trade-unionism, one should try to encourage unionists, as citizens, to take an active interest in political matters (4, I, 691; cf. 4, II, 887). The labor movement, he was convinced, encompassed three kinds of effort: education, organization, and agitation. More attention to the first would ensure better results from the other two. Like Post, he supported Henry George's views, and regretted that they were not endorsed by American workingmen generally (4, I, 708 ff.).

King was not in favor of producers' co-operatives because he felt that workingmen were not prepared for the kind of self-restraint required or for the kind of decisions involved. He observed that the conditions necessary for the successful operation of producers' co-operatives were such that they could exist only in a society in which the need for the co-operative would not be present. In response to a question about the educational value of co-operatives, he replied that trade-unions had a greater value.

We claim that the trades unions by their methods are a graded system of practical education for bringing the workmen, entirely self-consciously, up to the point where they will regard the good of all other workmen in their country and their trade as of as much importance as their own, and recognize the welfare of each as bound up in the welfare of others. . . . [The International Trades Union] begins at the lowest and most degraded kind of man, and is capable of lifting that man up by the practical education that it gives him, and we claim that cooperation is not capable of taking a man of that kind and doing anything with him. We claim that cooperation begins with principles of character that do not at present exist . . . [4, II, 889].

In answer to several questions aimed at undermining his praise of unions and his faith in them, King replied that a man who starts as a wage worker, joins the union movement, and progresses in his interest from his shop to his trade and from his trade to general economic problems, gets "a graduated system of education, which cannot be supplied by churches, by schools, nor by technical education. It is a graduated education in working together for impersonal purposes . . ." (4, II, 890).

Few of the witnesses gave testimony favorable to socialistic ideas. An exception was Charles Lenz, editor of the "capitalist" newspaper, *Capital and Labor*. Lenz reported that there was a fourfold division in the American labor movement: (1) the "old trades-union element," interested only in "the question of wages"; (2) a united labor party, "aimed at cooperation"; (3) the Socialistic Labor party in Chicago and New York City, organized on the principles of Lassalle and Marx; and (4) a numerically insignificant communistic element.

Senator Blair expressed keen interest in the program of the Socialists. "What," he asked, "is the socialists' idea of government? Where does the government originate and how are its functions to be exercised?" Lenz replied that the Socialists generally held that "the nucleus of society should be the trade unions," which would draw up proposals to be considered as national referendums. Representatives would be elected, but would be subject to recall.

In answer to Senator Call (1834–1910, Dem., Fla.), Lenz reported that a struggle was taking place in trade-union circles between the socialistic, public-ownership faction and the old wage-conscious faction. Lenz pointed to the ascendancy of T. V. Powderly, presumably a Henry George enthusiast, as an indication of the growth of the power of the reformist group.

Lenz was convinced that the existence of socialistic ideas was of little practical consequence unless "the so-called educated classes take hold of the [labor] movement," in which case "we shall be on the verge of a revolution." He added that the rise of a Socialist press and the appearance of books like George's *Progress and Poverty* brought socialism to the attention of the educated public. He went on to say, however, that the ideas of Henry George would be wrecked for a generation or two by the opposition of small farmers (4, I, 237–45).

Lenz concluded his testimony by recommending greater federal aid to the poor and extended federal control in the area of education. He advocated a uniform system of technological schools to educate mechanics, and assured the committee that control by the various states would not be successful or beneficial. He also noted in passing that there was a need for greater statistical knowledge of income disposition: he estimated that 24 per cent of the wages earned in large cities was spent in saloons. Thus some of his views were related to the need for institutionally controlled moral improvement (4, I, 256–57).

One witness who stressed the need for moral reform was Carroll D. Wright, at the time still with the Massachusetts Bureau of Statistics of Labor. He told the committee, ". . . I do not believe much in intellectual education without moral education. Moral reform must come from the top. Political reform comes sometimes the other end up, but moral reform must come from above." In this instance he felt that morality and moral discipline must start with employers, and for this reason the advisory powers of his own bureau were held to be models (4, III, 277–83, 432 ff.). The foundations of reform, he said, were moral restraint and education, higher intelligence and charity, and better conditions in the home.

And, finally, the committee spent most of September 18, 1883, hearing the views of the Reverend Dr. R. Heber Newton, pastor of All Souls Protestant Episcopal Church in New York City, who began by diagnosing the leading social ills and allocating responsibility for them. Labor (excepting skilled tradesmen), he testified, was at fault because of its slothful inefficiency, its lack of pride in work, its thriftlessness, its intemperance (in appetites for food, dress, tobacco, and excursioning), and its general reluctance to form trade-unions for reasons other than organizing strike actions. He also discoursed at length on the responsibilities and the failure of capital, philanthropy, government, and society at large (4, II, 576), but his greatest emphasis was on the necessity for the churches to minister to the poor and needy as well as to the rich and secure: "Original Christianity, as we are now learning to read the secret history of its origins, was also a religious socialism" (4, II, 594).

His stress on the social rather than on the more traditional scriptural gospel was not unique, and he told the committee of a recent church congress where his views had been endorsed. He also pointed to the London Christian Socialist movement, inspired by the ideas of F. D. Maurice and Charles Kingsley (4, II, 595). Thus the Reverend Dr. Newton espoused something like the classical Christian Socialist doctrine: repentance succeeded by good works, particularly producers' co-operatives.

By 1883, therefore, not only were industrial relations regarded as a distinct area of inquiry, but Congress had encountered at least three fairly distinct interpretations of the organized labor movement. The first was the theory that the union movement offered workmen an opportunity to better their moral as well as their economic condition by self-education and producers' co-operatives. The second suggested that through Socialist political activity the working class could eventually take over full control of the means of production and distribution. The third, unlike the other two, took the continuation of the wage system for granted, but saw unions operating within it, using mutual insurance and collective bargaining as the means of protecting the workers' economic interests.

It is not strange that many witnesses expressed more than a single theory of unionism in their one or more appearances before the committee. In most instances, every man who spoke as a representative of an organization had of necessity to reconcile the somewhat divergent views of that organization's membership. Few were as fortunate as Dr. Newton, who could take the point of view of a Christian Socialist without having to modify it.

Certainly, the Central Labor Union of New York City was an amalgam of "pure and simple" trade-unionists, Henry George single taxers, and Socialists. It espoused the socialization of some of the means of production, a Henry George land-reform program, and other general reforms, yet it also stressed quite clearly the limited, particularistic aims of the trade-unions. The union's ambivalent attitude toward politics, so clearly seen in the testimony of Edward King, no doubt grew out of the crushing defeat of its candidates in the 1882 Congressional elections. Yet the Central Labor Union within three years again resorted to political action, when Henry George polled 68,000 votes against Abram Hewitt's 90,000 and Theodore Roosevelt's 60,000 votes for mayor of the city (see 6, II, 450 ff.). The political "success" of 1886 led to division within the ranks of the Henry George–Central Labor Union fusion and eventually to the political reverses of 1887 and political oblivion somewhat later. Eventually, the trade-unionists went one way and Henry George with his supporters another. In time even the scientific Socialists, briefly associated with the trade-unionists, also splintered away. They rejoined forces again for a brief period in 1890, only to pull away once more after Gompers refused to seat Lucien Saniel.[1]

The ideas presented by the witnesses associated with the Federation of Organized Trades and Labor Unions seem the least novel. Unlike the other groups, they accepted the wage system, and their emphasis was on "becoming" (the bargaining process) rather than on "being" (the new society). They were comparatively sophisticated in their tactics, and their stress on the particular rather than on the general made them appear rational, sound, and comparatively conservative. This limited reformism was, however, a fairly radical innovation, for implicit in it was the realization that the industrial-relations problem was at least partly separate from all other problems.

Thus an understanding of the usefulness of union incorporation, the use of the patent clause in the federal constitution, and the prohibition of the importation of contract labor is actually only part of a more fundamental understanding, namely, an understanding of implications of the meaning of industrial relations and what is now called "collective bargaining." That the committee perceived this concept at all is more significant, in a way, than the fact that their realization of it was lost in a maze of testimony.

Originally the chairman's intent was to publish five volumes of testimony with the committee's recommendations included in the final volume. After the appearance of the first four volumes, however, his senatorial colleagues chose to withhold additional funds, since they were far from satisfied with the quality of the work. Senator Sherman (1823–1900, Rep., Ohio), in opposing

---

[1] In 1892 the Central Labor Union once more espoused political action and came under the influence of Daniel De Leon (6, pp. 461 ff. and 516 ff.).

further expenditure except on a one-volume summary, took a categorical attitude.

. . . I wish not to belittle the subject, but I have looked through these volumes as they came to my hands, and there is a vast amount of utterly worthless matter, entirely crude, that ought not to be published in any form, much less in a public document of the Senate of the United States. . . . To print five volumes of this work, which nobody can wade through, it seems to me is not a wise disposition of the public money . . . [8, XV, 5382].

In fact, Blair's only support in the debate was the limited answer to Sherman made by Senator Hawley (1826–1905, Rep., Conn.), who said, after agreeing with Sherman's view regarding the value of much of the testimony,

There are many things in these five [*sic*] volumes that the Senator thinks, and other Senators also think, are trash; there are embraced many foolish things and speculations, in our judgment, by people not well qualified: there are many wild speculations; but remember that one of the things that gives value to this book is that we know now just precisely what sort of wild speculations are going on, and what a certain class of people do desire to say [8, XV, 5382].

Hawley's judgment was undoubtedly even more precise than he may have realized at the time. In any event, he prevailed on his Committee on Printing to continue with the four volumes, a total of 25,000 copies of which were prepared.

In 1886 Blair reported that the fifth and last volume was nearly ready, but even though his colleagues gave him sanction to finish it, the project seems to have lapsed (8, XVII, 51–52, 7775, 7847, 7909). Blair remained in the Senate until 1891. Samuel Gompers understood that Senator Aldrich was responsible for withholding the volume (15, I, 446). The National Archives have to this day no record of the project (23).

The achievement of the Blair committee remained for the greater part unrecognized. Even such historians as Commons overlooked the valuable testimony it heard and could see only confusion in its findings (cf. 37, XXX [1913], 571–78). The only significant exception was Selig Perlman, who in his section of the *History of Labour in the United States* (6, II, 309 ff.) highlighted the Strasser testimony. But the gains in intellectual scope and understanding made between the 1879 hearings and the Blair hearings of 1883–86 are so significant that they deserve greater recognition.

The U.S. Industrial Commission, 1898–1901

The next major Congressional investigation demonstrated the development of a mature appreciation of the complexities of the problems of industrial relations. Dorfman, in describing the commission's work as the "keynote of the period," comments that "at one extreme it . . . recognized the need for the competitive system and for the removal of all clogs that might hamper its efficient operations; at the other, it recognized labor problems and the need for a solution to them. But how these difficulties . . . could be overcome was not very clearly determined" (10, p. 309). This investigation was begun only after a lengthy legislative struggle, for, in spite of the great and disastrous strikes of 1890 at Homestead, Pennsylvania, and 1894 in Chicago, considerable feeling persisted in Congress that there was no need to analyze industrial relations anew. Senator Hoar (Dem., Mass.) felt that members of Congress lacked the time to serve and that the use of nonmembers was not warranted. He also felt that Congress did not need aid to formulate proper legislation. Senator Hawley (Rep., Conn.) feared the alignment of the "lay" members against the members of Congress.

In 1896 the first significant attempt to get a commission appointed to examine the performance of the whole American economy was made by Congressman Thomas W. Phillips (1835–1912, Rep., Pa.). His bill, H.R. 9188, passed the House but was forced to hang over until 1897 in the Senate, where it was eventually amended and approved (8, XXVIII, 5960, 5989, 6059). A Senate-House conference prepared a compromise act, which was passed by both houses and sent to President Cleveland during his last full day in office. There the act died, the casualty of a pocket veto (8, XXIX, 2739, 2751, 2980, 2983). The measure then had to go once again through the whole legislative process. Eventually the Senate accepted an amended version of a House bill and sent the measure to President McKinley, who signed it on June 18, 1898.[2]

The Industrial Commission was directed "to investigate questions pertaining to immigration, to labor, to agriculture, to manufacturing, and to business . . ." and "to suggest such legislation as it may deem best on these subjects." Further, it was "[to] furnish such information and to suggest such laws as may be made a basis for uniform legislation by the various States . . . , in order to harmonize conflicting interests and to be equitable to the laborer, the employer, the producer, and the consumer." The bulk of the work was done by the nine presidentially appointed commissioners and a large technical staff, although for organizational purposes each subcommittee included members of Congress as well.

Among the commissioners appointed by McKinley were M. D. Ratchford (president of the United Mine Workers), J. L. Kennedy (once active in the printers' union), Charles Litchman (formerly secretary-treasurer of the Knights of Labor), and John M. Farquhar (once a member of Congress and a onetime president of the International Typographical Union). Litchman succeeded Ratchford in May, 1900. Samuel Gompers reported that he was offered membership on the commission by McKinley but declined (15, I, 523). Also appointed by the President was Thomas W. Phillips, who had sponsored the original bill in 1896 and who had subsequently retired to private life. Each house of Congress sent five members to the commission; the President appointed nine private citizens, making a total of nineteen (cf. 32). Of the

[2] During the 55th Congress, 1st session, S. 2253 was indefinitely postponed (8, XXX, 2664, 2809–10, and S. Rept. 384). At the next session S. 2253 was replaced by H.R. 4073, which eventually became Pub. Law No. 146 (1898) (8, XXXI, 13, 1486, 4861, 4875, 4984, 4993, 5086, 5800, 6060, 6061, 6206; also H. Rept. 353).

technical staff of twenty-seven experts, eleven were employed on specific subjects relating to labor: Miss Kate Holladay Claghorn (immigration and general statistics), John R. Commons (immigration and labor), J. R. Dodge (agricultural labor), E. Dana Durand (strikes and arbitration), Charles E. Edgerton (labor organizations), Samuel M. Lindsay (railroad labor), Victor H. Olmstead and William M. Stewart (prison labor), F. J. Stimson (labor legislation), Thomas F. Turner (Asiatic labor on the Pacific Coast), and Eugene Willison (mine labor legislation) (cf. also 30). The group supervising the hearings "on Conditions of Labor and Capital Employed in Manufacturing and General Business" included Ellison A. Smyth (succeeded by D. A. Tompkins in 1900), Senator Boies Penrose, Representative L. F. Livingston, S. N. D. North (replaced in June, 1899, by Albert Clarke), and John M. Farquhar.

In order systematically to encompass the field, five investigational syllabuses (lists of topical questions) were prepared and submitted to witnesses, with the specific instruction to testify "only with relation to *such topics as [you] are informed upon*" (44).

Ultimately the commission submitted nineteen volumes of carefully summarized and indexed materials, as well as systematic recommendations (41). Ten of these volumes relate in some way to the problems of labor; one contains the final summary. It is the substantive content of these volumes, rather than the legislation proposed, which represents the project's significant achievement. One of the commissioners, the eminent statistician and editor, S. N. D. North (1849–1924), noted in 1899 that in light of the diversity of labor legislation in the various states, the most the commissioners could do was to educate the public by providing the opportunity for reformers and carefully chosen representatives of labor and industry to give their views (30, pp. 711, 714, and 716). The *American Federationist* thought that the labor members, in a minority position, should see that no antiunion statements went unchallenged. "While we are not too sanguine as to the results of this investigation yet, we shall watch with a friendly but critical eye the progress which is being made, and from time to time record its doings for the information and edification of our friends" (1, p. 161). In all, approximately seven hundred witnesses were heard.

Each of the nineteen volumes contained a narrative description of its contents, followed by a summary digest of the evidence topically arranged with references to specific witnesses. After this came the testimony proper. Both the summary digest and the testimony were indexed under topical headings. The final volume contained a master index as well as the list of recommendations.

Most of the material on trade-unionism is found in volumes VII, XIV, and XVII; the two former, issued in March and December of 1901, respectively, contain the testimony of over 150 witnesses, and this testimony, following the lines of the syllabuses, covers the topics of labor industry, capital in industry, and proposed remedial legislation.

Of the many views the commission sought out, some are more relevant than others to our subject. For instance, George E. McNeill, by then one of the "elder statesmen of the labor movement," reported from the wealth of his own experience the positive changes that had occurred in the status of organized labor. Notwithstanding all of labor's progress, he expressed the conviction that "we are rapidly nearing a crisis of the wage system, when . . . the profit upon labor decreases and wages advance." Then he said, "The capitalist will . . . say to the laborer: We have been fighting it out on this line for a hundred years, now let us join our forces—your skill, time, and endurance with my capital—and we will divide the profits equitably" (41, VII, 119). Yet McNeill assured his listeners that organized labor did not want socialism and had no intention of replacing the private capitalist, even if it was in a position to do so.

The fact is, the laboring man is not qualified to conduct large enterprises, especially in the production of wealth. He can do better in the distribution of wealth by the conduct of the store than in pro-

duction. The trust is the school that is teaching . . . the advisability
. . . of conducting enterprises on a large and magnificent scale. The
day of small enterprises is gone. . . . The trusts are here to stay . . .
[41, VII, 121].

A second witness whose voice carried echoes from the past was
Jacob G. Schonfarber, a Baltimore printer and member of the
International Typographical Union. He appeared, however, not
as a printer but as a representative of the Knights of Labor.
Schonfarber's views contained much that seemed contradictory.
He preferred unions of various crafts, since "having men of
mixed trades on the committee gives it a broader view; [it gives
the men] . . . the opportunity of considering both sides of the
case with better facilities for reaching a settlement" (41, VII,
425), yet he was also an advocate of an unusual (for the Knights)
type of localism: he favored the handling of disputes by those
immediately involved.

In the Knights . . . we maintain strictly that the local assembly
has the right to settle all its own difficulties without interference
from anybody . . . until the time comes when they find that they
cannot settle it; . . . neither the general executive board nor the
district executive board has a right to interfere in a trade matter or
at a trade dispute so long as the local assembly or the local union . . .
does not ask for its assistance [41, VII, 426].

In addition, Schonfarber criticized the lack of power of AFL
international officers.

He also discoursed at some length on the reasons for the order's
decline in membership. He told the commission that too many
members were interested only in immediate results and not in
the program of general education that the organization sponsored; that the national officers had failed to use effectively the
membership's massed political power when the ranks were
swelled; and that, even worse, there was an inevitable tendency
toward dissension whenever political action was necessary, because the commitment of the Knights to political participation
required the endorsement of a specific candidate. He also believed

that the defeat of Henry George in 1886 had disheartened many of the novices (41, VII, 423, 428, 446).

Schonfarber endorsed the preamble of the Knights of Labor constitution once more for the commission's benefit, and spoke enthusiastically in favor of co-operation and land reform. He pledged his organization's faith in "evolution and not revolution" and ended his testimony on a cautionary note.

. . . We are afraid of great centralization of power. We are afraid that it will lead too rapidly to socialism, and we do not think that this country is prepared for extreme socialism yet. In saying that I do not mean to say that we have any horror of socialism, when the time comes for its adoption; but that is a long way off . . . [41, VII, 450].

Carroll D. Wright, the first witness to present his views on the condition of capital and labor, ascribed the decline of the Knights to a disregard of human nature and to too close an embrace of Socialist principles (41, VII, 9–10).

Adolph Strasser, then the examiner of accounts of the cigar makers' union, told the commission of the difficulties his union had with its socialistically inclined New York local. He spoke derogatorily of attempts ". . . to drag trade unions right down into partisan politics," where sooner or later they would be exterminated (41, VII, 259). Strasser continued his old argument against unlimited immigration, and stressed the desirability of an educational test for all immigrants. He added, however, that his views were not shared by all unionists (41, VII, 266).

Strasser reversed his old stand on the incorporation of trade-unions, saying that he no longer saw anything to be gained by it. He voiced the opinion that unions were better off when they did not depend upon state control, and added that he thought nonenforcible legislation was of little, if any, value. He feared that antiunionism in legislatures and particularly on the judicial bench was growing, yet he hesitated to make any predictions regarding the future. "At the present time," he informed his audience, "I would advise no trade union to incorporate, because they can not expect justice at the hands of the courts" (41, VII, 261, 262).

Strasser's close associate, Samuel Gompers, gave perhaps the clearest and most detailed statement of trade-union philosophy heard by the commission. After implying that the AFL belonged to the tradition of American unionism because of its descent from the National Labor Union, a reference which at best strained the historical relationship, Gompers likened its federal structure to that of the national government (41, VII, 596–97). (In this he was undoubtedly adopting Calhoun's view of the federal system.) He defended strike action and attempted to demonstrate its successful results. He discoursed on these results (41, VII, 619) and went on to stress the unselfish aspects of a form of unionism that sought to extend these beneficial results to the unorganized.

There is a difference between the contracted selfishness and the broad selfishness that finds one's good served by serving others; by benefiting others. We know that our movement is largely hampered, our progress is hindered, by the large number of unorganized men, and to bring the unorganized within the pale of the organization would make our effort all the more successful and the struggle less intense [41, VII, 642].

Gompers made a point of demonstrating labor's willingness to work with the trusts, but he made it clear that he had few illusions about some of the past treatment that trusts had given unions in the community as well as in the shop. In an exchange with Commissioner Farquhar, Gompers clarified this point.

Q. (*by Farquhar*): The testimony before this commission by leaders in the labor movement of this country has been both ways; first of all, that they were willing to cooperate with trusts, and they thought that trusts gave stability to wages and a better guaranty of continuous work than in the old way, and also that trusts, by taking in, as you state, the nonunion concerns, have unionized them. Now do you think that there is enough power in the organized labor of this country, backed by a fair, honest, and just public opinion, to keep the trusts honest in dealing with the workmen and with the consumer?

A. (*by Gompers*): To the first part of your question I should say, as to whether the trusts have made labor more permanent and regular and steady, that is still in a tentative state, that is yet to be demonstrated. . . .

As to the unionizing of establishments or trusts that have formerly been nonunion, that . . . has acted both ways.

And to the third proposition . . . I will say that there is a power inherent in organized labor to compel now and more effectively in the near future, fair treatment in the shape of fair wages and fair conditions of labor.

As to the power of organized labor to compel the trusts to deal fairly with the public as to the selling price of the product, that is not the province of organized labor. . . . Organized labor deals with the question from the standpoint of the producer; then as consumers they take their place with every other citizen [41, VII, 643–44].

Gompers' views regarding bigness of organization were consistent: he advocated farmers' organizations so that "they can take care of their own end of [the economic] controversy" (41, VII, 649).

He did not believe that an identity of interest existed between capital and labor; each had distinct and differing purposes. He said that those who thought that labor and management would come to recognize one another's rights and share identical interests were talking of something "very remote and very far removed," and he compared plans to achieve this end with the impractical panaceas "offered by our populist, socialist, anarchist, and single-tax friends" (41, VII, 655). Labor was ready to negotiate and to bargain, nothing more.

He went on to criticize those who considered the state to be the agency "to curb the growth and development or destroy the combinations of industry." He pointed out that in their ignorance of statecraft and economics, such theorists as these only succeeded in penalizing labor unions. Given a free hand, trade-unions would, of course, eventually reshape the fabric of industry, but they would do it gradually. In the meantime, he argued, governmental action should not be aimed at crippling the trusts, since the latter invariably outfoxed the reformers (41, VII, 655–56).

The commission also heard from other key unionists, many of whom described in some detail unusual problems in their own organizations. G. W. Perkins, president of the cigar makers' union, explained why compulsory voting was more democratic (41, VII, 177), and Samuel B. Donnelly, president of the International Typographical Union, reported on the use of the membership referendum in his organization (41, VII, 269). Both of these witnesses assured the commission that unions were "conservators of order," and that union progress was largely the result of self-help (41, VII, 172, 280).

This emphasis on the responsibility of trade-unions and their increasing willingness to work within the contemporary capitalist system was nicely illustrated by Bishop H. C. Potter of the Protestant Episcopal Diocese of New York, who said, in reference to the tenement occupants in his city: "Whether they are anarchistic or revolutionary in their tendencies, they find that their wage gives them a chance to put away some money, and the socialist and proletariat becomes [*sic*] conservative just as soon as he gets money in the savings bank" (41, XIV, 5).

During the last two years of the commission's existence there was increasing reliance on skilled, university-trained investigators on the commission's staff to supplement the time-consuming, often poorly focused public hearings. The staff assembled in a separate volume (XVII) all the material on labor organizations, labor disputes, and arbitration that was accumulated by the testimony and the staff's own research. Charles E. Edgerton (1861–1932) and E. Dana Durand supervised this aspect of the commission's work, aided by John R. Commons and others. In his autobiography Commons relates how Edgerton and Durand had to bring in a team of economists to complete the reports after the staff of politicians and newspaper reporters had prepared an earlier report, which was rejected (5, p. 75; cf. 11). The final version consisted of five parts, dealing with national labor organizations;

collective bargaining, conciliation, and arbitration; laws and court decisions as to labor combinations; statistics of strikes and lockouts; and an excellent 137-page summary and general discussion.

In the section on national labor organizations there were three introductory chapters covering the available history of early general movements (limited to a history of the National Labor Union and The Industrial Brotherhood), the Knights of Labor, and the American Federation of Labor. The second of these chapters reviewed the convention proceedings of the Knights and analyzed the reasons for the secession of splinter groups, the organizational structure, and the theoretical function of the administration.

The 27-page review of the AFL began with a short formal history, including some resolutions and a list of general aims; a statistical analysis of membership; a discussion of the handling of relations with Negro workers, the Knights of Labor, and similar "problem groups"; and a summary of union devices such as strikes, boycotts, and union labels.

It continued with nine chapters on unions in particular trades, each of which gave a short history and condensed discussion of the organizational structure of the union concerned. The chapters dealt with the textile and clothing trades (12 unions), the printing trades (6 unions), the building trades (12 unions), the glass and pottery trades (4 unions), the mine workers (2 unions), the woodworking and allied trades (6 unions), the metal and machine trades (16 unions), the transportation workers (5 unions), and miscellaneous trades (25 unions). These summaries, although brief and generally factual, gave a good picture of the relationships between various trade groups in the organized labor movement.

The next major section of the report dealt with the direct relationship between organized labor and the employers. It summarized nine national or general agreements and twenty-three local contract systems. In order to analyze this material, the writers made one of the first systematic attempts to define such processes as *arbitration, conciliation, collective bargaining,* and *mediation.*[3] They also drew a sharp distinction between disputes involving new contracts and those involving interpretation of existing contracts (41, XVII, 75). And, finally they took cognizance of informal methods of dispute settlement as well as of more regularized methods. This section on the relationship between the two segments of the industrial community concluded with a discussion of the handling of this relationship by the major American governmental agencies (federal and local) and by the governments of Great Britain, France, Belgium, Germany, Austria, Australia,[4] New Zealand, and Canada.

Volume XVII of the *Report* was undoubtedly the clearest factual discussion of the trade-union's role in American society published at the turn of the century. It lacked historical data, which led Commons and Ely to initiate the Wisconsin studies a short time later (see p. 34). Its handling of the devices of unionism revealed the gaps in research that were soon to be filled by the Johns Hopkins studies (see p. 26) as well as by Commons' own monograph on the restriction of output (7). But it was the only carefully prepared analytical study of the structure and methods of American unionism. No subsequent study has attempted so ambitious a project; later writers have concentrated instead on historical developments within the labor movement, the methods

---

[3] "*Arbitration* is the authoritative decision of an issue as to which the parties have failed to agree by some person or persons other than the parties." "*Conciliation* is a term applied very commonly by [the] English . . . to the discussion and settlement of questions between the parties themselves, or between their representatives, who are themselves actually interested. It is frequently used by State boards of arbitration as identical with mediation." (The commission, however, chose to restrict usage of the term to the settlement of minor disputes within an expressed or "understood" contract.) "*Collective bargaining* . . . [is] the process by which the general terms of the labor contract itself . . . are determined by negotiation directly between employers or employers' associations and organized workingmen." "*Mediation* is the intervention, usually . . . [proffered by] some outside person or body, with a view to bringing the parties to a dispute together in conciliatory conferences" (41, XVII, 75).

[4] More specifically, certain of the Australian colonies, since federation took place after the research was done.

and devices of trade-unionism, or, more recently, on the administrative structures found in labor organizations.

To satisfy public interest, the commission prepared a preliminary report of recommendations (Vol. V) in March, 1900. The formal statement of proposals relating to labor was contained, however, in the 234 compactly phrased pages of Volume XIX, released in 1902. Because the project was divided, the review prepared by experts and the commissioners' own plans for reform did not always stress the same points, nor was the legislative action suggested in the 1902 volume identical with that suggested in 1900 (cf. 11, pp. 573–75).

The 1902 summary prepared by the staff noted the growth of concentration in industry and the consequent polarization of the economic interests of management and labor. The commissioners, in their recommendations, went on to argue that most industrial-relations problems should nonetheless continue to be handled through private agencies, although they conceded that there were areas where vastly increased federal control would be more appropriate. Opinion was divided on what, specifically, these areas were (41, XIX, 723–24, 847–55; cf. V, 31 ff.).

The commission recommended, for example, that uniform laws be passed by the various states to regulate the hours of labor for adults and younger workers. (Commissioners J. W. Daniel, E. A. Smyth, and C. J. Harris dissented, arguing that climatic differences precluded uniformity. They were also vitally concerned that such legislation threatened the inviolability of freedom of contracts [41, XIX, 953–54].) The commission also suggested that factory legislation be enacted in those states where it had not yet appeared; and went on record as favoring the eight-hour day in all public employment. They recommended that Congress, under the interstate commerce clause, provide legislation that would call for the physical examination of locomotive engineers and firemen as well as prohibit the employment of juvenile railroad telegraphers.

Only 15 of the surviving 18 members of the commission, including dissents, signed the 1902 labor report.[5] Names of deceased members and one member who had resigned appeared in the 1902 list. Durand reports that among the members of Congress there were many who felt that the entire work of the commission had been colored by Republicanism—a charge that contained an element of truth (11, p. 578).

The attention of state legislatures was directed to ending the evil practices of truck pay and company stores. The problem of the abuse of equity court injunctions was considered, and the majority of the commissioners favored some form of limitation of the arbitrary judicial powers regarding procedure in contempt of court cases, length of imprisonment for conviction of contempt of court, and "blanket" prohibition clauses in injunctions.

Violations of the political rights of laborers were discussed, but were held to be a matter for the state legislatures. The great majority of the members of the commission went on record as favoring the growth of labor organizations, although they felt that every laborer should have the right to refuse to belong to unions. "The right to be employed and protected without belonging to a union should be preserved; but every facility should be given labor to organize if it desires, and the last vestige of the notion that trade unions are a criminal conspiracy should be swept away" (41, XIX, 951). Commissioners C. J. Harris and D. A. Tompkins submitted a vigorous dissent, stressing the curbs on individual liberty found in many unions "where the degree of intelligence is not high" (41, XIX, 954–55).

General recommendations in lieu of specific proposals regarding the union label, black-listing, labor spies, and the procedure for voluntary arbitration were also made. And, finally, reference was made to the need of policies for the standardization of laws in the many political jurisdictions.

Unlike those of the two earlier investigations, the Industrial

[5] Several members had resigned or died—S. N. D. North, M. D. Ratchford, D. A. Tompkins, Lee Mantle, and J. H. Kyle. The surviving members who did not sign the report or a dissent therefrom were Sen. Stephen R. Mallory and Reps. John J. Gardner, L. F. Livingston, and John C. Bell.

Commission's final report was published in its entirety. It far surpassed in magnitude either of the earlier publications, for the country which three decades earlier had been feeling its way and still borrowing from its European heritage had become by 1900 a young nation of growing industrial might and importance.

America's pride in its new-found intellectual independence and sense of its own importance was reflected in the attitudes revealed by the industrial investigation. American labor hailed the trusts' power, maintaining at the same time an awareness of its own strength. It was evident that a new "philosophy of labor" had appeared, and this appearance was in itself significant. Gompers in 1899 represented a vastly more stable labor group than did Strasser in 1879, or any of the various spokesmen in 1883. The conceptual clarity of the program of "pure and simple unionism," in which most of the commission and all of the investigational staff on record obviously believed, was based on a clear notion of the problems of industrial relations in a relatively free society. That change, too, is significant. The implications of modern industrial "bigness" were not readily observable when Hewitt or Blair held their hearings. They were quite evident after 1898.[6]

The very complexity of the new industrial society emphasized the inefficiency of a haphazard questioning of witnesses. Specialized and professional knowledge was required for a complete understanding of the issues, and the systematic examination of documents and records had to replace former attempts to collect opinions in a helter-skelter fashion. Durand, eventually the secretary of the commission, noted in this connection that

. . . with a witness who has something to conceal, who does not know what is wanted of him, or who is unskilled in expressing himself, the path of the questioner is devious and thorny. A high degree of expert knowledge . . . becomes essential. . . .

Unfortunately, too often the members . . . showed themselves lacking in the degree of skill needed. . . . Many a witness—a great labor leader, for example,—who would willingly have given a mass

[6] As a matter of fact, the sordid side of this bigness was discussed earlier in the two reports on the Homestead strike (see 20 and 35).

of valuable information if skillfully questioned, was allowed to deal merely in ill-expressed generalities or in insignificant details. . . .

Durand admitted, however, that *"the Industrial Commission probably compares most favorably with other similar bodies . . ."* (**11**, pp. 568–69; italics added).

The commission's increasing reliance on the reports of trained experts was an important step in the history of governmental research. Moreover, it is also significant that they took on the monumental job of summarizing and indexing all the material, which had not been done in the earlier projects.

Finally, the attention which both the commissioners and their expert staff paid to the problems in the organizational structure of unions and to actual historical experience contributed to a wider knowledge of unions. "What do you do?" and "How do you do it?" are every bit as useful questions as "Why do you do it?" On the negative side, there is perhaps the relatively small effect of the commission on the shaping of industrial laws. Even though the commission made a few recommendations for positive legal changes, it is significant that practically nothing was accomplished in the next few years. Perhaps the well-known dynamism of McKinley's successor and the death of Mark Hanna, rather than a failure of the reports themselves, serve as the explanation.

As happens with many governmental investigations, however, this one hesitated to consider the future of labor and of industrial relations in America. The "expert" volume and the testimony volumes all tend to be reassuring about the existence of imminent dangers, instead of warning the country of them. Thus the commission failed adequately to publicize the brewing discontent that was soon to erupt, first in the organization of the Industrial Workers of the World and later in the bombing of the *Los Angeles Times* building. Ely, in a long commendatory review of the commission's work, saw this fault at the time.

In a general way it may be said that the report deals with labor in its static rather than its dynamic aspects. The idea of evolution in labor conditions is suggested here and there, but not consistently developed, and perhaps to do so would not have been in harmony with the character of the work assigned to the Commission . . . [12, 249–50].

But little else critical was said about it. S. M. Lindsay published a brief but excellent summary of the commission's work in 1901 (28).

The U.S. Commission on Industrial Relations, 1912–15

The fourth investigation of industrial relations resulted from the direct political pressure of a group of social workers, university professors, and other citizens who had become alarmed by the prospect of further violence such as the bombing of the *Los Angeles Times* building. That incident, which occurred on October 1, 1910, killed 20 and injured 17. It grew out of a dispute between the National Erectors' Association and the International Association of Bridge and Structural Ironworkers. The particularly disturbing aspect of the bombing was not the simple act of violence so much as the discrediting of the established labor movement that came about when the leaders of the structural ironworkers' union were arrested, swore their innocence, and then suddenly, to save their lives, admitted their guilt (31, pp. 318–25; 9, pp. 177–78; 36, pp. 659–89). After the success of the open-shop campaign launched by the National Association of Manufacturers, the admission by these union leaders of a conspiracy resulting in violence and death had an adverse effect on the development of public policy toward unions and industrial relations.

A group of social workers, many of them associated with *The Survey* magazine, formed a committee to draft a letter to President Taft asking for a new commission to investigate the possibilities of greater federal control of industrial disputes. This letter, presented as a petition at the end of 1911, asked for a study of the situation in the structural-iron trade, for an analysis of the attitude of the courts in industrial problems, for an estimate of the economic and social costs of industrial disputes to the American economy, and for a comparative survey of the nature of industrial relations both with and without unions. In addition, the letter requested that studies be made of the role of existing American and foreign agencies and "economic governments for industry." Those who eventually signed included Miss Jane Addams, Miss Lillian Wald, Edward T. Devine, Paul U. Kellogg, Henry Morgenthau, Sr., Owen Lovejoy, Samuel McCune Lindsay, Arthur P. Kellogg, Stephen S. Wise, John A. Fitch, Miss Florence Kelley, E. R. A. Seligman, Louis Brandeis, George E. Barnett, T. N. Carver, Irving Fisher, Ernest Freund, J. W. Jenks, Alvin Johnson, S. N. Patten, E. A. Ross, W. F. Willcox, and Mary W. Simkhovitch. Adolph Lewisohn, Mrs. Emmons Blaine, and Julius Rosenwald gave financial aid in order to push the proposal along (37, XXVII [1911–12], 1407, 1430–31, 1563, 1587–88; 37, XXX [1913], 571–78).

Taft included in his 1912 message to Congress a proposal for a new commission on industrial relations. Six months later, on August 23, 1912, Congress passed Public Law 300, which established a new commission, to be composed of nine persons, "not less than three of whom shall be employers of labor and not less than three of whom shall be representatives of organized labor." The bill (H.R. 21094) replaced the Senate version (S. 5546) and was amended several times in the course of its consideration. Originally, provision was made for not less than two representatives each of organized labor and employing interests. Also, the initial appropriation was pared from $300,000 to $100,000. The final version permitted the hiring of experts at salaries not to exceed $5,000 per annum, although an earlier version had set the maximum at $3,000 (8, XLVIII, 2646, 2800, 6609, 9190–207, 9230, 9675, 10972, 11192, 11225, 11239, 11367, 11480, 11527, 11566, 11608, 11744; see also 21).

The commission's assignment, found in Section 4 of the Act, was broad enough to permit the examination, either by direct testimony or through research, of any phase of the industrial-

relations problems except immigration. Specifically, it was authorized to

> . . . inquire into the general condition of labor in the principal in-
> dustries of the United States . . . especially in those . . . carried on
> in corporate forms; . . . into the effect of industrial conditions on
> public welfare and into the rights and powers of the community to
> deal therewith; into the conditions of sanitation and safety of em-
> ployees . . . ; into the growth of associations of employers and of
> wage earners and . . . [their] effect upon . . . [industrial] re-
> lations . . . ; into the extent and results of methods of collective
> bargaining; into methods for avoiding or adjusting labor disputes
> . . . ; into the scope, methods, and resources of existing bureaus of
> labor . . . ; into the question of smuggling or other illegal entry
> of Asiatics into the United States. . . . The commission shall seek
> to discover the underlying causes of dissatisfaction in the industrial
> situation and report its conclusions thereon.

Taft's nominees for the commission were as follows—public
members: George Sutherland, Republican senator from Utah;
George B. Chandler, Republican from Connecticut; and Charles
Simon Barrett, Democrat from Georgia; employer members:
Frederick A. Delano, Illinois; Adolph Lewisohn, New York;
and Fred C. Schwedtman, Missouri; labor members: Austin B.
Garretson, Iowa, Order of Railway Conductors; James B. Lennon, Illinois, treasurer of the AFL, though recently defeated in
his own tailors' union for re-election as a union officer; and
James O'Connell, District of Columbia, vice-president of the AFL,
although he too had recently been defeated for the presidency
of the International Association of Machinists.

Some of these nominees, whose names were ignored by Congress, were considered poor choices by *The Survey* magazine and
the university groups who originally presented the petition. It was
noted that Taft had not chosen an economist, a social worker,
a woman, or even a trained investigator. Since Taft by this time
was a "lame duck," the petitioners had high hopes that the
President-elect would remedy these deficiencies (37, XXIX [1912–

13], 381–82). Wilson did not disappoint them, and though he nominated the same labor people, he strengthened the other two representative groups by including as public members Frank Walsh, Missouri lawyer; John R. Commons, Wisconsin professor; and Florence J. Harriman (Mrs. J. Borden Harriman), New York member of the Democratic National Committee; and as employer members, Frederick A. Delano, Illinois; Harris Weinstock, California, associated with the National Civic Federation and veteran investigator of California labor problems; and S. Thurston Ballard, Kentucky.[7]

Louis Brandeis had been offered the chairmanship, but declined to serve (17, p. 133). Through the offices of Senator Robert M. La Follette, John R. Commons was offered the chairmanship in June, 1913. He declined, but happened by coincidence to be in Frank P. Walsh's office in Kansas City when the telegram arrived from President Wilson offering Walsh the chairmanship.

[Walsh then] joined . . . in urging me to accept a membership on the Commission. I explained that I could not leave the University. It was finally agreed that I might put in my vacation periods with the Commission and organize an investigational staff other than the staff employed for the public hearings. So I wired from Walsh's office to Senator La Follette that I would accept membership on the Commission, and Walsh wired at the same time to the President accepting the position of chairman . . . [5, pp. 165–67].

The changes made in the commission by Wilson were apparently satisfactory to the *Survey* people, although one nominee was criticized. Paul U. Kellogg wrote:

The first impression of my social workers is that the Commission as nominated by President Wilson comes much nearer being [the proper] sort of group than that nominated by Mr. Taft. An especial reason for this impression they find in the appointment of Professor Commons, the one man in America, who, as economist and investigator has thought out industrial reforms, as statesman has drafted them into laws which would give them effect and as administrator

---

[7] Delano resigned and was replaced by Richard H. Aishton of Illinois on March 17, 1915.

has practically enforced those laws with the unexampled cooperation of employer and employee [37, XXX (1913), 452–53].

However, Mrs. Florence J. Harriman, in her autobiographical *From Pinafores to Politics,* remarks that Florence Kelley regarded her as too much of an amateur to accomplish anything constructive in this complicated area (17, p. 133).

Once *The Survey* had succeeded, albeit somewhat slowly, in getting the commission established, it published in its August 2, 1913, issue a symposium on what the commission should actually do. Twenty-one views were offered, to which Paul U. Kellogg wrote an introductory summary (37, XXX [1913], 571–88). John R. Commons' proposal is particularly noteworthy, although he did not know at the time he wrote it that he was slated to be a member of the commission. Commons emphasized the need for an operational approach and criticized the procedures of the earlier investigations.

The most important service of the Industrial Relations Commission, I should say, would be to bring about a better organization and co-operation of all state and federal agencies that deal with labor problems. We have already had two great governmental investigations of labor: one made in 1884, and the other that of the Industrial Commission in 1900. Each of these seemed to be merely an opportunity for all interested parties to get their opinions published, and it is difficult to locate any constructive work that these investigations accomplished. . . .

I should say the commission should start off by calling in heads of departments and their chief subordinates that have to do with labor problems, both state and federal, and find out why they have not taken care of their work. What are the obstacles in their way? Do they overlap? Are there gaps? Are they competent? Do they waste time on routine that could be given to essentials? What would they suggest to make their investigations and administration more effective? [37, XXX (1913), 578.]

Although Commons saw the immense practical advantage that public hearings would have in attracting public attention to the need for better enforcement of labor laws, he felt, above all, that those skilled in the technicalities of the subject would have to assume actual responsibility. In his own words,

These seem to me to be the first things to do—investigate the investigators, and get them to cover many of the subjects set up for the commission. Since appropriation is made for only one year, the commission ought to bring something to a head before the year ends, and something, too, that would last after the commission is gone. It, of course, should take up other important subjects assigned, but not to the detriment of this fundamental one, on which the others depend for execution [37, XXX (1913), 578].

Commons based his view not only on his earlier U.S. Industrial Commission experience, but also on the conclusions he had developed during his recent term of office (1912–13) as an industrial commissioner in Wisconsin (see 27, pp. 9–30).

Initially, at least, the commission's work was carried on in two ways, in public hearings and in research done by experts. Four areas, or "divisions," were established for the investigations by research: (1) methods used by public agencies to handle labor disputes; (2) collective bargaining, unionism, and disputes; (3) the industrial problems of unorganized labor; and (4) industrial relations and the courts. These areas were under the supervision, respectively, of F. H. Bird (a student of Commons from Wisconsin), George E. Barnett, Basil M. Manly (a special agent of the Bureau of Labor Statistics), and Mrs. Crystal Eastman Benedict (a New York lawyer who had done considerable work on the Pittsburgh study sponsored several years earlier by the *Survey* group). W. Jett Lauck (associated with the 1907–10 U.S. Immigration Commission) was the first director of research.

At the same time, in public hearings scheduled by Chairman Walsh, numerous witnesses were examined both by expert counsel and by the commissioners. As events developed, however, Chairman Walsh and the other commissioners took over more and more of the interrogation of witnesses, until finally they were doing it all.

The research operation was slow in organizing itself effectively, and in June, 1914, Commons induced Dr. Charles McCarthy (1873–1921), founder and director of the Wisconsin Legislative Reference Library, to take over the directorship.[8] McCarthy, by this time an almost legendary figure, enjoyed world-wide fame for the excellence of his work in analyzing technical data and presenting them in a form that made legislative action possible. *Survey* hailed the appointment of McCarthy:

> . . . It is an open secret that for ten months following the commission's appointment it floundered badly, without a clear-cut program of work, without clear-cut division of responsibility, and with great areas of the field before it practically untouched. The alignment . . . which brought the investigation into Mr. McCarthy's hands . . . for the first time gave promise of coherence enough . . . to allow disinterested observers to make sure of its [the commission's] trend . . . [37, XXXIII (1914–15), 54].

McCarthy set up field headquarters in Chicago and organized the research staff into nine substantive divisions and an editorial section. The nine divisions were: legal and legislative; labor organizations and collective bargaining; employment; labor problems in agriculture; education and industrial training; welfare and insurance; accidents, safety, and sanitation; underlying causes of industrial unrest; and women in industry. The legal division staff included Patrick Gill, B. F. Moore, Daniel O'Regan, David Saposs, Miss Inis Weed, and Edwin Witte. The division on labor organizations was headed by George E. Barnett, and the staff consisted of Ira Cross, F. S. Deibler, Miss Frieda H. Fligelman, Henry Hoagland, David McCabe, Selig Perlman, A. E. Suffern, and Leo Wolman. William Leiserson was in charge of the division on employment, and was aided by C. B. Barnes, Paul Brissenden, W. M. Duffus, E. A. Goldenweiser, Carleton Parker, and others. John L. Coulter and Charles W. Holman dealt with the section on agricultural labor, G. C. Sprague and Miss Anna Herkner with education and industrial training, and Selig Perl-

[8] For an interesting account of McCarthy's life as well as for his side of the impending dispute with Walsh, see Fitzpatrick, *McCarthy of Wisconsin* (14).

man, Miss Elizabeth Hyde, Edgar Sydenstricker, and B. S. Warren with the welfare and insurance division. F. H. Bird supervised the research on accidents and safety, and was assisted by Horace Secrist and Miss Hyde; W. Jett Lauck headed the section working on industrial unrest, and was joined by Ralph Fleming, Miss Fligelman, L. Magnussen, Sumner Slichter, and Francis P. Valiant; and the division concerned with women in industry was supervised by Miss Marie L. Obernauer, in association with Misses Gertrude Barnum, Nelle B. Curry, Elizabeth Hyde, and Inis Weed.

McCarthy also organized standard reporting and reviewing systems, and as the monographs came in they were systematically filed away. For a while it appeared that these semiauthoritative investigations might provide the backbone of a new *summa* similar to Volume XVII of the U.S. Industrial Commission's report (14, pp. 191–96). Some of the manuscripts proved to be almost the definitive works on the subject, for example, George Barnett's essay on joint agreements. Other excellent pieces among these forgotten monographs are C. W. Mixter's analysis of the areas of future *rapprochement* between scientific management and labor, Selig Perlman's essay on how to study industrial relations in a hostile community, and Edwin Witte's study of injunctions. These monographs, which run in excess of 20,000 pages, also show the intellectual development of such scholars as Carleton Parker, whose essay on how he handled a strike situation in Phoenix, Arizona, contains much of his social philosophy, and Leo Wolman, who started his study of trade-union membership on the basis of Barnett's research.

The research division was suddenly disbanded, however, and even though a pious wish was expressed in the final report that the monographs be published by the government, the few that were eventually published were done under commercial auspices (see 39, I, 14). Barnett's and McCabe's *Mediation and Arbitration* (2) was published in 1916, and Hoxie's *Scientific Management and Labor* (22) in 1915. Other manuscript reports underwent extensive revision or became parts of later books. (The manuscripts themselves are available on microfilm in the National Archives (40). A few authors continued their research after leaving the commission's employment, and their books were ultimately printed, for example, Lauck's *Political and Industrial Democracy* (25), Leiserson's *Adjusting Immigrant and Industry* (26), McCabe's *National Collective Bargaining in the Pottery Industry* (29), and Witte's *The Government in Labor Disputes* (43).

Commissioners Commons and Harriman were in sympathetic accord with McCarthy's aim to make the research projects the commission's major contribution (see **5**, pp. 171 ff., and **17**, p. 172), but Chairman Walsh had other ideas. Walsh was convinced that open hearings, generously publicized, would arouse sentiment against the iniquities practiced by employers in modern industrial society and would result in much-needed social reform. Walsh had little faith in experts and technical reports, but he had had a great deal of experience with political agitation. Consequently, he allocated the major share of the commission's budget to the hearings.

There were 154 days of hearings, held in Washington, New York City, Paterson (New Jersey), Philadelphia, Boston, Chicago, Lead (South Dakota), Butte, Seattle, Portland, San Francisco, Los Angeles, Denver, and Dallas. Seven hundred and forty "carefully selected" witnesses testified (see Table 1, p. 288).

The forty-six subjects discussed ranged from the selection of an appropriate agendum, on which sixteen expert witnesses gave 126 pages of testimony, to such varied topics as industrial relations in specific industries (almost 5,000 pages) and the areas in industrial relations affected by Rockefeller interests (1,600 pages). In all, there were close to 11,000 pages of testimony and exhibits.

Walsh was intent on demonstrating the general callousness of American industrialists, and evidently envisioned his role as that of a public prosecutor. He first demonstrated the comparatively reasonable attitude of organized labor by staging a public "debate" between Samuel Gompers and Morris Hillquit on the re-

TABLE 1

CLASSIFICATION OF WITNESSES UPON INDUSTRIAL SUBJECTS *

Affiliated with employers:

Employers, managers, foremen, etc.............	134
Representatives of employers' organizations......	37
Attorneys..................................	15
Efficiency engineers.........................	10
Employment agents..........................	14
Capitalists, bankers, directors, etc..............	20
	230

Affiliated with labor:

Trades-union officials.........................	135
Workingmen and working women..............	90
Attorneys.................................	6
Industrial Workers of the World...............	8
Representatives of the Socialist Party..........	6
	245

Not affiliated with either group:

Agriculturists...............................	22
Attorneys..................................	15
Public officials..............................	69
Representatives of civic organizations...........	24
Educators..................................	22
Economists and sociologists...................	20
Investigators...............................	11
Representatives of the press..................	14
Clergy.....................................	10
Physicians..................................	7
Unclassified................................	17
On Chinese exclusion........................	34
	265
Total.......................................	740

* U.S. Commission on Industrial Relations, *Final Report and Testimony*, I, 20.

spective merits of "pure and simple" unionism and evolutionary socialism. The debate was acrimonious in tone, and did not add to Gompers' distinction, as it probably was supposed to do (39, II, 1443, 1445, 1462–549, 1568–71, 1572–79). Fortunately, Hillquit was not a "fire-eater," and Walsh was not in the least personally embarrassed by the outcome, and certainly not by the many yards of newspaper publicity. Representatives of the IWW were invited to be present and were permitted to give testimony, but the commissioners paid little attention to their extremist views.

Mrs. Harriman later wrote of Walsh:

My opinion of him now is that he would have made a very good labor representative, but I still seriously question his suitability as one of the representatives of the public. He was, I feel, quite sincere in his desire to better labor conditions, but quite unjust in many of his conclusions about capital. He [was] a born agitator with a very engaging personality, and [had] his place, but not in the position of a judge. To me he was always . . . cross-examining as though capital were in the dock and always helping labor with the sympathetic spotlight. It may only be, of course, that he thought of himself as a French juge-d'instruction, who investigates rather than weighs [17, p. 136].

After examining industrial working and living conditions in the East and Midwest, the commission heard testimony on West Coast problems, including the smuggling of Asiatics and the controversial open- and closed-shop disputes in Los Angeles (see 16). They were also interested in the condition of agricultural labor.

The most sensational phase of their investigation concerned the "Ludlow [Colorado] Massacre," which was the name applied to "the gruesome burning of eleven children and two women in the Ludlow union tent colony" on April 20, 1914. The Massacre was part of the violence during a United Mine Workers strike at the Rockefeller-controlled Colorado Fuel and Iron Company. Repeated public appeals had been made to John D. Rockefeller, Jr., a major stockholder and company director, to intervene by directing the management to negotiate with the men, but these had failed, and Walsh sought to force Rockefeller to admit his personal moral liability for the situation. This Rockefeller refused to do and, instead, took the opportunity to lecture to the commission, and particularly to Walsh, giving his views of the limited responsibilities of both stockholders and company directors (see 37, XXXIII [1914-15], 480, 524-26, and XXXIV [1915], 461-72). A monograph, highly critical of Rockefeller, was published by the commission in 1915 (42).

To add insult to injury, Rockefeller organized an "independent" study of industrial relations, directed by William Lyon Mackenzie King, former Minister of Labor in Canada and later Prime Minister, and supported by the Rockefeller Foundation. King was aided by Clarence J. Hicks, a onetime Y.M.C.A. worker (see 18). The two research projects, one private and the other public, appeared to be competitive. Walsh, ever more intent on his campaign to discredit employers in general and Rockefeller in particular, took the opportunity to subpoena Rockefeller and King and hound them during their hours on the witness stand. Walsh's capture of newspaper space was spectacularly successful. During June, 1915, strong charges and even stronger counter-charges were aired.

To the charge and the argument of Henry Demarest Lloyd that the name of Rockefeller is that of a thief, Walsh added an arraignment for murder.

To the Ida Tarbell incriminations of Rockefeller as thief and liar, Walsh added an arraignment for the killing of women and children.

To the pile of proof which shows the Rockefellers double-crossing stockholders in Standard Oil and crushing all rivals by cunning and ruthless tactics, Walsh added the new charge that this Baptist family, for all its millions handed out to churches and the cross and Jesus, works in secrecy to beat down the organizations of labor unions even to the extent of using thugs and drunken soldiers to burn women and children to death [33, pp. 19-20].

Many editors and all employer journals naturally felt that Walsh's flamboyant search for headlines and his insensitive bullying of witnesses were totally unconscionable. The *Iron Trade Review* coined a new word, "Walshing," meaning "to bully, to rage against 'capital' and 'plutocracy'; having the characteristics of a devil dancer, dervishkearney, a Haywood or a flubdubber; used to rock a fellow on the 'money' boat." On August 18, 1915, a *New York Times* editorial writer likened Walsh's prosecution of the Rockefellers to that of a "sheriff's posse from Sandy Gulch chasing a couple of horse thieves." The next day the *Times* asked, "Upon what and whose recommendation, solicitation, or guarantee was this passionate Red appointed to the Commission as one of its 'impartial' members, supposed to represent the general public? Who is responsible for WALSH?"

Walsh replied to the criticism by training his sights on the tax-free educational and philanthropic foundations. This course led him into a public battle with the *Survey* magazine group, whose views, he charged, had been consistently prostituted to the Rockefeller interests. This charge was raised by George Creel, a close associate of Walsh. The allegation was later withdrawn, but the damage was done. Paul U. Kellogg, the editor of *Survey*, received scant consideration, although he was permitted a hearing in which he "bared *The Survey's* financial soul" (see **37**, XXXIII [1914-15], 541-42 and 561-64). The *Survey* group felt that they had created a monster which had turned on them (**37**, XXXIII [1914-15], 593 ff.).

During this period Walsh had a major falling-out with McCarthy. Their nominal difference was a disagreement over the research budget—Walsh, of course, had allocated the major portion of the budget to his hearings—but Walsh made much of McCarthy's old friendship with John D. Rockefeller, Jr., his Brown University classmate. Although he was completely unable to prove any unethical conduct on McCarthy's part, Walsh, taking full advantage of his powers as chairman, forced McCarthy out. Whether McCarthy was fired, or merely announced that he would no longer consider working with Walsh, is a moot point (**37**, XXXIV [1915], 40; also **37**, XXXIII [1914-15], 686).

Most of the research staff then resigned or were dismissed.

"Imagine the surprise of the Employers . . . and of Professor Commons and myself," wrote Mrs. Harriman,

when we learned that Mr. Walsh had summarily dismissed McCarthy and had put Basil Manly at the helm in his place. Those of us who had stood by McCarthy felt as though we were on a train that in some wayward fashion was tearing east just after the stationmaster had sold us tickets for a point west [17, p. 172].

Actually, after Walsh's *fait accompli,* Commons voted for Manly (5, p. 177).

It was inevitable that after this event the commission should produce no unanimous reports or plans. The *Final Report* (39) consisted of eleven volumes: 253 pages of recommendations, and the rest, transcripts of testimony. The commissioners' recommendations are divided into three groups: the "Major Report," so called although it was actually subscribed to by a minority; the "Commons Report," signed in whole or in part by commissioners Commons, Harriman, Weinstock, Ballard, and Aishton; and an "Employers Report," which elaborates the latter three's partial dissent from the Commons Report.

The Major or Manly Report was actually written by Basil M. Manly, but signed by commissioners Walsh, Lennon, O'Connell, and Garretson, and there were supplemental signed statements by each commissioner. It was devoted to a discussion of four main sources of industrial unrest—(1) unjust distribution of wealth and income; (2) unemployment and denial of an opportunity to earn a living; (3) denial of justice in the creation, the adjudication, and the administration of law; and (4) denial of the right and opportunity to form effective organizations. With regard to each of these four sources, in order, the Manly Report recommended (1) that Congress should enact a highly progressive inheritance tax, including a 100 per cent rate for all amounts over $1,000,000, to pay for the extension of education and the development of public works in co-operation with the states and municipalities. (2) That Congress legislate for the regaining of all land, water, and mineral rights "secured by . . . fraud," the establishment of land laws to include application of the doctrine of "superior use," and the taxation of all unused but usable land. (3) That Congress provide for further constitutional amendments to secure personal liberty and individual rights and the supremacy of the legislative product over judicial review, and that statutes be enacted to provide for a broad-base jury list and the regulation of private detective agencies, particularly in industrial disputes. (4) That provision be made for constitutional guarantees of the right to organize, that statutes be enacted to prohibit discharge from any job because of union membership, and to provide for federal prosecution, in administrative channels, for violations of a code of certain labor practices.

The basic assumption, made explicit at several points, was that an unhampered, free, trade-union movement was the only effective way to combat the evils of industrialism (39, I, 28 ff., 65 ff., 67 ff., 119 ff.). For example,

It is evident . . . that there can be at best only a benevolent despotism where collective action on the part of the employees does not exist [39, I, 64].

To suggest that labor unions can be effective if organized on less than a national scale seems to ignore entirely the facts and trend of present-day American business. . . . This does not . . . require that all employees in an industry . . . belong to a national organization, for . . . whenever even a considerable part are union members, the advances which they secure are almost invariably granted by competitors, . . . in order to prevent their own [nonunion] employees from organizing [39, I, 65].

The right to organize, Manly urged, must be protected, and he proposed that the Department of Labor be authorized to prosecute charges of unfair labor practices before the Federal Trade Commission, which was to sit in judgment (39, I, 67–68).

In addition, he urged the establishment of a federal mediation commission to handle all industrial disputes except those in public utilities. This mediation commission, which was to be completely independent of all other federal agencies, could intervene at the request of either interested party, at the will of its chairman, or by the direction of the secretaries of Commerce and Labor. Manly's plan also provided for co-operation between the mediation commission and such similar state instrumentalities that it was hoped would be established.

Walsh did not support Manly's plan for a new mediation commission. Instead, he expressed his conviction that the facilities existing in the Department of Labor were sufficient to meet all needs (39, I, 156). Commissioners Garretson, Lennon, and O'Connell, all union men, also dissented from Manly's report, which like Walsh they had signed with reservations, and took the occasion to express their faith in the Department of Labor as the sole agency (39, I, 158, 164–65). Thus on this point Manly, not even a commissioner, was alone. His view, however, was shared by the signers of the Commons Report (39, I, 206), except that commissioners Commons and Harriman (both public members) wanted to restrict the intervention of the mediation service to those instances when it was asked for by one of the interested parties. Commissioners Weinstock, Ballard, and Aishton did not wish to restrict entry thus (39, I, 232 ff.).

There are many aspects of the Manly Report which make its value somewhat questionable. The recommendations were often completely unsubstantiated by evidence, or evidence, even when alleged to be available, was not printed. Some of Manly's proposals were, in the light of historical perspective, on the bizarre side. For example, one of them reads: "That Congress immediately enact a statute or, if deemed necessary, initiate a constitutional amendment, specifically prohibiting the courts from declaring legislative acts unconstitutional."

Yet, for all the criticisms, the two basic ideas advanced by Manly and Walsh were recognized to have "theoretical" merit. These ideas were (1) that improvement in industrial relations must come, within the limits of the American cultural process, through unionism and collective bargaining, and (2) that the greatest help that the government could give unions was to publicize the unfair practices engaged in by employers. Their recommendations were made from this point of view.

By way of contrast, the Commons Report assumed that inadequate public administration was delaying the development of equity in industrial relations. (Commons' announced view was not in accord with most of the thinking he had done on the subject. It represents his fourth rather than his third "phase.") In his opinion, the solution involved the recognition of certain fundamental principles: (1) that there is a limited area of conflict in the fundamental economic interests of the wage earners and the wage payers; (2) that this difference can best be adjusted by voluntary, bilateral negotiation rather than by legal enactment; and (3) that the governmental role should be limited to one of encouraging the formation of, and then assisting, these bargaining groups. These principles were derived from his own experience, since he rejected the staff manuscripts, which he felt had not been critically cross-examined (39, I, 171).

Commons' considerable experience as an industrial commissioner in Wisconsin had convinced him that the Representative Advisory Council system, which he personally had established there, would be a satisfactory general solution. "The essential evil of bureaucracy," Commons noted, "is not so-called permanency of tenure, but the refusal of the official to take advice from laymen" (39, I, 182).

He suggested that one federal and many state industrial commissions be created. Their responsibilities would include the administration of the laws pertaining to industrial relations and any other activities that would smooth bipartite negotiation. They would also draft any remedial legislation mutually agreed upon by employers and unions. These industrial commissions, consisting of three public officials appointed by the Executive, were to have representative advisory councils consisting of twenty men each, representing employers, unions, farmers, and women. The councils would advise the commission, and would have no veto power.

Commons did not intend that the industrial commissions should replace the existing departments of labor (state or federal); the commissions would be limited to administering laws while the departments would handle all policy-forming functions. Only the departments, he thought, would be influenced by political considerations (39, I, 186–87). "The Industrial Commission is purely an administrative body not intended to promote new legislation, except where it is needed in connection with its administration of existing laws. Other new legislation gets its initiative elsewhere . . ." (39, I, 187).

The commissions, assisted by a civil-service type of staff, would issue technical rulings that could be contested, if it were so desired, in the courts (39, I, 199). These rulings would be made only after adequate investigation, and Commons assumed that they would generally meet with voluntary compliance. The commissions would also make technical studies, if so requested by the legislative bodies or the state supreme courts. Each year the commissions would publish reports on the conditions of labor, wages, and so forth. All technical reports were to be made public only after everyone on the Representative Advisory Council had had a chance to read them carefully and had noted any possible points of personal dissent. All in all, Commons wanted careful, patient analysis, subject to close examination at each step. "All labor legislation," he wrote, "all administration of labor laws, all efforts of mediation and arbitration, all recommendations of public bodies, go back, for their justification, to statistics and investigations. The money of the Government is worse than wasted, and the officials are discredited, if there remains any interested body of citizens who do not place confidence in these official statistics and investigations" (39, I, 193; cf. 5, pp. 171, 176–77). Commons' rejection of the uncriticized staff research reports, even though these were largely made by his former students, followed closely from this line of reasoning.

Commons argued that the reforms he suggested would strengthen unions at their weakest point, and that the traditionally divisive effects of politics and political ambition on internal union administration would be lessened. Through their representation on the advisory councils, unions would get a voice in the shaping of public policy. Moreover, the union representatives' personal ambitions would have no corrosive effects. "Under such circumstances [as those he advocated] there can ordinarily be no question of the union representatives 'selling out' to employers or politicians" (39, I, 191).

Commons made provision in his report for a mediation service that was to be insulated from the influence of the Industrial Commission. Each mediation service would have a chief mediator, assisted by a civil-service staff. The assistance of the service was to be offered whenever the chief felt it was needed. If agreement was not achieved through conciliation, voluntary arbitration was to be urged. If that suggestion failed, the parties were to be asked to agree to the appointment of a "Board of Mediation and Investigation" that could compel testimony, a power which the mediators would not have. What would happen if the parties remained deadlocked, or if they refused this final, fact-finding step, was not made clear, though Commons implied that a strike or lockout might develop. "It can not be expected that strikes and lockouts can be abolished altogether. Even countries with compulsory systems have not succeeded in preventing all of them. In our country, the voluntary method in collective bargaining avoids the much more serious evil of discrediting the agencies of Government . . ." (39, I, 213).

The second major part of the Commons Report recommended the adoption of legislation similar to that of the British Trade Disputes Act of 1906. Commons believed that all the devices employed by trade-unions and employers should be "legalized," since they were used anyway. Thus he came to sanction as legitimate the closed shop, boycotts, strikes, and picketing, as well as black-listing, lockouts, and the employment of strikebreakers. He believed that earlier laws restraining the use of these devices had had a pro-employer effect when they were enforced, and he wanted primarily to even up the struggle between labor and management. He was aware of union abuses, but believed that negotiation rather than law was the remedy.

Just as our earlier recommendations were intended, in part, to take the administration of labor law out of the hands of either side and to make it a joint affair, so this recommendation is intended, in

part, to relieve the courts of similar partisanship in matters of collective bargaining. *It is believed that strong organizations of employers and employees are much more capable than the courts of
holding each other in check and preventing abuses on either side*
[39, I, 215; italics supplied].

Manly, it should be added, supported Commons on this point.
The employers on the commission, however, did not.

Other items touched on in the Commons Report involved the
licensing of industrial police by the proposed permanent federal
industrial commission, a further investigation of the endowed
educational foundations, increased restrictions on immigration,
electoral and land reforms, and the extension of industrial education. Commons also advocated a progressive inheritance tax on
amounts in excess of $25,000 willed to direct heirs; the schedule
was revised upward in the case of remote heirs or strangers. The
revenue derived from this tax was to go to the federal government, although each state that repealed its own inheritance-tax
laws was to get 50 cents per capita per annum. These federal
monies were to be known as the "Fund for Social Welfare" and
were to be spent for the operation of the federal industrial commission and similar state agencies, for subsidies to the industrial-
education programs of the states, for the maintenance of state
and federal employment agencies, for the administration of immigration laws, and for various forms of social insurance and welfare.

The third report of the Commission on Industrial Relations,
the "Employers Report," is identical with the Commons Report
except for two major points. (1) The three employer commissioners dissented from Commons' opinion that secondary boycotts and allied union techniques were permissible, and (2) they
held that both sides did not have to concur before a fact-finding
board could be appointed. In the latter context they noted that
public opinion had become an independent element in the settlement of disputes and should be allowed to play a part, regardless
of the whims of the major parties (39, I, 232 ff.).

On the immigration question Walsh lined up with Weinstock

in opposing tighter immigration controls. This left the other commissioners (Commons, Harriman, Aishton, Ballard, Lennon, O'Connell, and Garretson) supporting increased restrictions.

Walsh wrote a supplemental report criticizing Commons (39, I, 153). The Commons Report, while not explicitly criticizing the Manly Report, nonetheless confirmed by implication the deepness of the split within the commission. The Employers Report did explicitly criticize the Manly Report (39, I, 233 ff.). Commissioners Garretson, Lennon, and O'Connell made a point of dissenting from the views of Commons (39, I, 158 ff. and 161 ff.). Commissioners Lennon, O'Connell, Garretson, Ballard, and Walsh also wrote a report on industrial education, a subject that had not been studied by the others (39, I, 255–61).

The confusion of opinions, dissents, counteropinions, and rejoinders made it impossible, of course, for anyone to take the whole *Final Report* very seriously. The Speaker of the House noted at one point in the discussions that the disposition of the mass of uncorroborated staff reports was a problem, "and somebody suggested that [they] be brought in here. There was not room enough in the well of the House . . . and the Chair ordered [them] not brought in. [They are] out in the lobby, and if anybody wants to inspect [them], he can go out there . . . (Laughter)" [8, LIII, 409]. Moreover, the European war overshadowed most peacetime labor problems. In any event, after some Congressional debate, the various reports and the testimony were ordered printed. These documents eventually found their way to the National Archives, although an almost complete set was given, presumably by Commons or McCarthy, to the Wisconsin Historical Society Library in Madison. They were for the most part forgotten.

Although the commission cost the taxpayers almost half a million dollars, it is not easy to point to many positive achievements. A follow-up committee was organized, but seems to have been ineffective (37, XXXV [1915–16], 155–56). A combination of economic and social circumstances, and especially the war, made it impossible for unions to capitalize on the publicity that Walsh had provided. For a variety of reasons, moreover, the Armistice gave new impetus to the employers' open-shop campaign.

In two minor senses, however, the commission did achieve success. In the first place, many of the staff members subsequently continued their work on the research problems assigned them by McCarthy. Studies in industrial relations by those whose intellectual and investigational careers were nurtured on this governmental project continued to appear for the next thirty years. And John Fitch, who reported the commission's hearings in *The Survey* magazine, prepared in 1924 a lengthy study of the problems of industrial relations in America (13). Fitch undertook this study because of his reaction to Ida Tarbell's panegyric of American industrial methods (38), and it reflected in great detail ideas that he had gained or had had confirmed during the hearings. While Fitch was writing he had the benefit of watching the postwar period and the adoption of the American Plan by much of industry; consequently he was much more skeptical about the future of American unionism than Walsh had been ten years previously.

The other small but undeniable success of the Walsh commission was in the educational effect of the reports. Two decades after their appearance Congress passed the Wagner Act, and endorsed policies encouraging collective bargaining. Unfair labor practices were defined and prohibited. Fact-finding investigations were later endorsed in the Taft-Hartley revisions to the Wagner Act.

In less than half a century (1879–1916) Congress had acquired a detailed knowledge of the problems of industrial relations in a complex, generally democratic, industrialized society. As is true with so many lessons, it took more time than this before the implications of this knowledge were fully understood. The evolution of the federal labor-relations policy after 1932 shows some of this knowledge at last being put to use.

The disorganized mass of material accumulated by the commission and the staff has been left relatively unexplored. The five basic theories of unionism that we have discussed in these chapters suggest a systematic way in which the conflicting estimates and attitudes in that material can be organized. Superficially, at least, the commission's material includes significant examples of the psychological, the socioeconomic, and the sociohistorical approaches to unionism. The work done by Parker and others on migrant labor is but one example of the psychological approach. The material on the Ludlow Massacre and on the economic misery found in tenements and in mining towns is a further example. As for the economic-welfare theory, Walsh was particularly impressed with unionism as a way to redistribute wealth and social power. Commons, directly concerned with the same problem, appeared to have faith in unionism only if it was assisted by governmental administrators. And Walsh's emphasis on bargaining by social groups approximates the social-institution approach. Many of the monographs are directed to detailed examinations of specific illustrations of unionism as a conservative and property-conscious movement. Elements of the other two approaches (moral and revolutionary) are also present, though they tend to be submerged. What had occurred during the years that led up to the establishment of the commission, of course, was the emergence of an American social structure in which these patterns could be distinguished.

What did the Commission on Industrial Relations have to do with the New Deal? The answer lies, partly, in the evolution of thinking made possible by the commission's employment and training of young experts, and partly in the clarification of concepts of industrial relations and unionism that resulted from the commission's activities.

References

1. *American Federationist,* V (October, 1898), 160–61.
2. Barnett, George E., and McCabe, David A., *Mediation, Investigation and Arbitration in Industrial Disputes.* New York: D. Appleton & Co., 1916.

3. Christie, Robert, *Empire in Wood*. Ithaca, N.Y.: New York State School of Industrial and Labor Relations, 1956.

4. Committee on Education and Labor, U.S. Senate, *Report of the Committee of the Senate upon the Relations between Labor and Capital, and Testimony Taken by the Committee*. 4 vols. Washington, D.C.: U.S. Government Printing Office, 1885.

5. Commons, John R., *Myself*. New York: The Macmillan Co., 1934.

6. ———, and Associates, *History of Labour in the United States*. 2 vols. New York: The Macmillan Co., 1918.

7. ———; Gray, John; *et al., Regulations and Restrictions of Output,* in Carroll D. Wright [commissioner], *Eleventh Special Report of the Commissioner of Labor*. Washington, D.C.: U.S. Government Printing Office, 1904.

8. *Congressional Record*.

9. Darrow, Clarence, *The Story of My Life*. New York: Charles Scribner's Sons, 1932.

10. Dorfman, Joseph, *The Economic Mind in American Civilization,* Vol. III, 1865–1918. New York: Viking Press, Inc., 1949.

11. Durand, E. Dana, "The United States Industrial Commission; Methods of Government Investigation," *Quarterly Journal of Economics,* XVI (1901–2), 564–86.

12. Ely, Richard T., "The Report of the Industrial Commission: I, Labor," *Yale Review,* XI (November, 1902), 229–50.

13. Fitch, John A., *The Causes of Industrial Unrest*. New York: Harper & Bros., 1924.

14. Fitzpatrick, Edward, *McCarthy of Wisconsin*. New York: Columbia University Press, 1944.

15. Gompers, Samuel, *Seventy Years of Life and Labor*. 2 vols. New York: E. P. Dutton & Co., Inc., 1925.

16. Grant, Luke, *The National Erectors' Association and the International Association of Bridge and Structural Ironworkers*. Washington, D.C.: [Government Printing Office?], 1915.

17. Harriman, Mrs. J. Borden, *From Pinafores to Politics*. New York: Henry Holt & Co., 1923.

18. Hicks, Clarence J., *My Life in Industrial Relations*. New York: Harper & Bros., 1941.

19. House Report 572 (46th Cong., 2d sess. [1880]).

20. House Report 2447 (52d Cong., 2d sess. [1893]).

21. House Reports 726 and 1233 (62d Cong., 2d sess. [1912]).

22. Hoxie, Robert F., *Scientific Management and Labor*. New York: D. Appleton & Co., 1915.

23. Hufford, Harold E., for Thad Page, Chief Archivist, Legislative and Fiscal Records Branch, National Archives, Washington, D.C., private communication, August 26, 1953.

24. *Journal of the House of Representatives* (46th Cong., 2d sess. [1879-80]).

25. Lauck, W. Jett, *Political and Industrial Democracy, 1776-1926*. New York: Funk & Wagnalls Co., 1926.

26. Leiserson, William, *Adjusting Immigrant and Industry*. New York: Harper & Bros., 1924.

27. Lescohier, Don D., and Brandeis, Elizabeth, *History of Labor in the United States*, Vol. III, *Working Conditions and Labor Legislation, 1896-1932*, with an Introduction by John R. Commons. New York: The Macmillan Co., 1935.

28. Lindsay, Samuel M., "A Colossal Inquiry Completed: The Three-Years' Work of the United States Industrial Commission," *American Monthly Review of Reviews*, XXIV (1901), 711-18.

29. McCabe, David A., *National Collective Bargaining in the Pottery Industry*. Baltimore: The Johns Hopkins University Press, 1932.

30. North, S. N. D., "The Industrial Commission," *North American Review*, CLXVIII (1899), 708-19.

31. Perlman, Selig, and Taft, Philip, *History of Labor in the United States*, Vol. IV, *Labor Movements, 1896-1932*. New York: The Macmillan Co., 1935.

32. Ripley, W. F., "The Work of Trained Economists in the Industrial Commission," *Quarterly Journal of Economics*, XVI (1901-2), 121-22.

33. Sandburg, Carl S., "The Two Mr. Rockefellers—and Mr. Walsh," *International Socialist Review*, XVI (July, 1915), pp. 18-25.

34. Select Committee on Depression in Labor and Business, House of Representatives, *Causes of the General Depression in Labor*

and Business, Etc. Misc. Doc. 29 (45th Cong., 3d sess. [1879]).

35. Senate Report 1280 (52d Cong., 2d sess. [1892–93]).

36. Steffens, Lincoln, *Autobiography*. New York: Harcourt, Brace & Co., 1931.

37. *The Survey* magazine.

38. Tarbell, Ida, *New Ideals in Business*. New York: The Macmillan Co., 1916.

39. United States Commission on Industrial Relations, *Final Report and Testimony*. 11 vols. Washington, D.C.: U.S. Government Printing Office, 1916.

40. United States Commission on Industrial Relations, "Reports." Unpublished research papers, Wisconsin Historical Society Library. Also available on microfilm, National Archives.

41. United States Industrial Commission, *Report of the Industrial Commission*. 19 vols.: I, *Trusts and Industrial Combinations;* II, *Trusts and Corporation Laws;* III, *Prison Labor;* IV, *Transportation;* V, *Labor Legislation;* VI, *Distribution of Farm Products;* VII, *Capital and Labor in Manufactures and General Business;* VIII, *Chicago Labor Disputes;* IX, *Transportation* (second volume); X, *Agriculture and Agricultural Labor;* XI, *Agriculture and Taxation;* XII, *Capital and Labor in the Mining Industries;* XIII, *Trusts and Industrial Combination* (second volume); XIV, *Capital and Labor in Manufactures and General Business* (second volume); XV, *Immigration and Education;* XVI, *Foreign Labor Legislation;* XVII, *Labor Organizations, Labor Disputes, and Arbitration. Railroad Labor;* XVIII, *Industrial Combinations in Europe;* XIX, *Final Report of the Commission*. Washington, D.C.: U.S. Government Printing Office, 1900–1902.

42. West, George P., *Report on the Colorado Strike*. Washington, D.C.: [U.S. Government Printing Office?], 1915.

43. Witte, Edwin E., *The Government in Labor Disputes*. New York: McGraw-Hill Book Co., Inc., 1932.

44. Wright, Carroll D., "Industrial Commissions in the United States and in Austria," *Quarterly Journal of Economics*, XIII (1898–99), 228–31.

Index

305

Ross, Edward A., 21, 24, 190, 280
Ryan, John A., 48–49, 224, 229
   his interpretation, 55–64

St. John, Vincent, 75, 83, 84, 86;
   see also Industrial Workers
   of the World
Saniel, Lucien, 262
Saposs, David J., 36, 66n, 285
Sartorius, August, 7–9
Schmoller, Gustav, 160–61, 174
Schonfarber, Jacob G., 268–69
Schumpeter, Joseph, 174
Schwedtman, Fred C., 281
Secrist, Horace, 286
Seligman, Edwin R. A., 7, 22, 280
Shaffer, T. J., 33
Shaw, Albert, 22
Sherman, John, 262–63
Sherman, William, 81
Shibley, George H., 32–33
Show, Arley B., 18–19
Simkhovitch, Mary W., 280
Simonds, John Cameron, 5–7
Slichter, Sumner H., 31, 286
Small, Albion W., 24
Smith, Adam, 50
Smyth, Ellison A., 266, 275
Social Democratic Party, 96; *see also* Socialist Party of America
Social-institution theory, 160–213, 236–38
   synthesized, 220–21, 226
Social-revolutionary theory, 66–119, 230–31
   synthesized, 216–17, 225

Socialism, 17, 53–54, 140–41, 224, 230; *see also* Marxism
Socialist Labor party, 53–54, 68, 69, 70, 74 ff., 76–81 *passim*, 259
Socialist Party of America, 71–74, 84, 87, 88, 95, 96, 101–6
Socialist Trade and Labor Alliance, 69, 76, 86
Sombart, Werner, 200 ff.
Sons of Vulcan, 10
Spargo, John, 71, 72, 74
Sprague, G. C., 285
Stewart, Ethelbert, 34
Stewart, William M., 266
Stimson, F. J., 266
Stone, N. I., 70, 102–3
Strasser, Adolph, 68, 246, 254–55, 264, 269–70
Studnitz, Arthur von, 5, 7
Suffern, A. E., 285
Sumner, Helen, 34, 36
Sumner, William Graham, 245
Survey magazine, 279 ff., 281, 283, 291
Sutherland, George, 281
Swinton, John, 12
Sydenstricker, Edgar, 286
Sylvis, William H., 1, 7
Syndicalist League of North America, 88, 89

Taft, Philip, 36
Taft, William H., 279, 281, 282
Taft-Hartley Act, 300
Tannenbaum, Frank, 120, 224
   his interpretation, 138–42
Tarbell, Ida, 290, 300
Taylor, John, 47